Archives Administration

**A Manual for Intermediate and Smaller
Organizations and for Local Government**

Archives Administration

A Manual for Intermediate and Smaller Organizations and for Local Government

Contents

Preface		viii
1	The archives office—objectives and structure	1
2	Records management	25
3	Operating a records centre	37
4	Appraisal of records	60
5	Disposal of records	78
6	Acquisition and arrangement of archives	95
7	Description of archives	114
8	Conservation of archives	135
9	Searchroom services in public repositories, I	144
10	Searchroom services in public repositories, II	160
11	Developmental services	172
12	Archives in education	183
13	Local archives services	199

Appendixes
A	Recommendations for British local archive services	202
B	Criteria for selection of public records for permanent preservation	206
C	A schedule of general conditions for deposit of archives	210
D	Regulations for readers	212
E	Access to public records in Britain	214

Abbreviations	217
References	218
Bibliography	228
Index	248

Preface

This book is one of the products of what has been called the 'archival revolution' which has been gathering pace since the Second World War. This 'revolution' has radically altered society's view of what archives are, and it has altered archivists' functions both in administration and in connexion with research. The main features of the archives world of today are that there is an almost inconceivably large body of records being produced, that the character of these records has changed from what it was before and is in process of changing further; and that the demands of both administration and research for access to the information in records and archives is rapidly growing and changing in character. All these features have led archivists to change their attitudes and their methods. Some of these attitudes and methods are the subject of this book and the changes are its justification.

It is no longer possible for one person to write a complete survey of professional practice in the administration of archives. Too many specialities have developed, and the scope of the work has grown too wide. This book is offered because it serves a practical purpose, and because it may help forward the processes involved in producing an adequate body of literature to support the art. It is offered in a spirit of respect to the leaders and elders in archives work, and in a spirit of encouragement and enthusiasm to those who are starting out.

The immediate objective of this book is to provide the basic information which will be needed by anyone starting or running a small or intermediate archives and records service. It is not based upon the experience of the larger national archives services, like most of the archival manuals published hitherto, but upon that of smaller and local ones. All complex organizations produce and need to manage records, and the general interest requires the development of archives services. Like all organized activities, these need resources of people, installations and finance. Therefore adequate services can be provided only by organizations above a certain size, and smaller entities will find it unrewarding to run their own: they may be able by co-operative agreements to make use of those of larger ones.

While accepting this situation, this book attempts to describe the activities, duties and standards of records and archives services run by organizations such as industrial or business firms or local government which are, in comparison with the national or international giants, small or intermediate in size. It confines itself to providing basic information, and in addition offers guidance through the bibliography on sources for further knowledge. Among the important subjects which are not dealt with in detail here are the technical aspects of conservation and repair (under this heading management aspects alone are included), technical developments and standards in description (cataloguing), computer programs beyond the merest outline, archival publication, the design and layout of archival buildings, and professional education. All these subjects call out for fresh literature, and in many cases it is difficult at present to suggest sources for newcomers to learn about them.

I should like to thank all those of my colleagues who have given permission for the inclusion of items from their work, or who have helped me with advice and information; they have been very generous. They include: the Keepers of the Public Records and of the Public Records of Northern Ireland; the Secretary of the Royal Commission on Historical Manuscripts and the Registrar of the National Register of Archives; the directors of national archives in Malaysia and Singapore; the county archivists of Cheshire, Clwyd, East Sussex, Gloucestershire, Greater London, Kent, Lancashire, Suffolk, and Worcestershire; the corporation archivist of the British Steel Corporation; and the Acting Director of the Borthwick Institute of Historical Research, York. In addition I acknowledge very gladly my debt to their respective councils or governing bodies for permission to reproduce or adapt documents. I should like also to thank the following for permission to reproduce documents at rather greater length: the British Steel Corporation for the retention schedule in chapter 5; Lancashire County Council for the version of their plan in chapter 10; the Public Record Office for their summary of archival values in appendix B; Her Majesty's Stationery Office for the extract from the Public Records Act 1958; the Schools Council and their project team on 'History, Geography and Social Science, 8–13' for the statement of objectives in chapter 12 and the Council of the Society of Archivists for the text of their *Recommendations* in appendix A. My colleagues at Liverpool, especially Adrian Allan, have been very understanding during a long period of gestation; Mrs Anne Oakes did a splendid job in the typing. Lastly I gladly advertise the fact that my wife and I have a very effective scheme for supporting each other in times of specially heavy work; I thank her especially for carrying it through in this case.

The University of Liverpool

MICHAEL COOK

1 The Archives Office—Objectives and Structure

It is particularly important that an archives office should have clear objectives which should be made explicit even in a small and informal organization. Common professional experience will often dictate standards, but there are situations for which past experience is not a sound guide, and where aims and methods must be thought out anew. From a general statement of objectives a series of programmes can be worked out, embodying decisions on priority, timetables and the allocation of resources. The evaluation of these programmes and their achievements is also important, and a regular review of policies should ensure credible objectives which are a source of good morale, high motivation and satisfaction in work well done.

The material which is the subject of an archives office's work should be defined. It is still not universally clear whether there should be, in the English language, any real distinction between 'archives' and 'records': the terms are commonly used interchangeably and imprecisely. In places where the British tradition in administration is dominant, it is still usual to refer to 'record' or 'records offices' rather than to 'archives', though this latter is increasingly the international term. International usage, however, stemming from the principal professional manual of recent decades,(1) indicates that records are papers (and other media of recorded information) which are drawn up in the course of business by any continuing organization, are kept for reference, and are of use in conducting that business. Archives are a specialized section of the records: those which, having passed out of currency, have been appraised and selected with a view to exploiting their use in research, or at any rate are actually held by an archives office because they are seen as valuable in a research context.

Archives are often confused with manuscripts. Anything handwritten (or by extension typewritten) is a manuscript, but the word usually suggests a document which, by virtue of the information it carries or of some other historical association, is worth collecting and keeping. Manuscripts are individual documents, or more or less arbitrary collections of documents, which are of interest for research but which do not have the essential character either of archives or of records referred to above—that is, they did not arise from, or have not been kept in, association with the conduct of business. It follows that manuscripts can be collected—by an archives office, a library or any interested person—for the benefit of research, but that records and archives can only be dealt with in some sort of relationship with, or with some sort of regard to, the organization which brought them into existence and for whose reference they were once kept. Hence one may speak of a collection of manuscripts, but of an archives or records service.

Archives are kept in buildings, and according to the dictionary these buildings are also called 'archives'. However, for the sake of clarity, the term 'archives office' is used here to indicate the institution which handles the archives, whatever name it goes by in real life. In Britain the term 'record office' is usual, and the prototype is of course the Public Record Office, which is the national archives; in the USA the more natural term is used.

Such titles are only there, however, for the sake of convenience. And there may be some advantage in discussing the operations of an archives office (a thing which we will not often meet with on public notice boards) in the hope that the principles suitable to such a place may be accepted for use in record offices and in other places where they have archives.

There are many different kinds of archives office. There are those which have been established by the organization which creates the archives, as a service to itself and others. The national archives belongs in this category, as does the archives office of a business firm, where such a thing exists. On the other hand, many institutions possessing collections of manuscripts should be included under the general heading of 'archives office'. In looking at the collections of such institutions as the Library of Congress or the British Library, one is immediately aware that several of them do have the essential characteristics of archives (that is, they are interconnected organic groups arising from a single organization) rather than of manuscripts (discrete items).

This book is concerned with records and archives, and the way in which they are administered in relation to their record-creating and employing institutions. The important thing about archives is their organic connexion with their creating organization, but it has always been accepted that they could be transferred to and administered by a separate institution. This is particularly so where the originating organization has gone out of existence. In this way an archives office can be appointed to carry out the duties of an archivist for the benefit of that existing or former institution. We may therefore find that archives of churches, estates, firms or local government bodies have found their way to libraries, museums or record offices without impropriety. The organic and continuing nature of the archives still persists, however tenuous the link with the originating organization, and marks the difference between series of archives administered through loan or deposit and collections of manuscripts deliberately built up and placed in the same institutions. The principle of deposit, or of the appointment of an archives office to administer archives for an institution, is an important one. Not every record-creating body can afford a proper service for their administration; so that, if the archives are to survive and are to be exploited, the services of an archivist must be obtained from outside. This will always be so, and it is the contribution particularly of the non-national archives offices to establish the pattern of the publicly provided archives service, willing and able to administer the archives of persons or institutions which can or will not do the job themselves.

In order that their significance as evidence may be preserved and exploited, archives must be arranged in a manner which respects their original order and the interdependence of component parts of the accumulation. By contrast, individual and unrelated manuscripts may be classified as if they were completely distinct units, as are library books. This constitutes a fundamental difference of procedure between libraries and archives offices, and the principle on which archives are arranged and interpreted is known as the principle of provenance.

The character and objectives of an archives office are deeply affected by the general state of society and its beliefs. Society no longer holds the same view of permanence and of its relation to posterity that it once did. Whereas our predecessors believed that their principal objective was to preserve valuable archives for ever, we of the last quarter of the twentieth century believe, rightly or wrongly, that posterity is close at hand, and that the useful lifetime of many informational instruments should be costed and calculated. The development of mechanical means of copying, of extracting information, the multiplication of documents and duplicates, the declining standard of permanence in the composition of paper and other media, and above all the sense of progress and change in the state of knowledge, have all eroded the sense of serving the long-term future, the uniqueness of the original document, the *species aeternitatis* which once we had.

This change of view does not, of course, mean that there are no precious original documents to the permanent preservation of which valuable resources should be given. Indeed it is important to perceive that the main archives of an organization ought to be preserved without excessive regard to technical and financial limitations, for the sake of the interests of society at large. But it does alter the particular quality of uniqueness which at least some archives have had, and it has made clear that there are degrees of value in the originals of any archive series, degrees which are measurable in terms of research use, intelligibility, content and form.

The view of society on what information should be compiled, and what limits it should have, has also changed. The collection of information has now become a vast international industry. Archives offices are specialized data banks, paralleled and supplemented by many other data banks. The information that goes into these is compiled by the investigations and activities of all sorts of corporations, governments heading the list. We have now reached the point where artifical limitations on the retention and use of information, at least as regards persons, are being discussed.(2)

Archives offices, like other data banks, exist for the purpose of reference and research. As will be seen below, they have functions in administration and the nature of the research carried on with the use of archival material varies widely. But archivists can hardly wander far from this fundamental aim, by which all their programmes should be judged. Within this general aim, the objectives can be classified into three broad areas of activity; these may be labelled 'acquisitive', 'conservative' and 'exploitative' activities. Much of the work of an archives office falls within programmes in the sector of acquisition, and the whole of records management may be included among these. Despite this, the statement of objectives should be made as simple as possible.

Acquisition

Essentially there will be a resolve to identify and acquire all the valuable material which is to be found in the records of the employing institution. This will imply (a) that the office will seek to discover what the records of its employing institution actually comprise; (b) that it will devise systems of selection and apply standards of appraisal to those records; and (c) that it will assume responsibility for all such records as are so judged to be worthy of treatment as archives. This last is a central principle of archive work, and it is a principle which (like the principle of arrangement by provenance) distinguishes it from library practice. There are values in archives which extend beyond the limits imposed by current levels of resources, and an archivist must accept—the planning of his professional work must take account of this— whatever material comes to him by strict application of the appropriate methods of selection. It is not acceptable that the long-term interests of society should be radically determined by current practical difficulties. Of course, practical expedients may be adopted to solve the problems posed by the intake of bulky series. It is often possible to deposit archive groups in temporary storage, and there are technical resources (discussed below) which may also help. It is clearly not a professional requirement that archive series must be accepted if they have to be stacked in the roadways: but neither should they be consigned to destruction solely because of present shortage of accommodation.

It is probable also that the objectives will include the acquisition of valuable (that is, appraised and selected) material which arises from some defined area of interest other than the employing authority itself. This area of interest may be territorial (for example a geographical region), connected with a particular activity or industry, or concerned with topic or subject. Difficulties arise with each of these.

Territorial. The aim here will be to acquire documentation offering a basis of evidence for research on any major aspect of the community, if that evidence exists. In acquiring this documentation, there may be conflicting jurisdictions or overlapping interests. In any given locality there is likely to be more than one institution concerned with the collection of material of research value relating to or arising from within the locality. There is usually a library or a university, for example, as well as an archives office, and national institutions may be interested. These difficulties are compounded in a situation where archives have acquired a market value, a situation growing more common. To solve these difficulties there is really only one solution: explicit determination of the interests and sphere of activity of each institution, backed by specific agreements and personal goodwill. Goodwill and co-operation in such cases are elements in professional conduct.

Another difficulty which may arise from territorially defined areas of interest is that the range of different types of archive may be too great for efficient servicing by the staff of one office. An examination of the intake of deposits by a county record office in Britain shows that almost any kind of document can be expected: church registers, business ledgers, architectural or engineering drawings, personal diaries, manuscript books, title deeds, proceedings in law courts, Acts of Parliament, tithe awards, Inland Revenue valuation papers, and so on. The range of period to be covered may also be great, which means that the archives office must possess the skills needed to interpret both medieval and modern documents. It is clear that one office will probably not have the range of technical expertise to provide all the necessary services, but to state the difficulty is not to prevent the activity. The solution to these problems no doubt lies in the recruitment of expert advice, whether by professional structures which have yet to be set up, or by local arrangement. For present purposes it is merely noted that the aim is valid if properly defined, and it is the designer of the programmes who must solve the difficulties and make the necessary agreements.

Specialized activity or industry. The objectives here will be to document the activity in question, but will be determined also by the nature of the archives office concerned. Where the office belongs to and serves an industrial or business firm, its objectives will be limited by the business interests of the firm, including consideration of competition. As an archives office, however, it will have professional standards which include service to research transcending the immediate interests of the firm, though these two are not necessarily—and actually are rarely—in conflict. A business or industrial archives office will have to define its objectives in relation to acquisition with three questions in mind: should intake be confined to material produced by the employing body only? If not, should it be supplemented by documentation useful for current reference? Should it be supplemented by 'historical' material for research use? In any case, there will probably be occasion for boundary agreements similar to those indicated above, but with the employing body's documentation centre, technical library, or museum, if these exist.

Subject. Possibly the greatest difficulties of all are encountered in drawing up practicable objectives for an archives office concerned with acquiring material on a subject. The subject interests of an archive office, in a classic situation, are determined by the content of the office's central accumulation of archives, which is that of its employing authority, and by its organic relationship with the creators of the record. In other cases, with arbitrarily formed collections, this principle may have been cut across. Some institutions have set out to acquire accumulations of archives with contents dealing with given subjects, such as educational administration or agriculture. In these cases some careful distinctions may be drawn. There are of course legitimate instances of subject collections planned on a national scale; these include: (i) cases where there is no other appropriate repository for a given group of archives; (ii) cases where the collector has in effect become the principal archives office for an activity or body; (iii) cases where centres of documentation based on means of reference, or on photocopies, have been established.

It is not always necessary that original archives must be drawn into one central place: if the objective is the establishment of a finding system so that a research project may make use of the information in a group of archives, then the construction of the finding system is more important to the institution than the possession of the originals. There is doubtless much scope for the creation and extension of registers of archives and similar finding aids.

The projection of new subject-based repositories—a thing of fairly frequent occurrence—tends to upset professional organizations of archivists, since the pattern of territorially based archives offices which exists in most countries seems to be threatened by them. Two principles must be insisted upon: firstly, that a regularly established archives office must be trusted to administer all archives that legitimately come to it, whatever the value of those archives in terms of market price or of international demand. There are not two grades of archive—a more valuable kind, of national or international import, to be trusted only to certain classes of archivist, and a less valuable kind, of local import, which may be relegated to other archivists. All archives offices ought to conform to professional standards, both in the training and provision of staff, and in the character of their accommodation and facilities. If they fall seriously short of normal professional standards, then they should think of alternative ways of administering their archives, perhaps by deposit in a larger office. But if the office does conform to those standards, it must be allowed to receive all appropriate materials. Secondly, all institutions which propose to accept archives, must accept them on the established principles of archive practice: the principle of provenance must be respected, archivally interconnected series or accumulations must be kept together (even where the limits of the institutions's subject interests are overstepped in consequence), and appraisal should be conducted archivally. Above all, the selection of some individual documents of particular appeal or relevance from a whole series should be avoided.

On the other hand, however, the purpose of research collections is reference. Therefore, if an institution can compile a reference collection which is of patent value, it should be welcomed as an addition to the nation's resources. A national archives service is normally confined to the administration of archives; this limitation is a natural one and assists its work because no reader expects to find anything but archives in it. But other types of archives office may find that a limitation of their holdings to archives or manuscripts is a narrowing of their research or reference function. Looking at great national institutions which hold archives collected on a subject basis— such as the Imperial War Museum or the National Maritime Museum—we may see how much the value of such places is enhanced by their possession of related objects and books. The presidential library system, which has obtained such a firm hold in America (and now elsewhere), is another example.

The principle then is that, in determining the field of acquisition of an archives office, the first question to be decided is that of its relationship with other research collections, libraries, museums, universities and so forth, both national and provincial. The circumstances of each case will differ, but the need for a radically thought-out objective and for clear agreements for its operation remains the same.

Behind all this there is one underlying principle, which must be considered and incorporated into the aims of the office. The overall aim must surely be the construction of an adequate and truthful documentation in the area of interest concerned. The limitations on acquisition which may be accepted are what really determine the nature of the acquisitive objectives of a particular archive office. If the office seeks only archival material, professional standards will require close and structured liaison with other offices holding material which will complete the documentation: documentation centres, libraries, museums, centres of oral investigation and recording, and technical records centres. Other limitations, perhaps to certain kinds of archive only, are clearly harder to justify in the abstract. All archives offices should ask themselves whether they have excluded any significant group of archives, the absence of which would invalidate their declared objective.

Conservation

Conservational aims cover the ordering and housing of the archives acquired so that they will be preserved physically from deterioration and be apt for the uses to which they will be put. Concealed within this last phrase is another of the basic professional duties of an archivist, one which was given by Sir Hilary Jenkinson the succinct title of the 'moral defence' of archives. By this he meant that the order in which the archivist placed the material, the numbers or codes which he allocated to it for the purpose of finding, and the way in which his descriptive lists were set out, had the effect of interpreting the documents in terms of their original purpose and of their place in the originating administration. If the order or listing of the archives does not demonstrate this original purpose, then the archivist has set up a situation in which they may be misinterpreted: he has introduced a bias which will be reflected in the research in which they are used. More positively, the arrangement, storage and numbering of archives should be carried out in such a way as to demonstrate and render permanent the relationships between archives and their original administrative structures. The moral defence of archives takes its place as one of the primary objectives.(3) It is of course for the benefit of the user, and is the main direct contribution of the archivist to research.

Exploitation

Programmes of exploitation are more easily postponed than those for acquisition or conservation, but the priorities of the service will still rank the exploitation of the archives as of equal value with the other operations.

There will be two groups of activities under the heading of exploitative services. These will be passive—the provision of facilities for readers to come and consult the archives—and active, the provision of instruments (publications and so forth) which will promote use of the archives in other ways. There is room for new and technical activity in this area.

The final objective, the achievement of which may be very remote, will be the establishment of such comprehensive intellectual control over the office's holdings as will permit the full exploitation of the whole accumulation in reference and research. Establishing an intellectual control over the holdings of an archives office involves all three facets of the office's work—acquisition, conservation and exploitation. In acquiring new archives, as in exploitation, instruments for control and retrieval are necessary, and the moral defence of archives includes the way in which they are listed and described, and hence their interpretation, and even the way in which they are sorted and stored. A statement of aims will override any subdivision of the office's work, and for this reason the overall planning and management of the archives service is as important as the successful achievement of any of its programmes.
Figure 1.1 may serve to give an overview of the interrelationships of objectives, programmes and service divisions which may develop in an office.

Legislation Governing Archives Services

Like all public functions, archives offices are regulated by statute and by various sorts of ordinance established by national governments, local authorities and employing authorities. In Britain the statutory and regulatory framework provided by these provisions is weak, and in contrast with other countries does not provide guidance or standards which cover anything like the whole field. Nor is the complete corpus of legislative or regulatory provisions known or easily available in reference works.

National archival legislation is not always suitable for the smaller organizations within the nation, either as guidance or as a supporting framework of law. However, it is always necessary for

EXPLOITATION ←——— CONSERVATION ←——— ACQUISITION

OBJECTIVES	PROGRAMMES	SERVICE DIVISIONS
IDENTIFICATION AND CONTROL OF ALL RELEVANT MATERIAL	INTERNAL SURVEYS RECORDS MANAGEMENT FIELD WORK EXTERNAL SURVEYS LIAISON	RECORDS SECTION FIELD SECTION
INTAKE OF MATERIAL	TRANSFER SYSTEMS DEPOSIT RECEPTION	REPOSITORY SERVICES
ORDERING, PRESERVATION REPAIR OF MATERIAL	ARRANGEMENT STORAGE REPAIR	TECHNICAL SECTION
RETRIEVAL OF INFORMATION FROM MATERIAL	DESCRIPTION DISPLAY	REPOSITORY SEARCHROOM } SERVICES
DEVELOPMENT OF POTENTIAL VALUES OF MATERIAL	PUBLICATION TEACHING SPECIALIST PROGRAMMES (EDUCATION)	PUBLICATION DEVELOPMENT } SECTION ADMINISTRATIVE SERVICES

ALLOCATION OF PRIORITIES AND RESOURCES

1.1 The Working of an Archives Office

an archivist to understand what the legal limitations on his work are, and it is usually useful for him to study archive law so that he can design his own operation in the light of existing structures.

The following are the main elements to be found in the archive laws of most countries.(4)

(i) The law defines the material it is to deal with: usually some

concept similar to 'public archives'. These are declared the
property of the nation and subject to regulation. There may in
addition be an inclusion of non-official or non-public archives
valuable to the country, and which may, or even must, be brought
into the field of operation of the archival authority.(5)

(ii) The archival authority is established, and its powers set out.
This may be an addition to the powers of a minister, or a special
public authority with a specific constitution. This minister, or
public authority, may be provided with an advisory council
containing representatives of interested or user bodies.(6)

(iii) Under the terms of these powers, a chief archivist is
appointed, and his qualifications and the kind of staff he is to be
supported by may be laid down.

(iv) The archivist's powers and duties are defined. These will
include powers to inspect and order the disposal of records and to
transfer them to his direct custody.

(v) Following this, the archivist's direct professional duty is
defined, and the work of the national archives as an institution is
authorized and directed: it will preserve, repair, describe and give
access to the archives. These duties may be specified in some
detail, and in some cases the positive side may be emphasized by
spelling out the archivist's duty to seek out relevant material and
to promote its use in relation to the nation's resources of
documentation or cultural materials.(7)

(vi) There may be an extension of these powers to subordinate
authorities and other branches of government, such as local or
State governments and cities, and to the legislature and judicial
branches of the central government. It is not always regarded as
essential that the national or central archives should be a single,
monolithic institution, though it tends to be so in the newer
countries.

(vii) Extensions of the legislative act might include the power to
make regulations in rather more detail and specificity, with
prescribed forms and procedures.(8)

One interesting case in which archival legislation has
developed somewhat differently from that of many younger
countries is Sweden. Here the archives law is central to public
administration since, under the law on the freedom of the press
(passed in 1949, but incorporating an older tradition), there exists
a right of inspection of all public documents which are not
specifically restricted on security or other grounds.(9) The
regulation of this considerable public right has given Swedish

archival law and practice a characteristic formation, both in the national and in smaller archives services, which is worthy of study.

Great Britain
England and Wales
The summary of archival legislation published in the international journal *Archivum* serves as a practical handbook to the law of archives in Britain, as it does to the law of archives of many other countries.(10) The legal situation in Britain is summarized here, as it may suggest comparable guidelines in other places.

The Public Record Office, founded in 1838, is today governed by the Public Records Act, 1958, as amended by a similar Act of 1967.(11) This 1958 Act incorporates the findings of the Grigg Committee of 1954 on the subject of the systematic disposal of government records which have passed out of currency.(12) It also introduces a definition of 'public records' which has proved of importance in the development of archive services apart from the central national service in the Public Record Office. These are defined as:

administrative and departmental records belonging to Her Majesty' whether in the United Kingdom or elsewhere, in right of Her Majesty's Government in the United Kingdom and, in particular,
(a) records of, or held in, any department of Her Majesty's Government in the United Kingdom, or
(b) records of any office, commission or other body or establishment whatsoever under Her Majesty's Government in the United Kingdom. . . .(13)

A schedule to the Act lists distinct and semi-independent 'bodies and establishments under government departments', and 'other establishments and organizations' whose records are 'public'. At the time of the drafting of the Act it was apparently the intention to include all bodies established under general Acts to discharge public functions, even where those bodies did not form part of the ordinary structure of government. For example, the British Museum, the National Coal Board, Remploy Ltd, and the Atomic Energy Commission were all included in the list. Since 1958, however, there has not been the same determination to bring the records of quasi-national bodies within the scope of the Act; thus the British Steel Corporation is not so included. The records of courts and tribunals, even those which function purely locally, however, are public records.

Public records of local provenance may be deposited locally, and for this purpose the Lord Chancellor may authorize a 'place of deposit'. It is customary for the Public Record Office to inspect any intended place of deposit before the official authorization is issued, and in many cases the physical standards of conservation available in these places have been improved as a result of the inspection. The Act, however, does not mention what the standards of a local archives service should be, and the duty of inspecting and reporting on places of deposit does not constitute a co-ordinating service covering local archives establishments.(14) Places of deposit for local public records include, besides local government archives offices, many libraries and some museums. The records concerned are usually those of local courts (quarter sessions, magistrates' and coroners' courts) but in many cases also include records of hospitals belonging to the former regional boards of the National Health Service.

The Act appoints a Keeper of Public Records, and outlines certain of his powers and duties. He is to 'take all practicable steps for the preservation of records under his charge', and 'shall have power to do all such things as appear to him necessary or expedient for maintaining the utility of the Public Record Office.' These things include: making indexes and guides to records, publications 'concerning the activities of and facilities provided by the Public Record Office'; regulating conditions of access by the public; making copies of records, accepting and keeping other records, making special arrangements for film or technically different records; and lending out records for exhibition.(15)

The 1967 Act reduces the general restriction on access from fifty to thirty years, and there are certain other provisions governing particular categories of records on a national basis.

Manorial records. Records of manorial courts, which often bear upon the title to private property, are private records, the property of the lord of the manor. However, since the Law of Property Act, 1922, they have been subjected to controls, and these controls have been codified in the Manorial Documents Rules.

All manorial records are in the 'charge and superintendence' of the Master of the Rolls, and may not be removed from England and Wales without his consent. Owners of such records must report their whereabouts, and a register of these reports is kept by the Historical Manuscripts Commission. Manorial records must also be kept in satisfactory conditions, and the Master of the Rolls may direct them to be deposited in suitable institutions, including local archives offices.(16)

Tithe records. Records relating to the commutation of tithe were also placed under the control of the Master of the Rolls by the Tithe Act, 1936. He has issued rules, and may direct such records to be deposited in local institutions, including archives offices.(17) A register of the records also is kept by the Historical Manuscripts Commission.

Archives of the established church. The Parochial Registers and Records Measure, 1929, established that the bishop of a diocese had some superintendence over the archives of his ecclesiastical parishes.(18) He may direct that these records should be adequately cared for, either in their parish or by a diocesan record office appointed by him. The bishop may also apply to the county court to oblige any person who has come into possession of parish registers of baptisms, marriages or burials to return them to their legal owners, the incumbent or churchwardens. Apart from this, the measure does not determine what diocesan record offices should do. In many cases they contain the archives of the diocese and other ecclesiastical jurisdictions, and frequently the bishop has appointed the local archives office for this purpose.(19)

Local government archives. Legal provision for these authorities is of two kinds:
(i) There is a general duty on the officers of local authorities to keep their records in a proper condition. This duty stems from a long tradition, but is specifically based upon successive local government Acts. For many years the principal of these were the Municipal Corporations Act, 1882, for towns, and the Local Government Act, 1933, for counties.(20) These Acts established that the clerk to the authority (Town Clerk in boroughs, Clerk to the County Council in counties) were the officers responsible for the custody of records. Clerks of other authorities were likewise considered responsible for the records of their councils, though in the case of the smallest sub-units of local government—the civil parishes—deposit of the records elsewhere was authorized. The Acts did not specify what activities constituted proper custody of records, but they were sometimes generously interpreted, and it is from these general powers that most local record offices originated. In other cases, the clerks did not interpret their powers and duties so widely, and have not conformed to adequate standards either in custody, storage or use of records. The

general provisions as to 'proper arrangements' for records of local
government authorities are continued under the ruling Act of the
present day.(21)

(ii)   Local authority record offices, that is, public archives
services for local areas, are governed by the Local Government
(Records) Act, 1962. This act authorized certain local authorities
to allocate resources to the exploitation of their own archives (by
providing for access, for lists, indexes and guides, publications and
exhibitions); and it authorized them to acquire, by purchase, gift or
deposit, records 'of general or local interest'. The powers under
this Act were restricted to local authorities of the highest class,
that is, counties and county boroughs—and in other cases those
authorities which had been specifically authorized by a statutory
instrument under the hand of the minister responsible (at present
the Secretary of State for the Environment). Under the Local
Government Act, 1972, the powers of the 1962 Act pass
automatically to the new counties and metropolitan counties,
other bodies being under the necessity of applying for orders from
the Secretary of State.(22)

   None of these provisions applies to the Greater London area,
where the ruling statute, broadly similar in these respects, is the
London Government Act, 1963. One difference is that in London
the Local Government (Records) Act, 1962, is modified to allow
both the Greater London Council and the London Boroughs to
exercise the specified powers.(23)

   At the time of the passing of the Local Government (Records)
Act, the responsible ministry issued a circular letter in which it
explained to local authorities its intention in implementing the
Act. In this letter advice is given which amounts to a recognition
that definite standards of efficiency and resources are expected of
a local archives office. Clerks of authorities are asked to ensure
that they have made provision for custody and preservation of
their most important records, allowing for future accruals. They
are urged to review their records, and to make selections for
retention and disposal. In these matters smaller authorities are
advised to seek the advice of archivists employed by larger ones,
and when access facilities are considered, there should be
catalogues and 'a well-staffed and well-equipped records
department'. The circular makes no specific requirements as to
the meaning of 'well-staffed and well-equipped'; but its advice is
good, and it is a pity that it has not been more widely acted
upon.(24)

Scotland and Northern Ireland

This exceedingly brief outline of statutory provisions for archives services in England and Wales ignores the rather different situation in Scotland and Northern Ireland, which have their own provisions. In Northern Ireland there is in effect only one archives institution, which combines the functions exercised in England by both the Public Record Office and the local record offices. The Public Record Office of Northern Ireland operates under the Public Records Act (Northern Ireland), 1923.(25)

In Scotland the origins of the Scottish Record Office are of some antiquity, but the ruling statute is the Public Registers and Records (Scotland) Act, 1948, supplemented by an administrative agreement of 1962 which brings in transfer and review arrangements similar to those operated in England. The Scottish Record Office, acting under an older Public Records (Scotland) Act, 1937, has customarily accepted on deposit the records of local authorities and other non-public records, including (under an agreement of 1960) many older archives of the established Church.

Nevertheless, the larger Scottish cities set up archives services of their own under general provisions of the Local Government (Scotland) Act, 1947.(26) A new form of local government has now been introduced in Scotland as a result of which several of the regions have assumed archival duties.(27) Meanwhile Scotland has developed regional surveys as an important archival tool, institutionalized in the National Register of Archives (Scotland).

Private Archives

Finally, although there is, apart from the special cases noted above, no statutory provision whatever for the disposal or maintenance of private archives, however valuable, there are three instruments bearing upon these which should be mentioned:

(i) The Royal Commission on Historical Manuscripts, established in 1869, now operates under the authority of a Royal Warrant of 1959. It has the general duty of inquiring into the whereabouts and nature of valuable deposits of private archives. The commission now maintains the National Register of Archives, a national documentation centre for lists of archive holdings, and also investigates holdings of archives in the hands of non-governmental institutions and individuals, and runs a publication programme.(28)

(ii)   Under the terms of various Finance Acts, it is possible for owners of accumulations of valuable archives to sell them to national or local institutions under special terms favourable to the institution which exempt the seller from payment of estate duty and capital gains tax. Such accumulations or collections may also be presented to the nation in lieu of estate duty. To this end, the Government has made available a fund which may under certain circumstances be drawn upon by archives offices (and other cultural institutions) if they find themselves able to acquire valuable collections by purchase.(29)

(iii)   There is statutory control over the export of manuscripts, including archives, through the Export Licensing Regulations. In this connection archives are not distinguished from other objects of historical or artistic value (including photographs), and the only restriction on their export is that, if they are more than seventy years old and worth more than £100, an export licence is necessary. Licences have usually been easy to obtain, and it is probable that many documents or collections have been exported without them. A proposal was made in the late 1960s for a statutory requirement that photocopies should be made of archives or manuscripts to be exported, and these presented to national collections; but it was not implemented, though it is surely along these lines that export control should be attempted.(30)

The legislative provision in the British Isles for archives is complicated because it has developed gradually from pre-existing practices; in other countries it has sometimes been possible to devise legislation *ab initio*. The archival legislation in force in most countries is set out in four volumes of the journal *Archivum*.(31) Internationally there has been a marked development in such legislation since about 1965, so that national peculiarities have been reduced, and there has been something of an approach to international standards. However, many countries still operate under archival laws which are outdated and do not offer sufficient guidance and protection.

Function and Control of Archives Services

Like all administrative services, archives offices are run under the supervision of appropriate bodies or officers in the administrative structure of their employing authority, and there must be some specific governing or controlling body in whose hands is the determination (after proper advice) of policy, scope of activities and finance. It is of major concern to the archives office, of course, that this controlling body should be properly advised, and that it should have the standing and resources, within the overall administrative structure, to allow the archives service to operate efficiently.

In central government, the national archives is naturally one of the responsibilities of a minister, who reports on its activities to the cabinet, or council of ministers, or to the legislature, in accordance with the constitution of the country. In many countries the archives come under the portfolio of either a minister with central controlling or co-ordinating duties, a minister concerned with leisure, cultural or amenity services, or a minister concerned with education. The basic choice is between treating the archives as an administrative common service, viewed primarily as part of the internal running of the government, and treating it as an educational, cultural or amenity service, viewed primarily as an institution for public resort, where research is carried on. A healthy archives service partakes of the character of both of these.(32)

In archives offices which are not those of central government the same dilemma arises. In smaller administrations, such as local government, the archives service traditionally has been the responsibility of one of the specialized committees to which aspects of the council's work has been delegated. Here again the choice has been between central committees concerned with common services such as finance or general management, public amenity committees, and specific programme committees, including those responsible for libraries or museums. The tendency of modern administrative theory, however, is to reduce the number of specialized committees, to subject their operations to the supervision of superior policy and planning bodies, and to confine their role to general policy formulation and financial planning, leaving the detailed administration in the hands of permanent officials.(33) The purpose of control structures, of course, is to see that a sound plan is adopted, and that adequate resources are given to its accomplishment.

To provide the proper specialist services, the archivist must be able to negotiate directly with departmental heads and chief officers in matters concerning the management of their records. Normally this would mean that the archivist should also rank as a

departmental head, where this term means that he controls one of
the many distinct units based upon function within the employing
authority. Where these are grouped into agglomerations of
services under general headings (social services, transport
services, administrative services, etc.), the archives will form one
section or division of (probably) the administrative programme
area, which will be appropriate because, in such an arrangement,
there must be considerable lateral communication between
programmes and departments. Lateral communication is indeed
of vital importance to a small common service such as archives.
For this reason such services do best in administrations which are
not rigidly hierarchical, but permit or promote communication
between departments at intermediate level.

Archives services within business organizations are in general
subject to the same principles, and to the same conflict between
administrative functions (often the responsibility of the central
administrative department) and 'cultural' functions (often the
responsibility of the public relations department). The services
offered to administration by the archives will be judged
particularly by their economy and general usefulness, and may be
run in close association with such services as technical
documentation and specialist libraries. The research and
exploitation side will be subject to the policy of the organization
which governs the allocation of funds to research or public
relations, and it is possible that this allocation may be made
capriciously, or may vary with the general financial state of the
firm or with the personal outlook of directors.

Since it is not really possible to conceive of an archives service
which is not fundamentally concerned with research and with the
exploitation of the archives, a business records service which did
not develop these aspects, or was subject to excessive financial
restraints on this side, would presumably look for some alternative
way of discharging the function. One way would be to delegate,
by deposit agreements or otherwise, the research and reference
function to a publicly provided archives office or institution, or
possibly to a university. It is possible, therefore, to divide these
two basic functions of an archive service—administration and
research—but clearly the success of this kind of arrangement
would depend on the firmness of the agreement and its
continuing nature.

It is indeed possible to divide an archives service even more
basically into its components, allocating each to a distinct

organization. Some of the possibilities inherent in such a division are discussed in chapter 13.

Staffing

Programmes are put into operation by distributing specific responsibilities and areas of duty among the staff. Each person should be given a field for which he is responsible. He should be clear as to what resources in personnel, material, accommodation and time are given him, but within these limitations a responsible worker should be left to carry out his programme in the best way possible. Close or interfering supervision is not necessary where there is adequate provision for disseminating information on the achievement of aims or the fulfilment of programmes, for criticism and advice on the effectiveness of the methods used, and for ensuring co-ordination between personnel.(34) An important part of the system is the establishment of regular staff meetings, at which detailed reports are made on the progress of the various sections and departments within their programmes, there is discussion of problems encountered, and timetables, priorities, and so forth are authoritatively adjusted.

Figure 1.1 (page 11) gives an outline staffing structure which provides for six service divisions or sections, in this case labelled 'records', 'field', 'repository services', 'technical', 'searchroom services' and 'publication/development'. This is therefore an example of an internal division of responsibility by function. In many ways this would seem to be the most natural way of dividing the office's work, especially since some of the more technical processes, for example repair, always have to have a separate functional division.

However, there are two drawbacks to adopting a staffing structure of this type. One is that there is a critical size: there must be at least one competent person in charge of each section, so that the model given demands a professional staff of a least seven (the six section heads and the director). The second drawback is best described by Posner:(35)

Archival materials cannot be subjected, like books, to the various necessary processes one after another in sharply delimited divisions, because in this fashion each of the divisions acquires only a partial knowledge of the unitary nature and individual character of the holdings that have passed through its hands.

The best alternative would seem to be to divide the work of the service into practicable programmes based upon archive groups. An archives office of this sort might be expected to have two major divisions, dealing with the official and the non-official (deposited) holdings of archives respectively. Further subdivisions might follow subdivisions of these holdings. It is frequently necessary, too, to modify these subdivisions to take account of the actual topographical arrangement of the archive holdings. Where series are housed in different buildings, it may well be necessary to divide responsibility for their processing in a parallel way (figure 1.2).

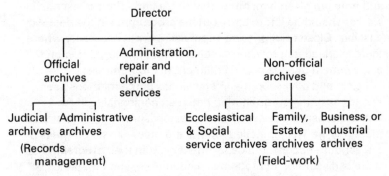

1.2 Staffing structure in a local archives office.

In very small archives offices still less administrative subdivision will be possible, and the staffing structure will be a simple allocation of duties so as to distribute the work-load suitably. A typical smaller archives office might divide its work on these lines:(36)

Chief archivist. Legal responsibility, planning and policy, general oversight, external relations.

Senior assistant archivist (deputy). Oversight of reader services, detailed work of assistant archivists, field programmes.

Assistant archivists. Each will have a work-load listing archive groups and collections, and maintaining reader services. Two special responsibilities are allocated to one assistant each:
    (a) copying facilities, library, publications
    (b) accession routines and progress.
All assistants undertake fieldwork and publications.

Repairer: repair, security, display.

Clerical assistant: filing, stationery, inventories, standby supervision of searchroom.

General assistant: production of documents, labelling, boxing, condition of shelving.

In deciding on a system of division of responsibility, important factors are the personal characters and interests of the staff. It may be true that an archivist should be able to undertake any legitimate task in the management of archives, and in particular should not become a specialist in any historical period; nevertheless, an archivist in post must necessarily become an expert in the content of the archives under his care, and must also be conversant with the research interests which depend upon these. In allocating the office's resources in personnel, therefore, it is often advisable to take into account the personal interests and knowledge of individuals, and to deploy them where they are happiest and most useful. In very large archives offices it is indeed often customary to divide responsibilities by historical period, having service divisions devoted to earlier, or to later, series of archives. But these divisions must be along the lines of archive or record groups or series rather than by date, and certainly not by the subject or content of particular documents.

There are two conflicting needs in archives work. On the one hand, archive groups are indivisible, and the archivist must be familiar with their make-up and content. On the other hand, the office needs its programmes to be developed by people who can give their full attention to their operation. In allocating the work, both of these needs must somehow be met.(37)

Budgeting

The Society of Archivists has recommended that 'the annual estimates should be drawn up by the archivist and, where the overall policy of the authority permits, submitted by him.'(38) This is an adaptation to British circumstances of the recommendation made by Dr Posner in his proposed standards for American State archives services, under the heading of budgetary requirements:(39)

1 Whether an independent agency or part of a parent agency, the archival agency should have a separate budget. . . .
2 The head of the archival agency should be permitted to defend his requests before the head of the parent agency . . . before the budget officer, commission, or other body of the executive branch; and before the legislature.

In drawing up his estimates, the archivist should ask his assistants and subordinates in the same office to prepare draft estimates so far as they relate to the different sections for which they are responsible. All archivists therefore should have some basic knowledge of the financing and budgetary systems of their employing authorities, and participate in them in due degree.

It is not yet possible to suggest a universal or standard size of budget allocation for an archive service in proportion to the income of a whole employing authority; this will depend on the nature of the programmes adopted. In his study of archival infrastructures, Delmas has attempted a relative standard in certain areas.(40) In staffing, he indicates: (a) an irreducible minimum of professional staff to deal with planning and supervising the service; and (b) a supplementary number of officers to carry out specific programmes. The number of these would be determined by the extent of the programmes and of the holdings of the office: perhaps one might arrive at a formula for this. There might, for example, be one professional archivist for each group of archive-creating agencies served, aided by one executive officer for each kilometre of shelving occupied. Building space is clearly related to the amount of material held, and technical services to the state of the documents and the degree of development in the exploitative services.

The fact that there is an irreducible minimum of staffing and other resources which must be achieved before the service can reach the stage of being staffed in proportion to the responsibilities developed demonstrates that there is a critical size both of an archives office and of the employing authority which has set it up. Employing authorities below this size will do best to delegate their archival work to agents where this is possible; archives offices below this size will not be able to discharge their professional functions. In some countries non-government archive services have fallen markedly below this standard. In Britain, for example, the Society of Archivists in 1968 found that(41) it may be taken that an:

annual cost figure of £15,000 to £20,000 was, at the time of the survey, no more than reasonably adequate for the average local repository, and it must be concluded that the majority have inadequate—often very inadequate— resources on which to function. This suggests that too many organizations are not adequately accepting their obligations; that too many archivists are too patient in endeavouring to make bricks without straw; and that some organizations cannot, on their own, support a repository, and should join forces to make more viable units. The further point can be made, that only a minority of local authority record offices have their own separate and distinct finances. The question arises as to how far this obscures their difficulties, and hampers professional officers in pleading a convincing financial case.

A viable service is one which can justify itself in financial terms, and which is given the opportunity to do so.

2 Records Management

Records management can be a very wide-ranging activity, covering the creation and design of records as well as their supersession and transfer to records centres or to the archives. A moderate and practical view of records management, however, is that its main concern is the control of the processes whereby records become archives. Withdrawal of non-current records, their handling and storage, and their evaluation as potential archives are the essentials of the subject.

The final objectives of an archives service are to do with research; but in the provision of a documentation of the past, as also in dealing with the economics of records storage, there are quantifiable benefits which may induce an authority to embark on records management schemes. Indeed a complex organization nowadays has little choice but to do so, for otherwise it will not cope with the jungle of information or the quantities of records it needs and generates.

The archivist should put the past at the disposal of the administration, which normally is ignorant of it, by providing a documentation as complete as possible on everything which, in the administrative records of the past, can assist in the solution of present problems. He should even shape contemporary administrative documentation in view of foreseeable needs of future historians.(1)

To cope with both these problems a records management system will set about ensuring that it does in fact come to hold all the documents it should, and at as early a date as possible. But management does not necessarily mean possession. Any responsibility exercised in practice for providing information will mean that records staff will become accustomed very rapidly to

finding out where groups of documents are originated and held
which record valuable information bearing on the activities of the
employing authority. They will find means to consult these
documents, even when they are not transferred to the records
centre, and in consequence there will be pressure on the creating
departments to transfer them to the centre, where they can be
covered by the system of finding aids. But it is not essential that
all records should always be transferred to the immediate control
of the records service; administration demands constant dialogue
between the staffs of related departments, including that of the
records service.

The records staff will make efforts to collect materials which
may be only peripherally records of the employing authority but
which are connected with it in some way and contain information
on its activities. These may include printed matter, publicity,
photographs, newspaper or other public comment, and
periodicals. A further development, which in some cases may be
vital, is the collection of quasi-private papers of staff or persons
connected, or formerly connected, with the work of the authority,
or even the collection of oral evidence, recollections by former
staff or people who are or were affected by the work of the
authority. Here there are direct parallels with the collection by
archives offices of accumulations of archives of non-official origin,
and with the collection of documentation by planning, research
and technical library services. Records staff should be allowed to
take part in the planning of future information and documentation.
services.

The consequences of not providing records and documentation
services centrally are the dissipation of resources in current
administration, and the devaluation of the cultural services which
are at the end of the line. If the records and documentation
facilities of the employing authority are inadequate for its needs in
administration and in policy-making, then the archives services
which, directly or indirectly, it provides or contributes to will be
inadequate for research needs. The long-term cost of this
inadequacy could be high.

Records management should therefore be a structured central
service with access to all the principal records of the employing
authority and with a programme for acquiring informative
material; with specific responsibilities for providing and exploiting
this material; and with a good relationship with other information
and documentation services in the same organization as

illustrated in figure 2.1. This implies that the archivist dealing with these matters must have a position in the staffing structures of the employing authority which will give weight to his opinion in the disposal and use of its records, allow him to make the necessary agreements with departmental heads and their staffs, and to acquire the necessary resources. It also implies that the records management system will operate within defined limits.

2.1 Relationships of records services

The range of activities to which records are submitted during their lifetime are summarized in figure 2.2.
In this range of activities there is a movement, running broadly from the top of the table downwards, from activities intended to refine and improve the quality of records as instruments of administration, to activities intended simply to control records as they are or happen to be. In selecting the point on this table at

Design of records systems (Paperwork management)	Design of forms Design of case records Abstracts of information Statistical reports
Operation of records services	Control of mail Filing systems and practices Circulation of papers Registry operation Organization and Methods
Retirement of non-current records	Record storage Retirement processes Selection Retrieval and reference Disposal processes Transfer to archives

2.2 Records operations

which his operations are to commence, the archivist is
determining the degree of influence he is to exercise on altering
(and, it is to be hoped, improving) the quality of the record. The
archivist has a professional interest in all these stages, but in all
the activities below 'retirement' they are direct and unavoidable.

Records management is undertaken for the benefit of reference
and research. It is an activity totally concerned with the needs of
communication and of scholarship. Though effective records
management may well lead to certain economies in the
administrative processes of the employing authority and in the
cost of storage, these economies are not the object of the
enterprise. Nor by itself is the achievement of greater efficiency in
the retrieval of information. The whole object of an archival
records management programme is the furtherance of scholarship
and the determination of fact. In this the archivist as records
manager is no different from the traditional archivist. If it were not
so, then records management work could be entirely left to
administrative personnel. But an archivist is specially qualified in
two things: the selection of material for its research value, and the
exploitation of material in research itself. If he is to be concerned
with current records at all, it must be in connexion with the
furtherance of research; and, conversely, this is the reason why
records management work should be done to the highest possible
standards.

Surveying Current Records in the Organization
Prior to all other records management work is a knowledge of
what records are to be managed.(2) This information is needed,
not only to plan the records programmes and to determine the
resources needed—for example, in space for storage—but also,
and more importantly, in making the appraisal and selection
which is the records manager's basic duty. Whoever draws up the
schedules, or whoever carries out the selection of records, should
first know what information is conveyed by the whole body of
records produced by the employing authority. It is clear that no
one, whether an archivist or not, would destroy a record unless he
first understood, at least in outline, the relationship which that
record bore to other records in existence. The kind of records
compiled by the department and the pattern of information stored
in them must be understood before any thorough weeding and
destruction of departmental records can be done.

Although a records officer must acquire and use this overall knowledge of his authority's records (and related records elsewhere), he can acquire the knowledge needed in one of two ways. He can get it by experience in sitting at the receipt of records and answering inquiries based upon them. To a large extent all records centres or archives offices, and their staffs, do acquire this working knowledge, and where the turnover of staff is not too great the value of it is hard to overestimate. There are circumstances, however, in which it is necessary to take deliberate steps to acquire it; these may include situations where the staff is new, or where responsibility for a particular group of departmental records is newly imposed, or where new or greatly developed functions or powers are operated in a department. Also it is necessary to find some way of initiating archive students or beginners in archives work. It is in these circumstances that a systematic survey of records might be considered; but, since the intellectual control of records is one of the objectives of the archives services, it is hard to envisage any circumstances in which a survey of current records would not be advisable, at least as an initial departure.

The survey on site

Work on a survey of current records begins by establishing an agreement with the head of the department whose records are to be surveyed, and in practice the agreement of the chief administrative officer of the department is desirable as well. At a preliminary discussion the archivist will outline his objectives and his methods, and the agreement which results should cover dates and times of day at which the survey will be made, the names of the records staff who will do it, and the order in which they will take the various offices.

The records staff will take the opportunity to obtain some basic information about the staffing structure and delegation of duties in the department to be surveyed, and relate these to the physical location of offices; there will be administrative diagrams and directories which can be used for this. They will also wish to be satisfied that the middle and lower grades of staff in the department are in fact informed and forewarned about the survey, and that they understand the objectives of it. If this is not done, there will be delays and inconvenience, and possibly suspicion or hostility. When this preliminary work has been done, the records staff will be briefed, and the work sheets designed and produced for them.

The work sheet to be employed will be adapted to suit the job in hand, but is likely to conform quite closely to existing models;(3) a specimen layout is shown in figure 2.3. A supply should be provided for each worker on the survey, in sufficient numbers to allow their free use.

Records Survey Work sheet	Department: Section: Office (Room No.):				Date	
(1)	(2)	(3)	(4)	(5)		(6)
Record series title and description	Date range	Status	Frequency of Reference	Type of Storage		Storage Capacity
	From	To					

2.3 Work sheet for records survey

Ideally, a survey should be conducted by as few people as possible. A quick job in a large department may necessitate the deployment of a number of staff; but, since the objective is to establish intellectual control over the records series found, the more it can be the work of one person, preferably the archivist himself, the better. On the other hand, adequate support or assistance is equally necessary, and this should mean at least one assistant to write down the surveyor's observations and file away the completed work sheets.

It is desirable that the survey should be completed within a relatively short time, and this is normally possible, since a properly planned survey is not a lengthy job. The survey working-team should probably begin in the mid-morning of each of the days agreed, so allowing the staff of the department time to complete their initial routines and to clear their incoming mail. Disruption of the department should not be great, but each office will need to supply one person to explain the nature and content of the various record series.

The survey may be taken section by section and office by office, either on a geographical basis (taking the next office according to physical location) or on a systematic basis (taking the next office in the departmental staffing plan), but care should be taken to see that each work sheet is adequately identified. The survey team will enter the main office of the division or section and make contact with the officer in charge there. With him, or with the person he appoints, they will go round the section describing on their work sheets each record series kept. Having completed the tour of the office, taking the record series one by one topographically, they will then move on to the next, the surveyor dictating to his assistant the descriptions to be inserted on the work sheet. Only one record series should be written on each work sheet: this is important.

A record series is a recognizable subdivision of records, with a title peculiar to itself which is commonly used in the office where it is kept.(4) Record series may vary greatly in size and character, one from another. A series may consist of one volume (perhaps a register of cases) or a whole filing-system containing many hundreds or even thousands of files, classified according to a filing scheme, and with a common finding system.

There is sometimes a difficulty in deciding which are record series and which are unrelated units of records. Although common sense may often dictate the decision in doubtful cases, as a general rule it is better to take a small number of larger groups of records than a greater number of smaller ones. But this rule should not be permitted to confuse under one title what are actually distinct record series with different uses and forms, for confusion at this point will lead to confusion in the archives later.

Distinguishing and naming record series demands the exercise of judgement, but in every case the actual daily usage in the office of origin should be taken as the guide. Archival lists and the labels given to different types of record should, if possible, always follow the administrative usage of those who created and used the record.

For speed and accuracy in using the work sheets, particularly when they are being written up in the bustle of a strange office, it is desirable to establish a number of conventions, which can be used by whoever writes down the information discovered. These conventions may include the following:

The date range (column 2 in figure 2.3) may be taken by whole years, earliest and latest document seen. Current files should be left with an open terminal date (e.g. 1972–   ). In some cases, such as regular returns or case records, a monthly, or even a weekly, date is needed. The simplest form should be taken, consistent with identification of the record's place in a series.

Status (column 3) requires a decision as to whether the record series in question is a main or original series, or whether it is a duplicate of another series held elsewhere. Some difficulty is found at times with this question, since an original file will of course contain many carbon or other duplicated papers, but will itself remain part of an original series.

The best example of original and duplicated series is the minutes or proceedings of governing committees or bodies. The original record is the main series kept by the clerk and signed by the chairman: this is the formal, legal record. The minutes, how-ever, are usually circulated to executive departments, so that a record of proceedings is available there and so that action can be taken. These are, of course, duplicate series, but a possible complication arises where these copy minutes are incorporated into a new, original series of records generated within the department.

Frequency of reference. For column 4 a classification should be established to provide a useful scale against which the degree of current use of the record can be judged. It is important for this scale not to be over-elaborate: in a sense the crudest judgement is the most workable. A four-part classification has been found to answer the various stages into which most records fall:

A indicates papers which have not yet become formal records, but which carry important information used in the office; examples are drafts, sketches or notes kept by executive administrators in and around their desks. At a certain stage these papers are systematized and placed upon the office's formal record, but prior to this they can be used by those who know their way around the office. The importance of papers in this category is that in loosely disciplined administrations, especially where (as in British local government or in business) there is no registry, many will never actually be incorporated into B systems. Wherever this happens, an informal system of recording and reference grows up in the office, additional to and by-passing the official record system.

B is the formal record, the current office record system. It will be a common resource which all in the department or section can call upon, and there will properly be some attempt to ensure that in fact all appropriate records are placed in it.

C indicates records which have begun to pass out of full currency, but which at times are still required for current reference.

D refers to 'dead' records which in practice are so rarely used for current reference, that their presence in the office is not justified. Typically records of this type are kept in closed record storage, and not in the working offices.

It is obvious that, unlike the others, category C is not always a direct physical description of a record series. Most usually a record series continues in use under B, but particular documents or files within it pass into category C with the lapse of time. Where this is so, the record series can be classified as BC, and this symbol indicates that the originating department has a records management problem to solve; that is, the regular closure of files or items from its current system, and their removal to store. In extreme cases one may see a current system which has been allowed to retain records which are grossly out of currency, in which case the symbol BCD may be used.

In using a four-part classification for frequency of reference, it is important to be clear that it is not a progression from constant use (A) through less constant use (B,C) to dead (D). In fact in terms purely of frequency of use, B should be the category most in use, and A merely indicates the presence of papers which may or may not pass into the record system, but which are of importance sufficient to be noticed.

Type of storage (column 5). This means the manner in which the record series is kept and operated; whether it is in volumes, cards, vertical or drawer filing, cupboards or parcels. Each of the most common types may have a symbol or letter to avoid having to write it out in full on each work sheet, and to avoid ambiguity it is best to work these out beforehand.

Space. Column 6 is an important part of the survey, since it is this which will allow a calculation of the bulk and cost of the records. However it is usually possible to insert the correct figures here at a later time since, if the information in column 5 is properly filled out, the application of a conversion factor will provide the figure for column 6.

Thus one standard four-drawer filing cabinet is known to occupy 0.35 square metres of floor space (in office management 0.6 square metres have to be allowed for these cabinets, since there must be space for the drawers to open fully); and to contain up to about one half cubic metre of records. Similarly the characteristics of other standard furniture is known. Where non-standard containers or equipment are used, some measurement is needed, and the surveyor should take tape measures with him. But even here, most records are stacked upon shelves or surfaces which have a standard capacity (one metre lengths, etc). Finally, there is an average relationship between square metres of floor space and cubic metres of records stored upon it, as in the case of the standard filing cabinets mentioned above. If the number of cabinets is known, the area of floor space is known, and from this multiplication by the agreed factor will produce a practical approximation to the cubic capacity of the records. Owing to the way records are stored in offices, a measurement of linear capacity is not normally meaningful.

Compiling the Report
When the work sheets have been filled in and the fieldwork completed, the records staff must set about processing the findings. The work sheets should be checked, so that figures are clear and unambiguous, the headings of the sheets filled in, and the figures for column 6 added. The sheets may then be sorted into different arrangements, to provide summary information in different forms, for incorporation into the final report. This report should contain a summary analysis of the record series identified, their size and characteristics, and an overall finding on the total quantities of records, their ranges of frequency of reference, the space occupied by them, with a costing of this, and recommendations as to disposal.

To establish a list of the record series identified, it is necessary to decide whether to make out the list as one long table, covering all records produced by the department, or in several sections, relating to the functional divisions of the department surveyed. There can be no rigid rule on which is preferable. Smaller departments which customarily act as a unit will demand a single unified list; larger departments where divisions have distinct functions may demand separate treatment for each. A decision must be made on this, which depends upon the way the records are actually kept and used and on the habits of work in the

department. In either case, however, the list of record series can
be made up by sorting the worksheets into the required order, and
copying the relevant information into list form, using appropriate
tabulations; once the sorting is done, this work is clerical.

There will be some worksheets which on final reflection seem
to describe peripheral papers of no continuing importance. These
can be dropped at this stage, so that the report can concentrate
upon the main series. It may also be found that complementary
series or sub-series of records occur in different divisions or
storage places. For example, the earlier files of one series may be
found in an office where the operating division once worked, and
the later files will be kept in the division's present offices. Many
series will be partly in closed and partly in current storage. These
cases will be easily identified when the worksheets are sorted,
and final tabulation will include a reference to the whereabouts of
separated sub-series.

At the end of this part of the collating process, a list of record
series arranged either in logical or in alphabetical order will
emerge. When this is done, the work sheets may be re-sorted to
collate other pieces of information: capacity of principal record
series, total capacity of all records, proportion of records storage
to overall office space by divisions, proportion of records in each
of the frequency of reference categories. A separate calculation
may be made of these factors concerning non-current records in
closed storage. Finally a figure for the annual cost of records
maintenance can be obtained by multiplying the figure calculated
for the area of floor space by the annual rent charged for the use
of this space; this latter figure can be obtained from the
administrative head of the department, from the land and property
department of the employing authority, or from comparison with
prevailing office rents, which are usually a matter of public
knowledge.

The report will conclude with recommendations for the
management and disposal of the records. It may be suggested, for
example, that non-current records should be transferred to the
records centre, and that semi-current records should be moved
out of current records systems. From this it may follow that a
process for identifying decline in frequency of reference, and
regular closing of files should be adopted.(5) In all cases the
recommendations may be backed by a comparison of the costs
involved.

The completed report will be submitted to the head of the

department surveyed, and its recommendations discussed with him; it may also have a wider circulation as a useful reference document within the employing authority, and there may also be a strong case for publishing it, since national standards are not as yet established, and records officers and archivists need to know a great deal more in detail about the work of their colleagues in other places. The report and the work sheets also form part of the control tools of the archives office; they will be suitably filed there for reference by the staff, and may be periodically updated.

3 Operating a Records Centre

When records are withdrawn from the systems used for current records, they must be sent somewhere where they do not clutter up current working space but where they can be stored usefully and cheaply for the remainder of their useful existence. In some cases it is possible to send them to the archives for this period; but this is not desirable, since archival storage must be constructed to high standards, and there will inevitably be a considerable mass of records of relatively low quality which have to be kept for a number of years for legal, accounting or other reasons.

The custom has developed of setting up an intermediate store for such non-current records; at one time this used to be called a 'limbo', but this designation is not satisfactory, as it implies that the records are necessarily inactive while there. In fact they are simply awaiting review or selection so as to pass into the archives (or to be destroyed) and are meanwhile quiescent. Such places are now called 'records centres'. Here the records retain their value to administrative departments, and their exploitation for other, research, purposes makes small beginnings, and for this reason they are increasingly referred to as 'pre-archival' records.(1) They are not, or should not be, simply dumped: they are centralized and administered, according to agreed methods, and the centre in which this is done has objectives and programmes which take their place with those of the archives service as a whole.

The following elements can be discerned among the objectives of a records centre.

Inflow. The records centre should receive and store all such records as are sent to it by the executive departments under arrangements made between them and the archivist, and it will aim at attracting the maximum quantity of useful records. This principle may well be modified in any particular case by special circumstances. The number and character of records sent in will be affected by such factors as cost of storage, availability of storage within departments, distance of departments from the centre, security or frequency of reference. In some cases ephemeral records could be economically disposed of directly by departments; in others the centre would receive these records too.

Reference. While they are in the centre, the records must be made available for consultation or issue to the originating department, or for consultation by such persons as the originating department may authorize (subject to the archivist's advice). Issue arrangements and accommodation for consultation *in situ* will obviously vary according to the facilities of the building. What is basic is that records in the centre must be accessible. Exploitation of informational values may be begun; in this case, the practice should be admitted as an objective.

Administration. The archivist will be responsible for the provision and working of finding aids relative to the records in the centre, provided that basic clerical work (essentially listing and boxing) is undertaken by the originating department as agreed with the archivist at or before the point of transfer. In principle it is immaterial whose staff carries out the routine work the records need: sorting, boxing, listing, registration, indexing, retrieval and return, and so on. The work could be done from start to finish by the archives (or records centre) staff, or, with somewhat less efficiency, it could be entirely done by departmental staff under the supervision of the archivist. But whoever does it must have the resources in staff and materials to do it.

It is assumed that in general the archives staff will be limited in relation to the tasks they have to do, and that therefore it is reasonable to expect the departmental staff to handle at least the bulk of the first listing. This leaves the archives staff to administer the records while they are in the centre. The division of labour seems reasonable, and this is a fairly usual system.

Outflow. No record should remain in the records centre permanently. The outflow of records should be governed by disposal schedules discussed and authorized by the employing authority. The archivist will be responsible for implementing these disposal schedules and for disposing of the records concerned. Of course, it is not necessary that destruction of records should be carried out by archives staff, if that is not convenient on other grounds. The essential is that drawing up disposal schedules should be the responsibility of the archivist. This is dealt with more fully in chapter 5.

Security. The archivist administers the records centre and associated services, but the records in it may be regarded as still the property of the originating departments, and security arrangements will be based on this principle. This again is a compromise. It would be perfectly possible for the records to become fully the 'property' of the records centre, and in smaller organizations this may indeed be the best policy. The practice of maintaining the 'ownership' of originating departments has the practical advantage that it solves a number of security problems, and tends to reassure the departments about the safety of using the system; though in respect of records generated by departments of one employing authority the terms 'ownership' and 'property' can only be used metaphorically.

The principles suggested here may—indeed will—be adjusted to meet particular circumstances. There are, however, five basic objectives which represent genuine archival requirements. To recapitulate briefly, these are that the inflow of records should represent the total documentation visualized in the archives plan; that records in store should be utilized to provide information; that records should be subject to control and should receive proper allocation of resources; that there should be a regulated outflow of records at the end of their administrative lives which will fine down the archival holdings to the most valuable core; and that there should be a proper attention to security.(2)

Physical Requirements and Layout

'Despite its importance, economy is not of course the paramount consideration in center operations. Safety of the records, particularly against their arch-enemy fire, is even more important. Furthermore, there would be no purpose in keeping the records if they were not usable when wanted. The standards that have been developed for judging the adequacy of buildings for center use in the United States reflect a merging of the need for economy, the need to protect the records, and operating needs.'(3)

Actually the paramount consideration in setting up a records centre may well be the site. In the USA the scale upon which the

National Archives and Records Service operates enables them to
have great freedom in deciding this. A federal records centre can
be constructed on a piece of empty land, near roads, and at points
which can be reached from all parts of the region served; but the
choice of actual site will be made on grounds of cheapness, and it
will certainly be well away from city centres. The user agencies
will have a constant traffic to and from the centres, using vans
and lorries. Elsewhere there is not the same scope for
constructions on this scale, or for decentralizing to this extent,
though industrial concerns organized on a large scale nationally
may approximate more closely to international patterns.(4)

In government the extent of the records to be administered has
meant that the costs of setting up a records centre within the
built-up area of the capital have had to be accepted. Records
storage is provided in Britain at the interdepartmental
intermediate record store at Hayes, Middlesex. Decentralization of
ministries to provincial cities, which is proceeding, introduces
complications, and may necessitate eventually some form of
regional records centre.(5) The same problems and solutions may
be seen in France, where the government has set up the *cité
interministérielle des archives*, in effect its principal records
centre, on the outskirts of Paris.(6)

In local government the scale of operation is of course vastly
smaller. This has its effect on the siting of records centres, for lack
of resources determines the extent to which the service can be
based upon transport facilities. To buy and run a van may mean
that the centre may not be financially viable. Where departments
are housed in old buildings in a city centre, they may find that they
have available accommodation which is suitable for records but
not for anything else; in this case the advantage of nearness will
outweigh any arguments the records centre might put up for
concentration of records. Where the authority is housed in a single
building complex, the records centre will tend to be part of the
complex, and will have its building standards dictated by those of
the main buildings: this again may cause difficulties in costing the
service, though it solves problems of environmental standards,
security, and the administration of reference services.

A successful records centre will necessarily be one that serves
a large organization, and there is a critical point of size; below this
the records centre will have to be integrated into the central
building complex, relying on its efficiency as an information
centre, and above it the centre may be external and relatively

remote, relying on the scale of the operation to justify itself. But it should not be forgotten that some form of records centre is necessary, even for quite small complex organizations, so that these problems cannot be solved by shelving them. It is of course possible to run a records centre jointly for two or more organizations, either as a commercial proposition or as a public service.(7)

It is necessary not to be doctrinaire when designing a records centre in circumstances where the size of the operation does not warrant a completely new construction situated in an open space away from administrative centres. It will probably always be best to accept and adapt existing buildings or parts of buildings, bearing in mind the three main considerations of storage space, ease of operation and cost in providing a service; of course certain minimum standards must be observed in all of these.(8)

The site and character of a records centre must be chosen by balancing a number of factors. Principal among these will be the cost of office space in executive departments, the degree of congestion there, the cost of space in fringe areas to which storage could be decentralized, the cost of transport to and from those fringe areas, and the degree of delay in provision of documents or information which is thought to be acceptable.

This last is a variable influenced by the size of the employing authority. Smaller organizations are less willing to accept delay in the production of records or information than are large ones. If it is acceptable for a requisitioned record to arrive, say, after two days, then a records centre well away from a city centre is reasonable. If it must arrive after some minutes or hours, then the records centre must remain near the central complex. Technological advances, such as the general installation of telex equipment, have mitigated the disadvantages of the remoteness of records centres out of town, but against this restrictions on traffic and the decline of postal services must be reckoned with. In view of all these things a successful choice of site is difficult, but this will determine the degree of success of the records administration generally for years ahead, and demands clear judgement and planning.

A records centre is basically a store, and for the most part it will be devoted to this function. However, it does need two other specialized areas, for the internal movement of records, and for administrative facilities. Since these two additional areas are essential, but occupy only a small proportion of the space (in the

USA about seven per cent of the whole floor space), it may be as
well to deal with them first.

Records movement areas

Records will be moved into the centre, to leave it at the end of
their allotted span, and from one point to another within the
storage area. Space must be allowed for this movement, including
space for vehicles (which may range from handtrolleys to fork-lift
trucks) to manoeuvre. Movement within the stacks is wasteful,
and the system should minimize it. But at the very least there will
be the movement associated with issue and replacement of
records on requisition.

On arrival records will have to be checked and undergo such
processes as labelling, perhaps reboxing, packing or cleaning,
before they can go to the shelves; there should be an area near a
loading entrance or bay, where they can remain while this is done.
Similarly records for disposal will have to be collected from
various points in the store, and taken to a suitable place to await
checking, amendment of lists, etc., and actual disposal. The area
where they wait should also, of course, be near the loading exit.
The design of these two places (which may not necessarily be
separate from each other) should allow for comfortable working
conditions for staff, and should be roomy enough to avoid
congestion and confusion.

Administrative areas

Office accommodation should receive the same design attention
as any central area office, and should conform to national
standards. The office will contain the apparatus for identification
and retrieval of records. It will also have any other facilities which
are necessary for utilizing the records and providing the service
required; these may include copying machinery, microfilm, basic
searchroom facilities either for officers of depositing departments
or for authorized searchers, and in some cases facilities for display
or exhibitions, a working reference library, or teaching space for
the instruction of records officers or clerks. The office area will be
so placed that it can command the entrance and exit, and so
control the use of the building.

In some cases, particularly with the records centres of large
industrial concerns or in regional centres, it has become
customary to provide high-quality archive storage conditions in
part of the building. This might include a 'vault' to contain

microform or non-documentary records such as magnetic tape, which require special storage conditions. There may also be a 'vital records' or a 'disaster plan' programme designed to ensure the preservation of the most important records in case of cataclysm. Similarly some centres contain laminating or other repair equipment. These facilities, however, are really archival, and normally should be provided in the archives building, rather than in the records centre. It is of the essence that records centres should be as simple as possible.

Storage areas

Most of the records centre will be taken up by storage. In planning this, regard will be had to capacity, environmental conditions, security, convenience of use and economy.

Typically, a records centre exists to receive retired records from a single employing authority and its departments. Since it is the duty of the archives service to know the contents and character of the records of this authority, it should be possible to calculate, within acceptable limits of accuracy, the likely intake of records over a given period. Allowance should be made for annual increases in the generation of records by departments, for the creation of new executive or research departments, and for increases in the proportion of records deposited by departments as experience and habit establish the use of the records centre.

Three factors need to be known in designing the services to go with the records centre: the size and rate of flow of the records coming in, the maximum storage required at any one point, and the rate of flow of records going out. Of these the most difficult to calculate is the last, and it cannot be undertaken until the disposal schedules have been completed. These factors also determine the answer to the question: How long must records remain in the records centre? The answer to this question also determines the standards accepted for environmental conditions. It is clear that some records (and these the most valuable, at least from a legal point of view) will have to remain there for many years, so that conditions must be reasonably good. The build-up of records within the centre will continue for a long time.

In theory there is a limit to the possible growth of a records centre, since every record in it will eventually go out, to make room for fresh records coming in. In practice, there is always a growth element, since the administration and activity of complex organizations always grows—there are always more records coming. Also, a well-run records service attracts more business as time goes by. There are always departments or accumulations of records which were overlooked in the original plan, and there is sometimes the possibility of taking records from external sources.

Planning the capacity of a records centre is therefore an imprecise business not even attempted in the standards for US federal centres, and the only clear principle is that it should have as much extra capacity (or, to put it another way, as many projected years of use before saturation) as possible. The longer the period over which the records centre will satisfy the needs of its records service, the more economical that service will be.

In actual practice, the size of records centres varies greatly. In the USA the official standards laid down by the national archives and records service provide that centres may hold up to two million cubic feet of records. A survey by Benedon in 1966 of six new records centres, which included a federal government centre, a state government centre and four belonging to private industrial corporations, showed that their capacities varied from 12,000 to 62,800 square feet of floor area, holding between 46,000 and 260,000 cubic feet of records.(9) The intermediate records store at Hayes for the British government contained, in 1971, 1,137,000 linear feet of shelving.(10) An example of a smaller purpose-built records centre is that of the Malaysian government, which can hold 21,930 linear feet.(11)

It is unfortunate that direct comparison of these two systems of measurement, linear and cubic, is almost impossible in the case of records centres, owing to the great variation in shelving types used. In settling the size of a new records centre, however, it must be possible to establish the ratio between cubic or linear measurements of holdings (whichever is used) and square measure of effective floor space. This means that the type of shelving must be determined at a very early stage in planning. Environmental conditions and security are subjects on which technical advice should be sought.

In shelving, the centre should be stacked out with maximum regard for economy, subject only to necessary access and working. Shelves should stand high and take standard boxes. It has been calculated that in records centre conditions, the ratio of cubic feet of records stored to square feet of floor space should be in the region of five to one. Since there will be an annual rent or charge based upon the square footage of floor space, which is directly comparable with the similar charge levied upon central office and storage space in central buildings, it is clear that the calculation of annual cost per cubic (or linear) foot of records can be directly and meaningfully compared with the costs of this in office areas. That this comparison should be a favourable one is, of course, most important to the success and usefulness of a records management scheme.

Figure 3.1 shows a model ground plan of a simple records centre serving the administration of a city: this is Singapore's record centre at Tanglin, using an adapted former military building.(12) A more complex records centre is that of the East Midlands regional records centre of the British Steel Corporation at Irthlingborough. This is also an adapted building, in this case a former miners' hostel. Figure 3.2 has been simplified.(13)

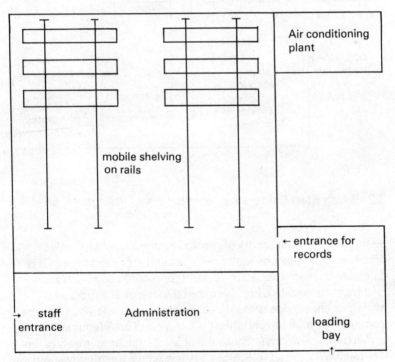

3.1 Records centre, Tanglin, Singapore.

Costs, Budgeting and Staff
Constructing a budget for a records service presents no special difficulties, and the only feature which distinguishes it from the budget of an archives service of the traditional kind is the need to

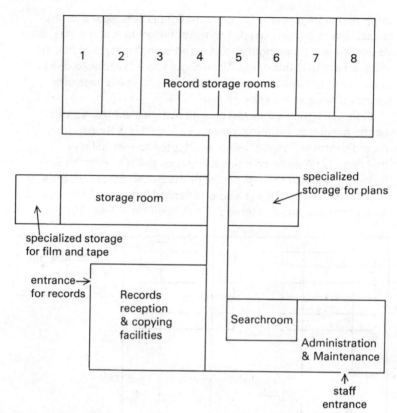

3.2 British Steel Corporation records centre, Irthlingborough

distinguish the basic costs of record storage in administrative
offices or buildings and in the records centre. For this reason it is
desirable to keep a separate account for records administration.

It must be recalled, however, that the object of a records
management service is the provision of a useful reference service
from records and, beyond this, the creation of an adequate and
comprehensive archive. These are objects valid in themselves, and
the machinery set up to achieve them is worth the money spent
on it. It is not desirable to proceed with any archives or records
scheme on any other basis. Cost-benefit analysis is a tool which
can be used to measure the efficiency of any particular means to a
desired end, but does not in itself establish what those ends
should be or what degree of value or priority they should have.

In the last resort, archives should be kept because, in the words of the Grigg report, 'the making of adequate arrangements for the preservation of its records is an inescapable duty of the government of a civilized state';(14) a duty, we may add, not confined to central government, or to government alone.

Nevertheless a comparison between storage costs of records in offices and in records centres (figure 3.3) will usually show a considerable margin in favour of the latter. With margins of this order the records centre has reasonable room for absorbing its administration costs into the savings offered.

In offices	In records centre
$1\frac{1}{2}$ c. ft average to 1 sq. ft floor space	5 c. ft average to 1 sq. ft floor space
@ £2 annual rent = £1.33	@ 50p annual rent = £0.10
@ £4 annual rent = £2.66	@ £1 annual rent = £0.20
@ £10 annual rent = £6.66	@ £2 annual rent = £0.40

3.3 *Direct storage costs* (1973 figures)

Records centre administration costs

Debt and amortization charges on capital investment.

Staff costs: salaries; insurance, superannuation; training provision.

Transport costs: capital charges and depreciation allowance on vehicles; maintenance and garaging; fuel; other transport charges (use of public transport, etc.).

Administrative costs: means of communication (telephone, telex, postage); office consumables.

Copying services: capital charges and depreciation on equipment; maintenance and repair; consumables.

Not all these items will appear, of course, in the annual estimates of any given records service. In many large organizations transport fleets are maintained for general purposes. A records centre may not have to run its own, or to have special transport at all, though it will have to provide for the movement of records and the issue of documents on request.

The other items in the budget are less avoidable, but the number of staff and range of communication and copying equipment will of course vary greatly from one installation to another.

There will be an important relationship between the size and complexity of the employing authority and the facilities it will find economical and convenient in its records services.

It is not normally possible to establish the true costs of the administration of records within departmental offices, even where there is a distinct registry. It is not suggested that removing semi- or non-current records will visibly diminish those costs, or will lead, for example, to staff reductions; though valuable space will be cleared, and departmental staff will be relieved of some difficulties. 'Financing documentation is the more difficult because the lack of it forms part of customary practice, and because the cost of non-documentation is invisible.'(15)

All functions of a records centre naturally require staff, and it is clear that there is a descending order of responsibility in the jobs involved in running the centre. The overall responsibility, which includes planning the centre, administering its budget, making the necessary agreements with departmental heads, designing the finding aids, developing the place as a centre of information, and drawing up disposal schedules, should be in the hands of an archivist and closely linked with the archives service. Nor is this a remote control, for some at least of the responsibilities indicated involve close work in the records centre itself. Below this level, however, there are many tasks which should be undertaken by clerical staff. These include checking transfer lists, filing them, allocating location codes, completing indexes to the transfer lists, registering inquiries, issues and returns, identifying records for transfer to the archives or for destruction, correspondence, etc. Below this again there are manual tasks: shelving, withdrawing and replacing records on issue or return, delivery of documents, and destruction or transfer.

In large organizations it may be that staff for some of these duties should be found by the originating departments; elsewhere existing facilities may be used (messenger services, portering staff, etc.). But no records centre can run effectively without a proper staff of its own, and a proper delegation of duties in accordance with a staffing structure (figure 3.4). It has sometimes been suggested that one records officer is needed for every 10,000 cubic feet (330 cubic metres) of records.(16)

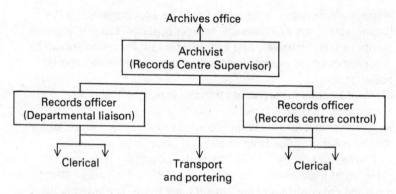

3.4 Staffing structure of a records centre

Inflow of Records
The flow of records into the management system, and hence into the records centre, in a sense begins with the initial surveys. When the time comes to begin actual transfers of retired records into the centre, the process may be speeded by the issue of a brochure setting out the objectives of the system and the advantages of the records centre, together with advice on how to use it. The brochure should be widely disseminated among the staff of the employing authority, and should also be distributed along with the stationery and boxes which are sent round to initiate the transfer of records to the centre.

A model brochure for a records centre might include the following elements:(17)
(i) A short statement of the reasons for setting up the records centre: ensuring a full and efficient archive; reducing the bulk of records kept; reducing the costs of storage; and increasing the ease of reference.
(ii) Advice or instructions to departmental staff on closing semi-current files and on sending them to the records centre. This may be detailed. It may be desirable to give precedence to clearing certain office storage space (for example, leased space).
(iii) Instructions on the specific procedures involved in transferring records. Existing containers may be reused, or new records centre boxes may be requisitioned. Ephemeral records whose agreed life is over, or nearly over, may be sent direct for destruction. Security classified files should be downgraded or treated separately. Stripping of individual papers from single files should not be attempted. Files should be packed neatly into the

boxes, in reasonable order, and should be accompanied by their
finding aids, such as indexes, wherever possible. Boxes should be
numbered unobtrusively and securely closed. Provision should be
made for oversize records (perhaps in separate parcels) and for
transport.

(iv) Instructions for preparing transfer lists, which should
accompany the consignment.

(v) Instructions for retrieving records in the records centre, or for
obtaining information from or about them.

The key to successful records centre operation is the proper
filling up of the transfer lists (figure 3.5(18)), which are in effect
the principal control and finding aid used there. The transfer list is
essentially a list of items (such as file titles) made out in accession
order. Normally these lists are made out on pads with
quadruplicate copies: the top copy is kept as main finding aid in
the records centre; the second copy is filed in destruction-date
order in the records centre to provide a disposal control; the third
copy is returned to the originating department when location
details have been entered by the records centre, for use as a
reference tool when ordering records from the centre; and the last
copy is retained in the originating department until the fully
completed third copy is received.

The instructions on the reverse for completing the form should
cover the following:

Consignment. Any group of records or boxes transferred by a
department at any one time and listed on one set of transfer lists.
Departments should number their consignments serially for
reference, beginning with the first consignment.

The *general description* should include information on: (a) the
administrative origin of the records transferred. The name of the
organization which created them, if different from the transferring
department, and any past organization changes affecting them
should be mentioned; (b) the relationship of these records to other
series of records; (c) the inclusive overall dates of the records.

Accessioning

On arrival at the records centre, the records transferred will
undergo an accessioning procedure. The consignment will be
checked, and the records staff will complete those sections of the
transfer list which are reserved to them. They will ensure that the
consignment has a proper reference code, as laid down in the

PART I: DATA SHEET	CONSIGNMENT NO:
CONSIGNMENT OF RECORDS FROM: DEPARTMENT SECTION OFFICE	DATE
GENERAL DESCRIPTION OF RECORDS (Continuation sheets provided)	
Additional data	
Storage accommodation cleared: Filing cabinets Transfer boxes shelving Cubic footage of records transferred:	
Departmental recommendations for retention	
Classified Confidential/Unrestricted	
Records transferred by: (Name) (Telephone)	

3.5 Records transfer list (to accompany or precede consignments of records)

transferring instructions: when complete, this will consist of the code for the transferring department, the consignment number, and the box numbers within that consignment. Since the transfer list itself can be retained as evidence of the transfer, there is normally no necessity for keeping a separate accessions register, as will be done in the archives.

Next, the boxes or volumes of the consignment will be found an appropriate place on the shelves, and the resulting location code written into the transfer list. The location code may be a simple box number, or it may indicate the bay and shelf where it is

PART II: TRANSFER LIST RECORDS FROM: DEPARTMENT SECTION OFFICE		CONSIGNMENT NO. _____ PAGE NO. _____			
Ref. Nos of items or boxes	Title and description of records	Inclusive dates		FOR RECORDS CENTRE USE	
		From	To	Disposal date	Records Centre Location

3.6　Records transfer list. Continuation sheet

placed, or both. Here there are broadly two alternative possibilities which determine the location of records in the centre. Each department may be given a certain area of shelving, and in this area consignments are shelved as they come in. This method is employed by the British government at the intermediate store at Hayes, but it must be remembered that Hayes is not a fully-fledged records centre: the departments themselves administer the records held there, and therefore they must each have their own clear space. However in other cases this method may be necessary: for example, where distinct departments produce vastly different types of record, or where the records centre is divided among different buildings parts of which are obviously more convenient for reference for different transferring offices.

The second alternative is to plan the use of shelving as a whole, and fill up spaces as and when they become available. In this method, no locational difference is made between records of different departments. Provided adequate lists are maintained, in an order which explains the significance of the administrative arrangement of the records, then it is not necessary to keep the records actually in this order. This principle is eminently suited to records centre operations, and allows the use of every little corner of space. The records remain in the technical ownership of the originating office; they are not being arranged as archives, and in any case they form an incomplete set coming in several consignments at different times. It is necessary only that any individual part of the records transferred could be quickly and accurately found. The records may then be stored in any convenient order, provided that an index of their location is added to the transfer list which identifies them. Probably a chart giving the allocation of location codes will be a useful addition to the equipment of the records centre. The location code, written into the third copy of the transfer list, is communicated to the originating department, and provides an additional record of it in case of loss. Loss by misplacement is the greatest single hazard facing records in a records centre.

When the location code is added to the transfer list, it should be written on to the box, or on to the storage box labels which can at this point be completed and stuck on to the boxes. Security is increased where no box labels are used, and boxes are identified simply by a location code; but, from a purely archival point of view, it is advantageous to have on each box a label which gives an accurate idea of what is in it, what has to be done to it, and whence it comes. It is also advantageous that this label should be completed by the records centre staff, so as to ensure uniformity and the correct use of conventions. A compromise between these two possibilities is a box label which identifies the department of origin but not the contents of the box (figure 3.7(19)).

Finally, the box label requires the disposal date, ascertained from disposal schedules, as detailed in the transfer instructions. At

Records transferred from	Consignment No
	Departmental box No
Location	
Disposal instructions	

3.7 Specimen records centre box label

this point the third copy of the transfer list may be sent back to the originating office, duly receipted, where it may replace permanently the temporary fourth copy which was the department's record of the transaction. The first copy is filed with its predecessors dealing with earlier consignments, so that there is one file of transfer lists for each participating department. The second copy is filed in order of the earliest disposal date on it, on a single large file which thus constitutes a reminder system in date order for disposal.

These processes complete the transfer of records into the centre.

Control and Retrieval of Records in a Records Centre

Departments of origin should be able to refer to records which they have transferred, up to the point where those records are disposed of by mutual agreement. The first aspect of control of records in the centre is therefore the retrieval arrangements which will allow for this reference.

The reference required may take one of three forms. A record or group of records may be requisitioned, that is, withdrawn temporarily from the centre and returned to the department for use there. The right of the orginating office to borrow back its own records in normal circumstances should be undisputed. The first requirement here is that there should be some means of identifying the record as one which has come from the records centre; therefore, it is usual to attach a small but conspicuous label to the front of records withdrawn on requisition (figure 3.8(20)). This label informs the user of the file where it comes from; it informs the records centre on its return that it is a record which is already on the books; and it gives the location code so that it can immediately be returned. The location code may also be of use to the searcher of the file, who can cite it when quoting.

```
This record has been issued by the
RECORDS CENTRE

Reference _____

Location _____
Please ensure that it is
returned
```

3.8 Specimen records centre issue label

A second requirement is a procedure for tracking outstanding issues. This may be done by filing requisition slips in chronological order. In some cases this can be backed up by issuing periodical reminders about outstanding records.

It is always worth considering whether it is not better to issue photocopies rather than original records. The danger of loss and the trouble of replacing records may be reduced by this means.

Secondly, the originating office may send someone down to the records centre to consult the files there. This may well be the best way to deal with a search which needs a number of files or records for consultation, or in which the questions are not definite. It is easier to send someone to the records than to demand the transport of large amounts of paper. In this case the records centre must provide the necessary facilities, which may resemble those of a searchroom in the archives; the basics will be suitable space to work, copying facilities, access to the finding aids, and the advice of the staff. In this case, however, (just as sometimes with archives also) it may be necessary to allow the department's representative a freer access to the shelves; it often happens that only a browse through files *in situ* will result in a quick finding, if the boxing and security arrangements permit.

The third way in which reference may be made is by passing an enquiry on to the records staff for them to answer. There are cases in which this is not legitimate; that is, where the enquiry is complex and the information central to the department's work. Then it is only right that the department should be asked to undertake its own researches. At other times, however, it is a proper practice; and the records centre, by taking custody of the records, has assumed a certain responsibility for the provision of information. This is particularly so where a quick reference to a specified document, readily available to the man on the spot, can answer the question, or where the wider knowledge of the records specialist or the archivist can add a dimension to the information contained in one department's records. There should be an allocation of manpower resources which will allow the records centre staff to provide such services at least within specified limits, and, of course, there should be a full provision of tools for the task, such as telephone or telex, a library of reference books, an indexed file of subject enquiries. For this purpose a formalized register of enquiries may be kept.

To facilitate any of these means of reference, it is necessary to have a retrieval system which will identify the record required, produce it, and ensure its return. This retrieval system must come into use at the earliest possible point after the record's arrival at the records centre. Fortunately, if the transfer list has been properly completed, it will provide a finding aid which will be sufficient for most purposes.

In filling up the transfer form, the one essential is that the titles of record series, or of files, should wherever possible be the ones used when the records were in full currency. This should present no difficulty to the office of origin, which of course holds a copy of the transfer list giving location codes. The main difficulty here is likely to be one which arises from poor filing practices in the originating department itself. If it cannot be certain that the papers required are on a given file, or if the file titles are not sufficiently exact, there will be difficulty. But then this difficulty would also arise during the records' currency, and could be avoided only by better filing practices in the administration.

Another difficulty with using transfer lists is that, as time goes on, a considerable file of them builds up, and to find a given record in the list may require a lengthy search through this file. So long as the searching is done by the originating department, this difficulty may be discounted. The department's staff will be familiar with the lists, and it is open to them to make an index if they wish; it is, after all, their responsibility to locate their own records. But if for any reason the onus is thrown upon the records centre, then leafing through transfer lists may prove very tiresome. The centre is likely to have not one, but perhaps fifty or more, thick files of transfer lists, a set for each department. It will need to provide itself with a key for finding and correlating information through the morass of these lists.

This can be done by building up a union index of subjects, persons and places as the lists come in. This will bring together references to information on subjects irrespective of their office of origin, and it will enable comparisons to be made between records which interrelate but which may never come together during their current lifetime. This has a bearing on destruction policy as well as upon the retrieval of information. It is a useful practice, as in all administrative indexing, to underline or mark on the main transfer list the words or concepts which have been indexed. If this is not done it is difficult to clean the index of obsolete items after disposal of the records. Further problems of indexing are discussed in connexion with archives.

It is also a useful practice to insist upon a system whereby

requisition slips are used wherever a document is to be removed
from the storage area. The system can be the same as that used
for the archives. The requisition slips if desired can be combined
with a slip for the registration of enquiries (figure 3.9(21)), and in
some organizations the records centre will be able to arrange for
regular collections of these slips and for deliveries of records
requisitioned. The purpose of the system is to prevent misfiling,
but it also provides a control of documents out, information on
their whereabouts, and on the size and nature of the demand
which the records centre is meeting. Three copies of the slip are
completed (using carbonized paper): the first is despatched and
remains on file in the records centre as long as the record is out;
the second is attached to the shelf in the record's location; the
third accompanies the record on its journey.

REQUEST FOR RECORD	Use a separate form for each request
Requested by (Address, telephone)	Date
Document requested, with reference and date	Location code
Information required	
Despatched: Date	Means
Received by requester	

3.9 Request slip for records or information

For record centres on a smaller scale, a layout for a simpler slip
is shown in figure 3.10. This is kept in duplicate only (for the first
two purposes above), without the 'information required' or receipt
sections.(22)

Security

It must be expected that the records centre will receive inquiries
from elsewhere. What is to be the attitude of the records centre to
research enquiries involving its records?

```
┌─────────────────────────────────────────────────┐
│ REQUEST FOR RECORD                                │
│ Requested by:                                     │
├───────────────────────────────┬───────────────────┤
│ Record required               │ Location          │
│                               │                   │
│                               │                   │
│                               │                   │
└───────────────────────────────┴───────────────────┘
```

Top copy
filed in records centre

```
┌─────────────────────────────────────────────────┐
│ RECORD REMOVED                                    │
│ Requested by:                                     │
├───────────────────────────────┬───────────────────┤
│ Record                        │ Location          │
│                               │                   │
│                               │                   │
│                               │                   │
└───────────────────────────────┴───────────────────┘
```

Second copy
attached to record location

3.10 Slip for requesting records

The records belong to the originating department. Therefore
that department can give such permission as to access as it
wishes, and no other department is so entitled. To this principle
the records centre staff must adhere: it is clear that access to the
records for purposes of research must either come through the
originating office, or at least be cleared with them before access is
given.

But it is not so certain that this, which has long been a rule of
records centre operation, will endure. It is now administrative
orthodoxy that central policy and research bodies override old
departmental boundaries. At times these have been far too rigid,
and now it is civic virtue to serve the local community by
providing as wide-ranging and rational a service as possible.
Moreover, requests for records or for information could well be
received from the chief executive of the authority or from research
agencies reporting to him, and in these cases, though surely it
will not be wrong to bring the originating department into full
consultation, it may well be right for the records centre to

undertake some degree of research and to provide an answer based upon a consultation of records from many sources. In this way it can benefit the administration generally or act in support of research enterprises which have been recognized (if not inspired) by it.

On the other hand, very serious attention must be given to the security of the records centre from unauthorized entry and from wrongful use. Many of the records in it will be of great sensitivity or deal with recent transactions, and in the ordinary way they would not be open for study for many years.

In allowing access to finding aids, it is important to remember that the records centre is simply for the storage in retrievable manner of records awaiting review; it would be unreasonable to set the records centre out as an alternative to the archives office as a place of public access.

In the provision of access to records or to lists the archivist in charge of a records centre should be prepared to accept considerable responsibility, as also he will in providing information direct to his employing authority. In making replies to official requests for information, sources of evidence should be provided for every answer from the records centre: if the inquiry was informal, then a written answer quoting the sources, with or without mechanical copies of relevant documents, should be sent on to the inquirer in due course. If this is not done, not only will the archivist or records officer have assumed an undue burden of responsibility (which, after all, may influence an expensive decision), but the degree of reliance which it is felt can be given to his replies may be impaired.

4 Appraisal of Records

Records which have been transferred to the records centre and administered there must be disposed of in due season. It is essential that there should be an outflow of records from the centre, as nearly corresponding in the aggregate to the inflow as possible; a choked and overflowing store is not a records centre, and, just as much as with the inflow of records, the outflow must be the subject of careful control.

The foremost consideration in disposal is that records which have completed their time in the records centre, both those which are to be retained permanently as archives and those which are to be destroyed, should be rapidly and easily identified at the appropriate moment, and should find their place in a smoothly working disposal machinery. The question of which records are to be destroyed, however, is one not so easily answered.

For the archivist to destroy a document because he thinks it useless is to import into the collection under his charge what we have been throughout most anxious to keep out of it, an element of his personal judgement; for the Historian to destroy because he thinks a document useless may be safer at the moment . . . but is even more destructive of the Archives' reputation for impartiality in the future; but for an Administrative body to destroy what it no longer needs is a matter entirely within its competence and an action which future ages (even though they may find reason to deplore it) cannot possibly criticise as illegitimate or as affecting the status of the remaining Archives; provided always that the administration proceeds only upon those grounds upon which alone it is competent to make a decision—the needs of its own practical business; provided, that is, that it can refrain from thinking of itself as a body producing historical evidences.(1)

Archivists should have final responsibility for judging the secondary values of records whether these are preserved as evidence of an agency's organizational and functional development, or for their social, economic, or other information.

... Through his training in the methodology of his profession, he knows the proper approaches to be taken in judging record values. He is in a position, moreover, to act as intermediary between the public official and the scholar in preserving records useful for research in a variety of subject-matter fields. If he is in doubt about the value of certain records for historical research, he can easily obtains the help of his professional *confrères*.(2)

These two quotations summarize the differences which emerged for a time between two schools of thought. Both statements reflect the circumstances and period in which they were written. Both lay down principles which are still valid, and which must be applied when there is question of evaluating records for destruction or for retention. The judgements made must be impartial (which is Jenkinson's main principle); the act of judging must be professional (which is Schellenberg's main principle). Since the archivist is part of the administration, it is not necessary to be conscious of a conflict between the two traditions.

It is clear that there must be destruction of a large proportion of records, both those which are to come in as backlog accumulations from the immediate past, and those currently accumulating. There are too many records; their bulk, their generally low level of informational quality, and the complexities of their interrelation, militate against their use for reference or research, and to keep them all would therefore not only bring about administrative costs quite out of proportion to the value of records in society as a whole or in administration, but would actually hinder the realization of research values. It is clear too that the process by which records are thinned out and disposed of should be a planned process, and not one left to chance.

The objective of the appraiser was stated by Jenkinson from the point of view of the employing authority. For him, the 'Golden Rule of Archive Making' was for the administrator 'to have [his papers] in such a state of completeness and order that, supposing himself and his staff to be by some accident obliterated, a successor totally ignorant of the work of the office would be able to take it up and carry it on with the least possible inconvenience and delay, simply on the strength of a study of the Office Files.'(3) The same idea was more charmingly and simply put by G. H. Fowler: 'Every administrator should have his records in such order that he can face sudden death with equanimity.'(4) The objective may be restated in this way: It is the compilation of a core of documentation which will give all necessary information on the origin and working of the employing authority and all important information acquired and used by that authority, and the exclusion of all other less valuable material.

Criteria

The rule upon which an appraisal system will be based must first of all be professional. That is, it should conform to what is being done in relevant fields by colleagues elsewhere. The time has now passed in which appraisal could be carried out entirely in isolation within one country or within one archives office. Therefore it is necessary to see that the appraiser has proper information.

In the international sphere, attempts are being made to see that he has. The International Council on Archives, backed by the resources of UNESCO, does attempt to disseminate knowledge of professional standards and programmes.(5) In Britain, there have been small beginnings.(6) It must be an important professional activity in the future to develop standards by which selection criteria can be compared. When this is done, it will be a test of the professionalism of an archivist that he has constructed an appraisal system which does pay regard to important areas of documentation outside his office, and does respect general agreement on important areas of documentation which he himself is expected to provide.

In the second place, the appraisal rule will be based upon a framework of knowledge of the contents of the accumulations being dealt with, of their administrative and legal context, of the contents of other records existing in the same subject field, and of published or other information.(7)

To be capable of sensible selection, reviewers clearly should have knowledge of the organization, functions and procedures of the department before, during and after the period covered by the records being reviewed. They should be aware of the importance of the function covered by the files in the total work of the department and of the whole machinery of government at the time. They should know something of the political, social and economic background. They should be familiar with the records themselves and with any related material, whether in records of the same or another department, and with any other associated sources, including printed material. . . .

The acquisition of a knowledge of a record group's content and of its context in the records systems of the originating department may begin at the time of the survey. It is assumed that the group being appraised forms a part of the compilations of such a department. This assumption is still correct even if we are considering private records (records of external origin), for one must assume that not every paper is being sent in to the archives office, there must be some administrative current files. If a formal survey is not being done, the same basic information must be obtained by informal inquiries, coupled with discussions with the officers concerned with the creation of these records.

The next step is to find out the relationship between this record system and the larger world. The originating department will not have been acting in isolation: if it is a government department, it will act in concert on certain matters with other departments, and there will in most cases be a reporting system at policy-making level which governs the information officially supplied on the work done. If it is a local government department, it will be acting in concert with a government office, perhaps both a central and a branch office, and it will have relationships with other departments in the same authority, particularly in regard to policy-making, observance of law and financial control; it may be also in concert (or even in conflict) with neighbouring local authorities. If it is a department of a business or industrial organization (whether private or publicly owned) it will equally have some relationship with relevant government departments, local government authorities, the other departments of the same organization; and it will be working in parallel with other organizations in other industries which have a share in supply of materials, design or marketing, or which form part of the same economic system.

It is now necessary to evaluate the content of the records to be appraised. This must be done by some form of review, or series of reviews, in which the records in their series are tested against a set of criteria which will determine their value and their fate in the next stage of their existence. The manner in which these reviews are conducted will vary according to the size and nature of the employing authority, and a digression to look at the history and existing nature of review procedures in British government will be justified.

The Grigg Report

The report of the Committee on Departmental Records under the chairmanship of Sir James Grigg in 1954 was an event of central importance to archives and records management in Britain and elsewhere.(8) It resulted in the passing of the Public Records Acts which govern the procedures adopted since then in British government for the appraisal and selection of public records. These establish the professional responsibility of the Public Record Office over the processes of appraisal, ensuring that records of value are sifted into the national archives. On the strength of these powers the Public Record Office has set up arrangements which closely follow the Grigg Committee's recommendations.

Having observed that previous arrangements under earlier acts failed because they confused two kinds of value, 'historical' (the potential use of a record for some kind of research), and 'administrative' (the need to keep certain records for legal reasons or for reference in the course of business), the committee thought that they might solve the great difficulties involved in selection by dividing the determination of these two values into two processes.

All records were to be reviewed, and they laid great stress upon the necessity for this review to be carried out under the supervision of a senior administrative officer (the departmental record officer). This review should occur, they thought, when the record was five years old—that is, five years after its closure. Review therefore depends on the regular closure of files, and is, as the report says, 'an extension of, rather than a superimposition on, [a department's] registration system'.(9)

At this first review, the departmental record officer will be concerned only with administrative value. He will mark on a list for destruction all records which appear to have no further value for the current business of the department, or which need not be kept to satisfy legal requirements. If a record has no further value to its creating department when it is only five years out of currency, then it is very unlikely that it will turn out to have any long-term value.

But the committee added three provisos:(10)
(i) The first review, at which the question, 'Is this department likely to require this record any longer for its own departmental purposes?' is put, must be held soon after the end of the record's currency, since a long lapse of time during which, for various reasons (including inaccessibility, no doubt), the record has been inactive and unused will affect the validity of the judgements made.

(ii) There must in fact be *some* historical awareness on the part of the reviewer; for the report remarks that if a department ceases to carry out a particular function it will have little administrative use for the records of that function (except as possible precedents); but the record of that function may well be of great interest historically.

(iii) 'Particular instance' papers form a separate problem.

These three provisos, if taken at the theoretical level, are a considerable infringement of the basic principle of the separation of administrative and historical criteria. The reviewing officer at first review is really considering historical value, at least, as the report says, 'by indirect means'. One must admit, however, that it is a practical method which seems to work where the record system is orderly and the supervision at first review is responsible.

The report goes into some of the main difficulties found in ensuring that record systems are in fact orderly. To review large series of records, the unit must be the file, and not the individual paper. Therefore titles must genuinely reflect the contents of the files.(11) Following from this it observes that staff of sufficient status and education must be used for the management of records and registries, and of course in the post of departmental record officer.(12)

Records which have passed the first review then remain in the custody of the department, though in a non-current condition. This may mean that they are deposited in the intermediate repository at Hayes.(13) There will then be a second review, which might take place when the record is twenty-five years out of currency, the object of which will be to determine its research value. At this point the appraisal process is completed, and records which pass this test will then go into the Public Record Office as archives.

Even when speaking of the second review, the Grigg report still sticks to its indirect approach. According to it, the decisions at the second review will still be taken by the departmental record officer, 'in conjunction with a representative of the Public Record Department', and although 'it should be possible for the historical criterion to be exercised *directly* in relation to these papers . . . the criteria for preservation at the Second Review will be both administrative and historical'.(14) No further detail is given about the application of the historical criteria, though elsewhere in the report the case is argued that this should be by the experienced staff of the Public Record Office, acting with advice.(15) In particular, the report dwelt on the need for the Public Record Office to develop as 'a repository for the National Archives in the true sense.'(16) By this is meant that a comparative evaluation as well as an absolute one should be made in the case of the records of each department.

The departmental record officer might be able to make an effective appraisal of his records, but he would not be able either to assign them a value (that is, essentially a research value) in relation to the records of other departments, nor would he be able to judge whether the total holdings of the Public Record Office amounted to an adequate overall documentation. The point is not dwelt upon, but the assumption here is that not only is it a fundamental function of a national archives institution to see that its documentation does in fact include all significant aspects of public activity, but that, even if it does not apply historical criteria directly to the records of any given department, it must still provide an overall evaluation in which an element of cost-benefit analysis comes in.(17)

For the resources available in total at any given time are always limited. The best use of them must be made and, when we are speaking of records in store and the use which is to be made of them, this means applying a comparative criterion which must inevitably be imposed upon the departmental record officers, but even more upon the national archives itself, and upon all who are carrying out appraisal exercises in particular cases.

It must therefore be recognized that it is the central archives and its staff that must advise, not only on questions of research value, but also on questions of cost and the allocation of resources to particular record series.

The Public Record Office

Since the acceptance of the Grigg proposals, the Public Record Office has put the system into operation by developing its records administration division, and the departments of government have done so by appointing departmental record officers. The Public Record Office has issued at three points in time a booklet giving advice and instructions to the departmental record officers.(18) It is instructive to notice the development of the attitude taken in these booklets to the application of the 'historical' criterion. In the provisional edition of the guide in 1958 there is a long section summarizing this, which attempts a radical analysis of the various criteria possible. It divides the demand for the consultation of records into three groups: from government, from 'ordinary members of the public', and from academic researchers. Four years later, in 1962, the long analysis noted above was modified. The 'criteria for selection of public records for permanent preservation' now occupied only just over two pages, and probably reached a degree of effective condensation which cannot be much improved upon. It is accordingly given in full in appendix B.(19)

In the years that followed, the Public Record Office built up its experience in the appraisal of records, and its small staff of inspecting officers began to take a more active role. Consequently, when the next edition of the departmental record officers' guide appeared in 1971, the theoretical analysis of historical criteria had disappeared; in its place a much briefer 'Guidelines for selection of records for permanent preservation' merely lists thirteen categories of papers under general headings, which are likely to be the most worthy of preservation. The introductory paragraph remarks that 'Appraisal criteria . . . should take into account not only the value of records for the long-term purposes of government or of the department but also their value for much wider research needs.'(20)

This is the extent of the booklet's discussion of historical criteria. It is no longer considered necessary to teach departmental record officers to recognize potential research value, since the inspecting officers, some of whom are now specialists in certain technical areas of knowledge, have in effect shouldered this burden. The establishment of research values has come into the professional area of the archivists, who therefore do not have to try to teach any person outside the office the elements of this essential function.

Other Criteria

Though the Grigg system of appraisal, based upon two reviews, both carried out at the executive level by responsible officers of the creating departments, has been adopted in essence by the Greater London Council and by Kent County Council (among others), an inescapable feature of it is that it is a system which can be operated only by a large and very complex organization. In smaller organizations it may not be possible for the archivist to shift the administrative burden of reviewing on to the shoulders of lay officers in the major departments, and equally it may not be possible for him to rely on the orderliness of the record-making and keeping systems which those departments will use in the normal course of business; the smaller the organization the less likely it is that high quality staff will be there to interest themselves in record systems, in retirement of files, or in reviewing them. In these cases it is clear that the archivist must develop these procedures himself.

The classical analysis of appraisal criteria has been provided by T. R. Schellenberg, in his book *Modern Archives*, and in his staff

instruction paper to the United States national archives.(21)
Schellenberg first accepted a distinction between primary
(administrative) and secondary (research) uses in records, but he
continued with a further distinction within the category of
secondary uses. This distinction is now established in technical
terminology in the English language, and is between two basic
kinds of research value in records, which he labelled 'evidential'
and 'informational', and he admitted at the outset that these are
technical labels with no meaning outside the jargon of the
archives profession. 'The terms "evidential" and "informational"
are meaningless if taken literally and if unexplained.'(22)
    Since the distinction is vital, the technical meaning of these
words must be understood.

Evidential values reside in records which document the origin,
development and functions of the creating department: they are
'evidence' for a study of the department itself. The principal of
these are the records which would normally always be kept: the
foundation document, the acts of the ruling body, policy papers,
reports and instructions. These records fall naturally into
arrangement by archival series, and document the work and
nature of the department itself.
    In assessing the relative value of records from the evidential
viewpoint, the essential task is to know the structure and history
of the creating department. Broadly speaking, the higher up the
structure, the more important is the office, and the more
important and worthy of preservation are the records. Further
down the structure the records will be increasingly concerned
with details, with the practicalities of daily operation, with internal
arrangements, and with housekeeping. But where records with
great evidential value occur in lower echelons of the departments,
they will be identified by applying the criterion: 'Do they document
an important development in the structure, character or work of
the department, which is not better set forth elsewhere?'
    In the case of these records, there is a strong coincidence
between administrative and research values. Consequently, when
research values alone are being considered, it is natural to think of
this material as being part of the institutional history of the
country. 'The event which is important to the research worker will
also have been important to the Department, and the information
which the Department regards as unimportant will not be of great
value to the researcher.'(23)

Informational values. The number of research workers who attend archives offices to undertake direct histories of departments or their functions constitutes only a very small proportion of the total. The great majority of researchers are attempting to co-ordinate scraps of information gleaned from the records of a variety of organizations, which will give them a picture of a certain event, person, place or subject. These researchers are looking for documents with 'informational values'—that is, records which contain information gathered by the creating department in the course of its activities, but about persons or things outside itself.

Future Research Needs

To decide whether or not a record series is worth keeping (irrespective of other factors) by virtue of its informational values, it is necessary to be able to forecast the research demands which may be made of it. This means that the archivist must be able to predict the course of future research in respect of the records he is appraising.

To attempt to prognosticate future possible research uses is to enter on most difficult ground. The scope, character and size of the research industry has changed enormously since the days when archive work first became systematized. Everyone knows that papers that were despised in late Victorian surveys are now prized as evidence in new and often most important research, for example into questions of social history. Research activities are likely to increase rather than decrease, and new subjects , or new inter-disciplinary relationships between subjects will continue to appear.

A common conclusion is that it is impossible to predict what kinds of record are going to have research value in the future. It must of course be accepted that the research project at present unknown may arise, and that it may be important. But in fact we are in a much better position than were our predecessors to predict future research possibilities, if only because we may take the trouble to do so.

Before we can predict future developments in research, we must naturally know what they have been in the past and what they are at present. This can only be done by deliberate investigation, and by taking measures to see that current knowledge is communicated to the staff of the archives office. Current periodicals and reports of research in progress, booksellers' lists and bibliographical material should be regularly received and circulated; and it is desirable that there should be regular meetings between the archives staff and those in higher education. These contacts should if possible not only be with individual members of university and college staffs, but also with boards of studies and administrative committees of university departments, polytechnics, schools and colleges or other research institutes.

In its effect upon the use of records, research must be considered, not only in its pure academic form, but also in its applied form as exploitation of particular records. What fills the searchrooms of many archives offices is the large number of readers who are engaged in exploiting in one place archives which have already been opened up in another, or in introducing archives which have been used in research to new students or in new applications. The post of archivist for academic liaison is therefore one which should be established in far more archives offices, on the model of some of the Canadian federal and provincial archives.

In addition to academic research, archives offices have to provide for individual requests for information on particular people, details of whom may appear in the records. These are the 'ordinary members of the public' referred to in 1958,(24) and their needs may be in connection with some legal right or claim (establishment of citizenship, right to pension, etc.), or it may be genealogical research undertaken for private reasons. The Grigg Committee determined that no record should be kept for genealogical purposes, or for that matter historical purposes, alone.(25) In the circumstances of government, where enormous quantities of records incidentally touch on individuals, this is no doubt a wise decision; but in local circumstances the needs of individuals and of local studies should receive a higher priority.

Since so many different disciplines, periods, places and subjects are concerned, it is hardly to be expected that any one archivist will be able to master sufficient expertise, even after study, to carry out appraisal or to advise departmental record officers in all situations. In many cases it is certainly his duty to seek for technical advice from academic or other institutions. In receiving this advice, the archivist must still weigh up the other considerations which are involved in an appraisal exercise. After all, the academic adviser does not have to undertake the burden of administering or storing the archives he has advised on, and he may have a direct personal interest in some particular research topics. Nevertheless it would be irresponsible of the archivist not to seek advice and, where appropriate, public discussion, where there is question of the disposal of a quantity of records which might have some academic or local significance. Consultative or liaison committees may provide a machinery for discussion and advice.

The Cost-Value Ratio

When all investigations have been completed, the archivist is in a position to approach his appraisal decisions. There is one further factor against which he must weigh these decisions: the cost-value ratio.

The overall view is that papers with definite archive quality should be preserved at whatever cost. The point of these slow and responsible operations is that research value (in the widest sense) is the primary object: there is no rational basis on which an archivist can say that a given group of records are of value, but that they cannot be retained simply because of financial or administrative limitations. In real life, however, the situation is never so clear-cut. Values are always relative, and in the case of records they are relative, above all, to bulk. In an ideal world, records might be appraised on the basis of their content alone, and not on the basis of their quantity; but in practice the size of the collection does make a difference. A very small quantity of records can be preserved on the strength of doubtful research value, 'just in case'. But if the series is large, the archivist will ask himself if its value is so overwhelmingly clear as to demand that it should be preserved at the cost of a major reallocation of resources. The idea of such a major reallocation should not be dismissed without thought. As a comparison, the appearance of the large-scale open-air museums and regional museums in the late 1960s represents one response of the museum profession to the plain fact that enormous artefacts—far beyond traditional museum objects in scale—needed to be housed and preserved. But in answering the questions raised by the evaluation of very large series of records, some attempt must be made to establish a cost-value assessment.

Particular Instance Papers

The difficulties involved in this are illustrated best by a discussion of the problem of 'particular instance papers'. The phrase was established by the report of the Grigg Committee, and it is now the standard usage in the Public Record Office. It is somewhat wider in meaning than the alternative 'case papers', which might be more readily intelligible elsewhere. Particular instance papers are series of papers which have the same general subject matter, but relate it to different instances. Thus, in local authority terms, the applications made by individuals for action under a particular statute are filed together as a group of particular instance papers. In government terms, such papers may also relate to individuals (as in the registration of individuals for purposes of national insurance) or to local authorities, or to business concerns.

Particular instance papers vary greatly in their content, but most, or even all, public bodies maintain them; in some cases, such as hospitals or universities, they constitute in bulk at least the main records of the institution. Typically these series constitute very large quantities of records, the chief value of which is the detail given of particular cases. It is likely that the informational value of each single file or item may be small, and the record will include much common form with only small sections for detailed information on the case in question. But the series as a whole may well be of great interest, amounting in the aggregate to a record of the effect of government upon whole social classes or sections of the population. They may be particularly apt for quantified and mechanized methods of research. These large classes of particular instance papers undoubtedly constitute the main practical difficulty which faces the appraiser of the present day.

The Grigg report itself contains a brief summary of certain of the most important particular instance papers existing at that time.(26) It recommended that there should be a committee under the auspices of the Public Record Office to conduct a survey of particular instance papers, and that the creation of new classes of particular instance papers should be accompanied by the advice of the Public Record Office on their form and retention value. Otherwise the only technique considered was that of sampling. Grigg did not favour microfilm as a possible solution to this problem.

The investigation and report, prior to 1954, was made before the computer had arrived as a common tool in either administration or research, and it consequently made almost no attempt to consider the possibility of preserving the essential record in statistical or quantitative form.(27) Such techniques will doubtless be a major resource of archivists in the future. The omission of the computer in research was more serious still, for it led the Grigg Committee to undervalue the research demand, and the capability of researchers to work on large series of particular instance papers.

An Example of Disposal.

A glance at the fate of one of the major series of particular instance papers referred to in the report is instructive. The crew lists and agreements of the Registrar of Shipping and Seamen was a very large accumulation of records (300,000 linear feet of shelving in 1954), the rate of accrual was very considerable, and the informational quality of the individual records was low. The series presented a classic case for appraisal.

The Public Record Office took deliberate action. First it refused to allow destruction, and then took advice from an academic body. Finally it announced a decision which at first looked as if an acceptable procedure had been found. The earlier series of crew lists, prior to 1861, would be kept entire. Of those between 1861 and 1913 (the effective dates covered by the appraisal exercise), a ten-per-cent statistical sample would be kept, together with lists relating to certain noteworthy ships, and a second ten-per-cent sample of the remaining documents 'on a chronological basis' was sent to the National Maritime Museum. The remainder was offered to any other archive repository which declared that it had an interest, provided that certain administrative charges were met by receiving offices.

The practical effect of this dispersal was that further statistical samples were sent to the Public Record Office of Northern Ireland, the University of Exeter, and Liverpool Record Office; and selections from the remainder, chosen from ships registered at the relevant ports, were sent to local record offices in some maritime areas. Most of the residue, amounting to about 70-75 per cent of the whole, was transferred to the Maritime History Group of the University of Newfoundland, who have devised a computerised retrieval system for controlling it.(28)

Two criticisms, with the benefit of hindsight, may be made of this procedure. One is that the principle upon which the selection of vessels for distribution to maritime record offices was made was insecure: a ship registered at a particular port has no necessary connection with the trade or life of that port, but it does have a connection with the maritime life of the nation. Local interest was therefore adopted as a criterion, but incorrectly applied. Secondly, as soon as the proposed destruction or distribution became known publicly, it appeared that there was a strong body of opinion which held that the records should have been kept. In fact, the Public Record Office itself clearly had suspected the existence of this body of opinion, as it offered samples to outside bodies. There is of course no reason why an archives office which is embarrassed by lack of resources to deal with a particular record series should not offer it on deposit to some other suitable institution, but one would normally expect this transaction to avoid splitting the series.

The final result is that, after all the thought and consultation that was undertaken, the record series has been so split up that, if any researcher were eventually to try to reconstitute it, he would have to work in dozens of institutions, widely separated one from another, and would in the end find that there was a residue which had been destroyed. Though it is still not clear that there will be in fact a serious academic demand for research into this class of records, it would seem that the operation of an appraisal process has resulted in the violating of some very basic rules of archival arrangement and administration.

Would it have been better if the bulk of the records had been disposed of silently? Presumably not, for, though the records have been scattered, their research value can now be put to the test. In the end, hiving off much of the cost of storage and administration has perhaps been the best solution.

The episode should be kept in memory, however, as an instruction on the pitfalls which await those who must make irreversible decisions, and the changes which mechanized tools of research might make possible; and it is a good illustration of the complexity of some appraisal exercises.

Other Considerations

The techniques of sampling and of microreprography, which may in many circumstances be specially applied to the problem of particular instance papers, are dealt with separately. If the only objection to microfilm as a solution to storage problems is cost, the true costs of alternative measures must be correctly calculated.

The final point to be made under the heading of appraisal is the question of validation. 'A means of testing efficiency is, we consider, an essential element in any satisfactory system.'(29) In the Public Record Office system, there is a regular series of 'test checks', both by departmental record officers and by inspecting officers, with the object of determining whether enough or too much is being destroyed, and whether the right things are being kept. It is not easy to suggest objective standards by which these things can be measured. The test of administrative value can be applied relatively objectively. If a record is in demand and proves to have been destoyed, then perhaps it should not have been destroyed, and vice versa. But the fact that a record which has been disposed of is occasionally requested does not by itself prove that it should not have been destroyed. There is a balance of advantages and disadvantages, and it is not necessary to retain a record series on the chance or even the certainty of occasional references, if there is no other case for its retention. It is the research criterion which is the more important, and which is the more difficult to subject to test checks. After all, some research undertakings are thought to be more valuable than others: who shall judge this scale of values? The existence or otherwise of a demand for a certain record series by researchers is often the result of the state of the publications regarding it: a valuable group of records may remain unused simply because it is not known.

Summary and Conclusion

In Britain, appraisal operations are dominated by the findings of the Grigg Committee, which determined the framework of law and custom within which the national archives operates. Nevertheless the archives staff have built up a tradition of work which resembles international practices more and more closely.

The appraisal system depends on a system of review procedures in which administrative values are theoretically treated separately from research values. Records series undergoing appraisal are therefore subjected to two sets of inquiry. In the first, after five years, the question is put, 'Is this record of further value for administrative reference?' To answer this, the appraiser must understand the significance of the record in its context. In the second, after twenty-five years, this question may be asked again, but supplemented by the question, 'Has this record any value for research?'

In answering this second question, the appraiser must have some notion of the kind of values which would be looked for in research. These values may be 'evidential' or 'informational'. Evidential values are concerned with the documentation of the creating department, its origin, functions and development. To preserve this information, a list of the main governing and operating series of records will be made, based on an analysis of the management and operating structure of the department. Informational values however may be discerned only by looking at the record with the eyes of a researcher seeking information incidental to the main operation of the department. This kind of information may relate to persons, places or subjects, and to obtain a comprehensive documentation will normally involve considering records from various sources.

The appraiser of records must have two areas of specialist knowledge, which may be supplemented by expert advice. He must know the content and structure of the records of his department in their context, and the extent of the information they give. He must know the research uses which have been or are being made of these records, and his acquaintance with the course and means of research must be such that some prognostication may be made of its future application to his records.

In addition, the appraiser must bear in mind the cost-value ratio in his records. He must be able, again after advice if necessary, to assign a realistic cost factor to the administration and storage of his record series, which may be balanced by their actual or likely usefulness in the future. This cost factor must be related to the resources which the archives service possesses, so that a judgement on the future of a given record series will involve a decision on the priorities within the archives service and the allocation of resources. However there is always a basic proviso that record series which are clearly judged to be of archival quality should, as a matter of professional ethics and national interest, be preserved and administered, whatever the financial implication.

In solving problems arising from such situations, archivists may of course call in help from research or other institutions, wherever that is possible, not only to give advice but in certain cases to take over the administration and exploitation of particular record series.

It is clearly not desirable to allow the appraisal of records for selection or destruction to occur by chance, or without proper knowledge and system. It is the function of an archives service to ensure, as far as possible, that it receives all records which provide a basic documentation for both administrative and research purposes within the area of its activity, and that records which do not come up to this standard are disposed of suitably. Though the administrative work involved in appraisal (and in other aspects of records management) may if appropriate be delegated, the final judgements involved can only be made by those who have an overview of the nature of the records, the various uses they serve, the demands of research and reference, the resources available for servicing records and the demands on those resources. These things are the professional concern of archivists.

5 Disposal of Records

Disposal Schedules

The bulk of records, and their variety, is such that it is vital to reduce decisions on their disposal as much as possible to routine. The instrument by which this is done is known as a disposal schedule. This is a list of all continuing and regular records series which can be clearly identified and labelled, which allocates to each series an appropriate life-span; once this is done, it should be possible to arrange for the automatic implementation of the terms of the schedule without giving the records further individual consideration. Clearly the drawing up of the schedule will demand professional attention, and there are problems both in drafting it and in implementing it which call for discussion.

The Grigg system of two reviews does not remove the need for disposal schedules and for the routine disposal of all the easily recognizable ephemeral series of records. In 1958 the Public Record Office's guide instructed departmental record officers to draw up 'classified lists' of regularly accruing classes of record, and assign to each, with the agreement of the inspecting officers, a definite life-span. In the 1971 guide, a further step has been taken towards using these schedules as an instrument of overall control of the disposal of records of all kinds:

The Disposal List need not be confined to records which are to be destroyed after fixed periods. Departments should consider the value of a Disposal List which sets out a complete programme for dealing with all its records, giving directions for disposal of each kind or series not only by automatic destruction but by normal review and other procedures. For example, disposal instructions can be 'Destroy after 3 years'; 'Consider at First Review'; 'After 2 years move to Hayes, destroy after 5 years'; 'Destroy after 5 years, subject to sample'; 'Preserve permanently', etc.(1)

The first requirement of a useful schedule is that it should set out under recognizable headings the records which are at that moment accruing in the department. There are three sources from which an archivist can get preliminary guidance at the first stage.

(i) There are exemplars of parallel or related records available from other sources; or, if not this, there are examples of similar schedules constructed by records managers elsewhere. It is a matter of professional concern that retention standards should be co-ordinated over the nation, or even internationally. Even if there is no schedule which deals with records in a related subject or type area, there is still value in basing new schedules on existing models, since this will lead to standardization of nomenclature, layout and periods of retention.

(ii) The analysis of the structure and functions of the creating department and its divisions will assist in providing a framework for the schedule of records which each produces. Some such analysis is needed in any case, because without it the appraisal of evidential values is impossible. Since the administration of records in the records centre is usually based on the principle of keeping the records of departments separate one from another, there is a practical as well as a theoretical advantage in drawing up the control lists on an analytical model which distinguishes departments, divisions, sections and offices in order of their chain of command, their rank in the hierarchy, and their functions.

(iii) In the same way, the survey of current records series, where it has been done, should provide both an analytical study of the administration of the department and a physical study of the records it holds.

The schedule then should be arranged under the headings of the creating offices, but it should itself be a list of record series. If the current records survey cannot be used, one way of drawing up such a list is to use the transfer lists, where a sufficient quantity of them has accumulated to provide a reasonable certainty that a representative quantity of records has come in. The draft schedule can be compiled by making a pilot index on slips from the transfer lists. The only difficulty which may arise is that of establishing what is properly a record series. Typical pilot index entries are given overleaf.

When the pilot index is reasonably complete, that is, when it contains entries relating to most series of records, the slips can be sorted into the order required. Then the information on them can be typed into tabular form, and the resulting document is a

| Development applications
1948-1969
*Planning
    †Central filing | Title deeds (corporate property)
various dates to 1970
*Legal adviser
    †Conveyancing |

* department of origin   † section or division of department

5.1 Specimen pilot index entries

draft schedule. On to this can be marked the suggested life-spans
or disposal instructions against each record series.

It is useful to allocate records series to one of a number of
categories of regular life-spans, rather than to invent a particular
life-span for each one. Thus there may emerge groups of record
series which are to be kept for one, seven, ten or fifteen years
respectively. Into one of these groups almost all records for
ultimate destruction can be placed. This is preferable to giving
each series a period of its own; this would produce a list full of
idiosyncratic periods, none similar to another, where life-spans
cannot be defended on strictly scientific grounds, and where the
resulting list is untidy administratively.

In allocating a life-span to each category of record, five
symbols or notes of instruction may be needed. These will
distinguish the following types of instruction:

(i) *Permanent preservation.* This in itself is inadequate as a
disposal instruction. Normally the record so designated will spend
a period in the office of its origin and a further period in the
records centre before being transferred to the archives. There
should be an instruction governing the date of these transfers.

(ii) *Indefinite retention.* This category is sometimes useful for
records with a long administrative (or legal) life but with small
archival quality; but it may also be used to allow a longer time for
appraisal. Clearly there must ultimately be a disposal decision.

(iii) *Retention for a stated period of years.* Here again it may be
convenient in certain circumstances to indicate the length of the
period during which the records should be held in departmental
storage, followed by the length of time it should spend in the
records centre.

(iv) There will inevitably be a category for records which are not
suitable for routine disposal, either into archives or to destruction.
This category will have to be marked 'for review' or the equivalent,
and it will doubtless be convenient to indicate in the schedule the

point of time at which these reviews should occur. The difference between the treatment of records in this class and those in (iii) and (v) is that they are appraised by the record unit (typically the individual file) rather than by series. Reviewing is required wherever the series cannot be appraised as a whole.

(v) There may be a category of records so ephemeral that it is a waste of effort to bring it into the records centre. Where this is so, destruction directly from the department at a given date will be authorized.

In all cases the point of time from which the instruction laid down in the schedule should operate must be clear. In many cases this will involve determining three stages in the life of the record: (i) the point at which the record was closed, or retired, in accordance with registry or filing centre standing instructions; (ii) the date of the last current entry on the record; (iii) the point at which the record was transferred to the records centre. Disposal (or in the case of archives, access) instructions will operate by calculating from these dates.

The next stage consists of the consideration of the draft schedule by interested parties and its authorization in final form. The draft should be seen by representatives of the chief executive and his central office services supervisor, of the central financial authority, of the legal department or adviser, and of the head of the originating department. Their comments may be invited; these will generally have the effect of increasing the proposed life-span in some cases.

It is rare, in practice, to find the situation where the archivist has to defend a class of records against an office determined to destroy; but where this does happen one may see the archivist's professional authority most clearly at work. More typically, however, the originating office will often suggest prolonging the life of an ephemeral record, 'just in case', against the archivist's more radical proposals. However, usually it does not matter too much whether a record series is moved from the seven-year to the ten-year category as the result of a departmental suggestion; provided that disposal is regularly carried out according to the schedule the records centre ought to be capable of handling the records. So long as the outward flow of records is maintained, the problems posed by growth in the creation and storage of records will be small compared with the growth (however much restricted) of the archives proper. But cases where retaining records for a year extra involves tangible costs are not difficult to find. In these cases the archivist will be able to support his proposals by quoting precise costs and applying a cost-benefit test.

Draft schedules should not receive too general a circulation, though they should be seen and commented on by all who have a genuine interest in the working of the system, and who are experienced in the operations recorded in the documents under discussion. Once the schedule has been agreed, however, it should be formally authorized by the controlling authority; from this point it should receive as much publicity as is possible within the employing authority, and it should become available (unless there are special factors of security or confidentiality) for guiding the appraisal and scheduling work of archivists elsewhere.

Schedules should have authority; they should be binding upon those who work in registries or filing centres. The whole point of them is that they reduce to a routine the disposal of the larger proportion of records produced without allowing elements of personal interest to come in. A specimen page appears in figure 5.2.(2) But the fact that a schedule is an official document or regulation, perhaps partaking of a legal status in some cases, should not allow it to become fossilized in a state in which it no longer refers to the records series actually being produced. The functions of departments change over the years, sometimes suddenly and radically, sometimes slowly and imperceptibly; in either case there must be reappraisals of the records scene, and redrafting of the schedules in the light of experience. An inappropriate schedule, full of references to dead record series or using obsolete titles for them, is not useful as an instrument for the control of records disposal.

If it is to be used to the full as an instrument of control of records, the schedule should include records which are current and accumulating in departments, as well as those which have been retired (or withdrawn) and are in closed storage or in the records centre; it can be closely associated with a register of current records series, if one is kept. It is not necessary to emphasize that the schedules will cover records destined for permanent retention as well as those destined to be shortly destroyed. In this context the word 'disposal' can be taken to cover disposal into the archives as well as disposal into the incinerator, and there should be no implication whatever that a disposal schedule is a list of records for destruction, rather than a control list of all records, arranged in series.

	Finance Department, continued	
Item number	*Title of record*	*Retention Period*
(9)	*Cash Received Sheets* To meet legal requirements.	C+6
(10)	*Cheque Payment Sheets* To meet legal requirements.	C+6
(11)	*Main Cash Books* To meet statutory requirements and reference needs which are infrequent but important.	P
(12)	*Journal Ledgers and Journal Vouchers* To meet statutory requirements and reference needs which are infrequent but important.	P
(13)	*Nominal and Private Ledgers* To meet statutory requirements and reference needs which are infrequent but important.	P
(14)	*Profit and Loss Accounts* To meet statutory requirements and reference needs which are infrequent but important.	P
(15)	*Sales and Purchase Ledgers* If dated before 1967 If dated later	 Indefinitely C+6
(16)	*Plant Register*	Indefinitely
(17)	*Income Tax Records*	Indefinitely
WAGES DOCUMENTS		
(18)	*Clock Cards*	Audit
(19)	*Pay Advice*	C+1
(20)	*Payroll, Payroll Control* The payroll and payroll control should be retained for ten years for reference purposes for possible legal action, tax queries, certificates of earnings, common law claims, etc.	C+10
	Where summaries of annual earnings of each individual are kept, Payroll and Payroll Control may be kept for a shorter period. Viz. Payroll and payroll control	 C+6
	Annual Earnings Summaries	C+10

Meaning of symbols
P—permanent retention.
C—current financial year, plus a number of years indicated.

5.2   Specimen page from a records disposal schedule(2)

Reviewing

Records series marked for review in the disposal schedule will
normally be those which intermingle important and unimportant
material in their make-up. The most typical example is a filing
system. This is an organized group of files constituting the formal
central store of working records for one particular office or
department, having an analysis or index which determines what
file titles should exist, and therefore on what file any given paper
should be placed.

There are several methods by which a filing system may be
subdivided, but common to all these systems is the fact that there
will be some files which contain important papers (for example,
papers recording major changes of policy), and some files which
contain only or mainly unimportant papers, such as duplicated
letters or circulars, letters arranging minor meetings and so on.
The object of the review procedure in these cases is to determine
which files have archival quality and which do not. All the
problems of appraisal centre upon the recognition of this quality in
an objective and systematic way.

Who is to do the reviewing, and when? In large organizations
the Grigg Committee's solution may be accepted: that there
should be two reviews, one by administrative personnel of
responsible rank, at a relatively early period after retirement, the
object of which is to weed out those files which have no further
administrative value; and a second, in which an archivist takes a
more prominent part, which seeks to recognize continuing
administrative values and archival values. The process is
illustrated in figure 5.3.

'A programme of records management [includes] . . . a continuous
appraisal of records during the first twenty-five years of their
existence, with a general shift of emphasis from the administrator
to the archivist.'(3) This states the principle, and indicates the
division of labour between the administrative appraiser
(departmental record officer) and the archivist. The smaller the
employing authority, the greater will be the role of the archivist,
and in many cases he may have to take responsibility for the
whole process.

There must be a means of control whereby records proceed
through the planned process in an orderly manner. This may be
done by marking the actual records, on the file covers, with
disposal instructions: review at (dates); to records centre (date);
destroy at (date); to archives (date); etc. More probably, however,

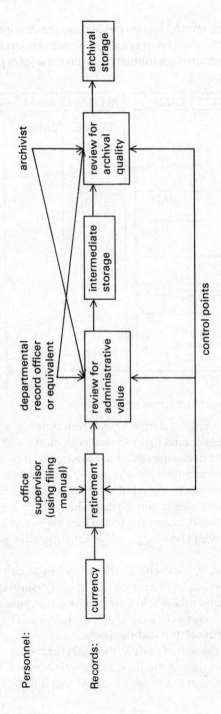

Personnel:

office
supervisor
(using filing
manual)

departmental
record officer
or equivalent

archivist

Records:

currency → retirement → review for
administrative
value → intermediate
storage → review for
archival
quality → archival
storage

control points

5.3 Stages in records disposal

some more central control will be needed, so that the information
necessary for control will be available at a central point for the
clerical staff. The control instrument may take the form of a card
(figure 5.4(4)).

RECORD PROGRESS CARD		RECORD ISSUED TO		
DEPARTMENT		OFFICE	DATE OUT	DATE IN
SECTION				
SERIES				
FILE REFERENCE				
FIRST REVIEW DATE				
TRANSFER TO RECORDS CENTRE				
SECOND REVIEW				
DISPOSAL INSTRUCTION				
NOTES				

       FRONT   BACK

5.4 Specimen record progress card

The reviewing archivist should have a committee of some kind
to support him. This should meet to deal with matters either of
policy or of specific decisions which are referred to it by the
archivist. Standing committees, where they exist, should no doubt
contain representatives of the administrative, legal and financial
authorities; in other cases it may be desirable to have *ad hoc*
committees composed, according to the records which are under
review, of people with knowledge in the administrative and
subject area.

Wherever possible, the archivist should be free to call for
advice or upon persons from outside his employing authority;
these outside consultants would normally be either academics or
professional colleagues with a parallel responsibility. The latter
practice is not yet usual, but it should become so.

In carrying out the actual review, the main technique is that of
comparison. An analysis of the filing index will show which
sections of files contain the most important material. But the

archivist will also apply tests with the object of discovering 'informational' values; and compare the make-up and content of other record systems within and without his employing authority or the department in question. It is this careful comparison of records from different sources which is the essence of good records management in the field of appraisal.

It often happens that points of policy of long-term significance are actually decided during the course of a particular incident, or during the deliberation upon one particular case. It is not always possible, therefore, to be certain that the most important policy papers are upon files with self-explanatory titles. File titles also tend to fossilize, and after a certain time files with one title tend to contain papers upon different matters. This is a question of good or bad filing practice. It is self-evident that archivists depend greatly upon the standards of current administration in records, both in appraisal and in retrieval of information, and they have a strong interest in the maintenance of good filing and recording methods.

There should be a rule which will deal with the situation where a file contains a few important papers and a number of ephemeral ones. It was the decision of the Grigg Committee to treat files as single units for appraisal purposes.(5) The work involved in stripping unimportant papers from a file is usually too complex to be worth the trouble of doing it. It should be done by someone responsible who understands the import of the whole record; the stripping of files by juniors is as bad a practice as appraisal by juniors. Moreover it has often been emphasized that the survival of unimportant groups of papers, casually or systematically, has an important place in appraisal systems: such papers are necessary to give a rounded view of the original system in operation.

The doings of the reviewing officer or committee should be recorded in sufficient detail to allow a later investigator to be certain that particular files or record series received a particular judgement. This may suggest that a destruction register should be kept; but this is necessary only where the records series destroyed can be easily identified by title, and where there is patent legal or administrative reason for the registration.

Sampling
Sampling is sometimes possible where otherwise total destruction of a record series would be necessary. It is a

mathematical process which demands technical knowledge, and no sampling exercise should be undertaken without expert advice. In some cases it may be that this advice can be impersonal and general, but these cases will be few; if the record series which is being appraised is being considered for sampling, it must have some possible archival value, which is brought into question only because of its bulk. A very bulky series may have considerable potential importance, especially where there are local considerations. In most cases where sampling is brought in as an appraisal resource, the particular advice of statistical experts should be sought.

Three types of sample are possible: the random, the selective and the representative.

The random sample. The object is to give a future researcher the material on which he can construct a statistical view of the operations recorded by the series in question. It will provide averages and other figures which may have a mathematical accuracy, subject to the size of the operation documented, with some calculable meaning. Calculations based on the sample will not provide historical accuracy, in the sense of tying the creating authority's operations to particular cases, but they should give an accurate overall view of the effect of policies or the extent of problems.

The selective sample. The aim here, on the other hand, is to provide an accurate 'historical' picture of the authority's operations at important preselected points. Thus in sampling from a long record series it might be decided to retain all records in the series from certain date ranges: those prior to a specified date, those which correspond to wars or periods of crisis, or, in a more common variant, it might be decided to retain the records for regular periods at specified intervals. A common method is to keep the whole record for one year in every five or ten, for example. Alternatively certain cases might be retained, where the authority was dealing with particularly important people or events. In a series of case files, for example, those relating to people mentioned in *Who's Who* might be retained.

The representative sample. Sections of the record are selected in order simply to represent the ordinary operations of the authority without regard to particular cases or to periodic developments. The most common form of representative sample is where

representative sets of forms are kept to show how the authority
designed its work and operated its papers.

Some Examples

In 1969 the Public Record Office was faced with the problem of
the crew lists. It commissioned a study by the Institute of
Historical Research of London University to establish a scheme for
sampling these records. Data was extracted from records covering
two years over the period 1861-1913, and this was analysed by
computer to determine the reliability of the sample. A conclusion
was that an overall ten per cent sample, to be made according to
specific rules, would give statistically reliable results.(6) Where
series are primarily important for statistical information, the
French national archives service has the practice of sampling by
preserving a tenth, twentieth, thirtieth, hundredth or a thousandth
part; but it also undertakes sampling by retaining files which
concern selected cases.(7) Similar practices are widespread in all
countries.

A Warning

But 'the size and character of a sample are determined by the uses
that are made of it; there is no such thing as a statistical sample of
general utility. For this reason the archivist must consider very
deliberately the types of use that he intends to serve before he
attempts to fix on a sampling formula.'(8) If this is true, it lays an
impossible burden on the archivist, who must foresee not only the
subject-fields into which research will develop, but even the uses
to which particular kinds of information are to be put.

The problem must for the moment be left in suspense. It is
mainly the relatively well-endowed national archives services
which are faced with the truly enormous series of records which
might be suitable for sampling, and it is to their investigations that
the profession must look. Records of the future may be provided
with a statistical record built into their operational programs.
Meanwhile it is not advisable for other archives services to resort
to sampling without specialist advice.(9)

Outward Movement of Records

Movement of records away from the records centre at the
termination of their stay there is a process which should be
controlled, just as is the movement of records into the centre.

Before any records can be transferred out, they must be

identified. This may be done by arranging a list of records held in order of their disposal date. A suitable list is provided by the second copies of the transfer lists. The disposal date which determines the order of these transfer lists will be the earliest disposal date on the form.

When one item has been disposed of, it can be crossed off, and the form refiled in the place dictated by the next earliest date on it. A records clerk can then take the second-copy transfer lists indicating due disposal dates, identify the records by the locations given, and remove them from the storage area. They then go for destruction, for further review or for transfer to archives as indicated.

Removal for disposal should take place at regular intervals, the frequency of which will be determined by the size and character of the records centre.

Records removed for disposal will leave a space available for new records. Normally it is advantageous to ensure that only complete boxes are sent out. This may be the subject of an instruction at the point of the inward transfer. If particular items within boxes are due for disposal, but the remainder of the box's contents are not, it is for decision within the records centre whether it is more worth while to destroy the item due, leaving the rest to wait until their time comes, or to leave the item until the whole box becomes due. Clearly the space cannot be utilized until the whole box goes.

The records clerk will keep some reminder of boxes which have been disposed of, leaving spaces available, so that these locations can be allocated at convenience. He will also erase from the main index any records which have gone, and he will keep a register of records disposed of which will be sufficiently detailed to clear up any doubt subsequently as to whether or not that particular series of records was disposed of and at what date.

As with the receipt of new records, it is probable that there will be some delay while consignments of records are collected and made ready, and therefore there should be adequate space for this work, suitably accessible from the loading bay or exit.

Destruction

Disposal of records scheduled for destruction poses some practical problems. The records centre may decide to undertake their destruction itself, or it may contract with some external agency for this. Again, destruction should be arranged either for the whole output of dead records from the employing authority, or only of those records which have gone through the records centre (where these are not the same).

Before making a decision on these points, some consideration must be given to the degree of confidentiality which the records may possess. Almost all records have some degree of confidentiality in that they give details of transactions which, however neutral in their content, are private to the creating authority. Some records may be highly and explicitly confidential because of a relationship with a client (as many of the records of a bank, otherwise uninteresting, may be), or because of a decision taken, or because of the personal character of the information. Some records may have been declared secret under public statutes or because they deal with industrial processes. Most records occupy an intermediate status between the poles of definite confidentiality and definite openness, and records for destruction will probably include some at least which are duplicates of papers of the highest importance which are recent. It cannot be assumed therefore that all sensitive and important material in the records centre will automatically go into the archives rather than into the destructor.

The main advantage of a records centre itself undertaking responsibility for destruction is that of control, including control not only of the circumstances of destruction (so avoiding accidental breaches of security) but also, more firmly than otherwise, over what is destroyed. If the records centre does the destruction itself, then one can be reasonably sure that no records of importance are destroyed casually and without consideration.

In any case the records centre will have to find a way of disposing of records for destruction, either by coming to an agreement with a waste-paper merchant or through the works department of the employing authority. A figure to cover any expenditure under this agreement should appear in the budget of the records centre, as will one for the receipts obtained from the sale of waste material. An important consideration today is that used paper should go for recycling.

Commercial Records Centres and Some Developments
Records centres may be observed in operation in many countries; their management has been discussed in the light of several actual institutions, in central government, local government and industry. There is one other type of records centre in existence

which may deserve attention, and that is the commercially based private-enterprise records centre of which there are examples in Britain, Israel, and the United States, among other countries.

The commercial records centre offers its services to any customer on a basis of payment for linear measurement of shelving space; this charge will cover such services as are provided. Basically these are very simple, and amount simply to storing such records as are sent in, and retrieving and issuing items on demand, using the initially supplied transfer lists as the basic finding aid. Destruction or other disposal is undertaken when instructed by the customer, and this service will be charged for. It is therefore entirely up to the customer to evaluate the cost of the service as against the saving of space in central buildings, and he has the responsibility of seeing that only valuable records are sent in.

The services in such a records centre are therefore a response to the situation of businesses in central city areas, where the cost of office accommodation is high; but they fall very far short of the services which should be provided by archives offices and by the records centres which are part of them. The achievements of the commercial records centres can therefore be used as a control, by which the achievements of public service or directly established archives offices can be judged.

A possible future development is the provision of records management services by archives offices on a contractual or agency basis. Regional or other large archives services might have on their staff a records management officer who would give his services to any authority or institution within his area, on a basis which would include an agency fee. The services offered would include oversight and planning of records management operations, and either the oversight of a records centre set up within the client organization and staffed as to clerical and manual personnel by them, or storage and management of retired records in a central records centre on a basis of payment for shelving occupied.

The services administered in either type of centre would go further than those at present offered commercially, and would approach a service much nearer that of a technical library or documentation centre, in this case a library of information and records. The construction of schedules and the systematic improvement of documentation would be a natural part of the service.

Nor would it be inappropriate for a public service archives office to undertake it (if a satisfactory financial basis could be found), for the object of the service, the improvement of documentation for reference and research (the creation of an effective archive)—is entirely in accord with the objectives of archives offices and the ideals of the profession.(10)

Microreprography in Records Management(11)
In certain circumstances a records manager may decide to use microfilm in some form as an alternative to the retention of originals; the main objective which he is likely to have will be the saving of storage space. There are undoubtedly some circumstances in which this device may be used, and many public authorities have taken steps to ensure that they have the power to employ it, without reducing the legal validity of the records on film. However, if this service is indeed restricted to space-saving, its costing will be a matter for careful consideration.

The cost of reducing records series to film, including their arrangement and indexing, checking and maintaining the film to proper standards, is such that savings will be evident only where the costs of storage are extremely high, and where the records are expected to have a lengthy retention period. These conditions will normally only be found where the employing authority is situated in high-cost central accommodation without the possibility of using records centre accommodation elsewhere.

However, the costs of using microfilm for this purpose may be mitigated if the operation can fulfil other objectives than this one of purely space-saving. There are two methods by which a records manager may reduce the specific costs of a microreprographic programme:
(i)   He may add an additional objective to the programme as originally conceived to save space. Thus if the microform adopted can be used to disseminate necessary copies of the record, or to provide additional points of access to it, the savings to the employing authority, though difficult to calculate, might be more attractive.
(ii)   He may add an additional objective to a microform programme which has already been designed for use in administrative departments for their current business. This will probably be the provision of a record copy at an early stage, which will be usable for reference elsewhere, and which will avoid the need for processing records and intermediate storage.

microreprography

There is one special case in which a microfilm programme should be planned between the records centre and the creating departments. This is the case of maps, plans, and architectural or engineering drawings. A modern administration produces these in very large numbers; their storage and conservation is unusually costly, and a high proportion are on unstable materials. 70 mm. or 35 mm. aperture cards provide what is probably the best method overall for conservation and reference, both during and after currency.(12)

As in the case of destruction, there may be a case for bringing the microreprographic equipment and service directly under the responsibility of the records centre. The costing and implications of this are discussed in a later chapter, since it is likely that such a service will have archival objectives. If this course is adopted, naturally proper accommodation must be provided, and there are special requirements for the storage and administration of records in microform.

6 Acquisition and Arrangement of Archives

The distinction between the management of archives and of records is not a clear one. A records centre will tend to look like an archives office, and will tend to develop archival functions; an archives office cannot avoid an interest in the intake of records from currency, and will tend to develop records functions. The healthiest situation, in principle, is one in which the two are formally interrelated.

Acquisition

An archives office naturally receives its accessions of new archival material because it belongs to or maintains a direct organic relationship with the archive-creating body. National archives institutions always belong to this group, as do the archives offices of local government and of businesses.

There has already been much discussion of the problems and procedures involved in transferring the records of the employing authority out of currency into the hands of records services. In considering the ultimate transfer of records from those services, or from the executive departments of the authority, into the archives proper, it is necessary to stand back a little to consider situations where regular records services have not been created. There are three possible kinds: where there are no established records services, and records are transferred to the archives in large closed backlog accumulations; where there are no records services, and records pass to the archives in regular direct consignments from closed records stores; where there are good records services, and records pass through an appraisal screen and are transferred to the archives as part of a worked-out system. In all circumstances, however, an archives office will seek to bring these accessions into a system, and to establish procedures for selection and transfer with creating departments.

The collection of non-official archives may obviously take many varied forms, and there is room for both a passive and an aggressive policy. Either may be defended in particular circumstances, but normally an active or aggressive acquisition policy will be appropriate for non-official sources; any other policy would require careful justification with regard to the office's objectives (rather than to its resources).

It is a general aim of any repository to build up, within its defined area or field of activity, a documentation which is sufficiently complete to give a true and balanced finding to a research enquiry. If an office is to collect from sources outside its employing authority's records—that is, non-official archives—it must take measures to see that the intake is representative and full. To do this it must set up appropriate structures, and assign the necessary resources from its own stock. A repository will need a section devoted to field work, working in parallel with the records management section.

It will be the duty of the archivist who is the field officer, firstly, to know his field—the record-creating agencies within it, their history and functions, their relationships with government or parallel bodies elsewhere, their whereabouts, and their likely plans for the immediate future. The principal difference between this work and that of an inspecting officer or records manager within departments of the employing authority is that a field officer will not usually be able to call upon any statute or regulation which gives him any status in the record-creating institutions. Typically, the work will be recognized on a voluntary basis by those organizations, and therefore the field officer will depend on his persuasiveness to convince potential donors of the values offered by his service, and he will depend on his energy and perhaps even on his social acquaintances to make the initial contacts.

Systematic search, using all available means of reference, will enable the field officer to maintain lists of sources of archives. The relationship between the archives office and record-transferring agencies is a businesslike one, and will involve appraisal and transfer arrangements broadly similar to those appropriate for official records. The underlying professional requirement to know of and manage all appraised and relevant material remains. The fieldwork side of an archives office must acquire the standards and competence of the records management side, and, of course, it deserves a suitable allocation of resources, particularly in personnel.

The analogy between archival field officers and records managers extends also to the education of their clientele. The owners or holders of accumulations of archives need to be enlightened as to their value and as to the proper means of dealing with them.

A programme of advertisement may be needed in some form, as part of a programme of search and acquisition. There are several such programmes in operation at present, funded by research foundations and by voluntary bodies such as the British Records Association and the Business Archives Council.

Conditions of deposit

When archives are acquired, there will be some form of agreement as between the archives office and the creating department or body, whereby questions of control and ownership are determined. Because of uncertainties in establishing legal ownership of non-official archives, archivists have in the past been unwilling to go deeply into such matters; the tradition of allowing deposit of such material has become common. In this context, 'deposit' means the placing of archives in the custody of an archives office without causing the legal ownership to be transferred to it: the legal owner, whoever he is, retains the right to withdraw the material, subject to any conditions which may have been laid down in the agreement by which the deposit was made.

A form of deposit agreement is given in appendix C.(1) Deposit agreements of this kind must be formal to the point of legal enforcement: that is, there must be a clear contract. Whether this contract is expressed by a formally executed agreement or it is recorded in officially registered correspondence is a matter for decision on particular occasions.

It is probable that the agreement for deposit, though it has been the usual method of transferring private archives to the custody of publicly provided archives offices, should become less common. Other methods of transfer, chiefly donation or sale, might become more common in their place. With the application of increasingly professional standards of conservation and management, the cost to the public of maintaining archive collections has grown. Equally, the value of such collections has grown; the public gets an adequate return for its investment from the use which is made of the archives. On both counts it is desirable that the public should be secure from the danger that depositors (or their successors in title) may withdraw archives for sale or dispersal, after a period on loan, during which they were professionally administered.

It is not always possible to negotiate donations, still less to purchase, and it is not desirable to stimulate the market in archival material. The practice of depositing will therefore continue, and in these cases it is desirable to strengthen the sanctions against withdrawal which are contained in the deposit agreement. These are usually contained in the clause which allows for reimbursement of expenses in conservation, and the calculation of these could be stated to include a share of the cost of staffing, accommodation and management as well as of actual repairs undertaken to specific parts of the accumulation. The cost of managing records in records centres is usually calculated on the basis of a figure per annum for linear measurement of shelving occupied. It should not be difficult to calculate a similar figure for archival storage, which should be higher (though the figure should reflect the actual costs according to the standard of conservation given). It is not suggested that this figure should be charged to depositors as the annual cost of maintaining their archives: it has generally been agreed that this is a charge the public will bear. But a formula can be arrived at by which the compensation due on accumulations of archives withdrawn after deposit can be calculated. A clause providing for photocopies in case of withdrawal might also be considered.

Initial controls
As with a records centre, it is important that an archives office should establish control over its incoming material at the earliest possible point, so that the standards of conservation can be established and the initial processes leading to exploitation can be begun. The processes are registration, initial physical treatment, and notification of the character and whereabouts of the new material.

Archives may be received as backlog accumulations or as transfers forming part of regularly accruing consignments. The treatment accorded to these two kinds of transfer will differ somewhat, but in each case allowance must be made for the likelihood that the consignment is not complete in itself. It may form part of a series, and there may have been earlier transfers of related records, or there may remain material for later transfers.

Backlog Accumulations

Traditional descriptions of the procedure for accessioning archives have referred almost always to backlog accumulations; that is, groups of papers which have been allowed to rest forgotten or unused in closed storage (or, in extreme cases, are discovered where they were not known to be), until they were entirely dead from the point of view of current administration.

The discovery and treatment of such accumulations is like an archaeological excavation: a whole new area of knowledge comes to light. It is important that the find should be properly dealt with and interpreted; wrong treatment at the point of discovery will lead to irrecoverable losses of information. At this point the archivist will seek primarily to recover and record all evidence of the original arrangement of the archives, and of the administrative system which controlled their creation and use. Eventually this system or order must be recorded or re-established when the accumulation has been fully treated archivally.

Consequently the order of the archives in the storage place in which they were identified, or when they are received in the archives office, and any indications of a previous order, are matters of importance. If possible, the archivist responsible for receiving and accessioning the group should see it in its original store, and should there record its arrangement (in bundles, on shelves, etc.) by allocating temporary numbers, unobtrusively and impermanently, by which the order in which they were stored can be determined later. Alternatively, in preparing the consignment for transport, the bundles or other units used then can be made up in a way that indicates at the point of receipt whatever original system was apparent before the transfer. In the case of consignments of very old archives, any original order may require some research to discover; in the case of more recent papers, the order may be apparent from the reference numbers written on the files or containers. In either case there may be no apparent original order at all, and a logical or methodical order would have to be adopted on the basis of the functions of the organization whose archives they are or were. Appraisal will have to be undertaken, except where the accumulation has reached such an age that it is accepted on this basis alone.

Transfers
Transfers of archives under records management arrangements
may be either from official or non-official sources, according to
the programmes of the archives office. Transfers may also be
initial (perhaps with some backlog element) or second or later
transfers in a continuing flow. In any of these cases the aim is still
the re-establishment of the original archival order, the order
imposed upon the archives during their period of currency.

Registration
On arrival at the archives office, the consignment will first be
accessioned. The details of the accumulation are entered in a
register designed and maintained by the office. A separate series
of registers may often be kept for official and for non-official
accessions, but this is not always necessary, as one of the
functions of the accessions register is to record clearly their
provenance, both immediate (where the consignment has just
come from) and ultimate (where these archives were created). A
secondary function of the register is to initiate control procedures,
so that the accumulation's orderly progress through the various
processes in the archives office can be ensured. A third function is
to provide for a receipt to the donor/transferor of the archives.
    A register need not be a volume, and nowadays it probably will
not be; more likely it will be a binder into which predesigned
leaves can be placed. The leaves (or forms) can be duplicated, so
that each entry can be sent to different destinations or used for
different purposes. An example appears in figure 6.1.(2)
    At this point of registration it is usually convenient to allocate
to the consignment an accession number by which it can be
identified. This can be written on labels or on boxes in which the
newly accessioned group is kept, and the archivist in charge of the
operation is then at liberty to store the group away under its
accession number, if that is the most convenient thing, until such
time as further work can be done on it. However, the registration
process should now be completed far enough to attain its
secondary objectives: control of processing and notification; and
to make retrieval possible.

Notification
As important as registration is the notification to interested
parties of the arrival and accessioning of the archive
accumulation. The donor, depositor or transferor of the group

ACKNOWLEDGEMENT OF ARCHIVES RECEIVED.	
Source: Donor/Depositor/Transferor . . . . Address	Accession No: Reference code: Date of deposit/transfer Terms of deposit
Description of archives:	

Dates	Description Provenance

6.1 Specimen accessions form

should always be told formally of its accession, and should be given a record of the transaction which will allow him to trace and identify the archives in the future. This may conveniently be done by providing a second copy of the register entry, which may be sent to the donor as soon as the entry has been made. If it is to be used for this purpose, the copy which goes to the donor must contain some simple explanatory wording such as the following:(3)

The following archives are now stored at the Archives Office under the terms specified. Any enquiries concerning these archives should be addressed to the Archivist, quoting the accession number.

This means that this wording will appear on the second (duplicate) leaf of the register. Since carbon will be used, naturally the spaces for written information must correspond.

In some cases it may be thought preferable not to use the registration form in this way, but to delay notification of any description of the archives until a list or inventory has been made. In this case, the donor may be sent a simple form letter of receipt at the time of accession. It is important that some clear receipt, identifying and showing the whereabouts of the archives, should remain with the donor. This is not only to satisfy the requirements of good public relations, but also as part of the moral defence of the archives.

The archives office will consider whether any other body should
be notified of the receipt of this particular archive group at this
point; possible recipients of notification might be bodies whose
records interlink with those of the donor, neighbouring or
associated archives offices, national collections with associated
interests, research bodies interested in the field, and the National
Register of Archives. Certain categories of records must be
notified to the proper authorities.(4)

Retrieval (Preliminary)

The next stage is to see to the physical safety of the consignment
by putting it through the fumigator, or by otherwise cleaning,
unfolding and repacking its constituent parts until it can be safely
assumed that the new arrival is not going to import contamination
into the storage area; that there will be no active deterioration of
the material; and that the processes to be undertaken by the
archives office are under control.

The work card or sheet to record progress (figure 6.2(5)) will
contain an analysis of the principal steps in the archival process,
omitting those better dealt with separately. It should not be too
detailed; if it is there will be a strong tendency for the working
archivists to omit entering the dates and initials in the right hand
columns. Something must be left to the individual's ability to
remember what he is doing. On the other hand, enough should be
included to allow the work card to be used as a genuine control,
particularly where a team is involved and all processes are not in
the hands of one person. The work cards should be filed in such a
way as to enable any colleague to see the stage each archive
series has reached, where it is, and what remains to be done; and
also to enable the chief of section to see what overall progress has
been made against the section's programme. It may be possible to
include deadlines, or expected target dates against the principal
groups of activities, though here again too much complexity
should be avoided.

At the end of the accessioning process, the archives are packed
and stored, identifiable by the description entered in the
accessions register, a record of their location is made, interested
parties are informed, and a control of further processes
established. The archives can now await the moment when the
office's programme can resume to complete the work which
remains to be done on them.

ARCHIVES CONSIGNMENT WORK CARD	LOCATION		
Accession details:			
		Date	By whom
Accessioning processes: registered donor notified register indexed entered in index of donors boxed and stored location registered summary list completed distribution of list			
Description processes: Sorting carried out draft inventory coding, marking final location guide summary index			
Typing and distribution: inventory to typist typed and corrected distribution			
Temporary accessions (where applicable) entered in temporary accessions register register indexed boxed, labelled with temporary accession number location registered returned to donor/ transferred			

6.2 Work card to control processing

Arrangement
Putting archives into their proper and final order is termed
'arrangement', although an alternative, 'classification', is still in
common usage. There is an important difference between the two
words: to arrange things is to place them in an order relative to
each other (this is what is done in archives work); to classify
things is to allocate them to categories previously established
(librarians classify books in subject categories which have been
determined to cater for a wide field of knowledge(6)).

Every archive accumulation is unique, and the way in which it is arranged must be determined after a study of its composition. However, there are classes of archives which bear a strong family relationship to similar classes elsewhere. For example, the staple group in every British county record office is the archives of the court of Quarter Sessions. Each county's Quarter Sessions archives are in a real sense unique, not only because each document gives unique information, but because differences in procedure, custom, etc., give each one unique characteristics which will certainly be reflected in the archival arrangement. But, on the whole, one series of Quarter Sessions archives looks like another, and can be explained almost entirely in terms of statutes or practices operating over the whole country. The county record offices have therefore been able to develop what can truly be called a classification scheme for Quarter Sessions archives,(7) and if a new accumulation of county Quarter Sessions papers were now to come to light, it could no doubt be classified, that is, sorted into the various categories established by usage, because the expectation would be that this arrangement would be found to suit the original administrative system which created the archives. There would no doubt be idiosyncratic sections for which new categories would have to be devised, but on the whole this classification would correspond to and explain the administrative origin and working of the archives, and would make the accumulation comprehensible, at least to those who are used to working with Quarter Sessions material.

There are other possible examples of a similar kind, where similar groups of archives appear in different areas and where they may be fitted into a classification scheme; but it is important to remember that classification schemes such as these are based, not on subject categories, but on an analysis of the functions and divisions of the originating body, which followed organizational patterns in local administration.

The Principle of Provenance
The object is to reconstruct, if that can be done, the arrangement of the archives bequeathed by the administrative machinery which brought them into existence. Since in many cases the place from whence the archives come into the archives office is not actually the place where they were brought into existence, the archivist is usually obliged to look behind the order in which he finds the

archives, to a possible earlier order of their creation. It is this primitive order which we usually seek to restore or to preserve, or at least to record, and the final archival arrangement will be one where the archives are placed with 'the last Administration in which it played an active part',(8) but where earlier arrangements are recorded and set out in the finding aids.

To establish what this arrangement should be demands investigation and analysis. 'Basic to practically all activities of the archivist is his analysis of records. This analysis involves him in studies of the organizational and functional origins of records to obtain information on their provenance, subject, content, and interrelations. . . . Analytical activities are the essence of an archivist's work; the other activities that are based on them are largely of a physical nature.'(9)

But *seul compte l'intérêt de l'histoire.*'(10) The principle of provenance is adopted, not for its own sake, but because it is the only satisfactory way of interpreting series of records as material for research. But there are situations in which provenance by itself is not sufficient guide to the detailed arrangement of archives, and where this is so, different methods (chronological, alphabetical, etc.) may be used. But underlying all these methods is the fact that archives belong essentially in series explicable only in terms of the administrative system which was using them. Whatever method of arrangement is used must set forth the original meaning of that system.

In establishing a 'pure' archival arrangement the archivist is safeguarding the historical authenticity of the archives; he is performing for the user a vital function, though it may not always be appreciated. Before he can exploit a document for its historical information, any historian must evaluate that document by placing it in its original context and by analysing its characteristics by reference to that—its author, his purposes, its readers, the action from which it sprang and to which it gave rise, the structures within which the protagonists acted, etc. It is the archival arrangement of records which preserves and explains this original context and its implications. In all but most complicated cases, this arrangement and exposition is done by the archivist: that is his function. Jenkinson called it the moral defence of archives: 'the only correct basis of Arrangement is exposition of the Administrative objects which the Archives originally served.'(11)

Other Principles of Arrangement

Arrangement by subject is not permissible, since it is not compatible with the moral defence of the archives: in the words of the French manual, it is *'dissolvant'*, disintegrative. Two other alternative methods may be considered: by *form* (like kinds of document placed with like kinds), and by *function* of the original administration.

Arrangement by form is commonly met with in archives offices. In the Public Record Office at one time this was carried to the length of bringing together like documents from different departments or places of origin. This is the cause of certain artificial groupings such as Ancient Correspondence.(12) Such categories are not permissible because, in making them, clear administrative distinctions were ignored. Thus arrangement by form must always be secondary to arrangement by provenance, and can only be used when provenance will give no further guidance.

The principle gives a good deal of latitude in practice. For example, at the present day the India Office Records operate a scheme of arrangement which depends to quite a large degree upon form: indexes, for example form a distinct series.(13) A problem is that arrangement by form often looks deceptively like arrangement by administrative origin.(14) Prior to the invention of the typewriter, many offices did in fact keep their papers, for administrative purposes, in three chronological series based upon similarity of form: in-letters, out-letters and internal memoranda, and until very recently documents were often filed in law courts according to their form—writs with writs, affidavits with affidavits—and were not grouped in cases, which would have facilitated access to the recorded information.

In setting out a principle, however, the principle of administrative origin must be taken as the guide. Sometimes arrangement by form is more convenient in use, sometimes it corresponds, in fact, with original administrative systems. More often, however, arrangement by form may stand in the way of exploitation and reference. But the moral defence of the archives, by exposition of original relationships, stands above convenience, both of storage and description and of reference.

Another alternative is arrangement by function. The Quarter Sessions classification scheme already mentioned is an example of this. Since a relatively primitive system of archive making in an administration with few staff and without strict management did

not, as a matter of historical fact, introduce sufficient functional
subdivisions in creating record series, we have now to introduce
these subdivisions in order to make the total archive intelligible.
Arrangement by function is a way of doing this, in preference to
an arrangement which would have been nearer to the original
administrative order, but much less valuable to us: arrangement
of all the papers as a miscellany, bundled session by session.

It may be accepted, then, that in many cases the principle of
arrangement by provenance can be compromised in certain
directions, subject to certain safeguards. No original bundle, file
binding, or grouping may be broken up without record. The overall
object is to allow the archives to support and explain each other
by setting them in a mutual relationship determined by the
operations which caused their creation.

Physical Arrangement and Listing Arrangement
It is assumed above that there is only one order possible, into
which the archivist has to arrange his archives. Physically, of
course, this is true; but, as Jenkinson recognized, there may be
one order into which the archives themselves are sorted, and
other orders into which the lists and inventories may be arranged
in response to particular needs. Jenkinson insisted that the order
of the archives themselves must be that of provenance, whatever
was done about listing.(15) Other archivists have noted that,
provided sufficient record is kept of what has been done, the
archives themselves can be sorted into any convenient order, and
the actual 'archival' order can be preserved on paper, in the
central list.(16)

Handling and Control
The process of sorting incoming consignments of archives
proceeds at two levels. At the deeper of these, the archivist is
analysing the documents in order to discern their true archival
order and significance. At the more superficial, he establishes a
suitable physical order in which they can be boxed and shelved
(figure 6.3).

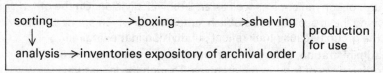

6.3 The initial sorting process

One rule of Jenkinson's is very wise: the archivist should place with the archives he is working on a note or notes, signed and dated, indicating what he has done. The habit of leaving such notes, either attached to individual archive items or to whole groups, or in the record of the archives office itself, should be widely cultivated.

Archive Groups and Series

A mass of archives must be subdivided in order to make it intelligible, and to control it as it goes through the various processes (figure 6.4), and so that it may be effectively described and put to use. The whole mass must be analysed in order to determine what these subdivisions should be.

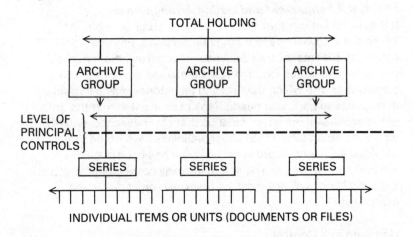

6.4 Control subdivisions of an archival accumulation

The archivist's work suffers from an unresolved conflict in recognizing subdivisions in an archive group. On the one hand, he is seeking to control the group by breaking it up into units of convenient size; this is true too of the archive group itself: it is a unit of convenience as well as an 'archival' division. On the other hand, he is seeking to establish subdivisions which are natural to the group because they reflect subdivision in the original administration, differences of function in that administration, or differences of form in the archives. Though these 'natural' subdivisions are what is aimed at archivally, the satisfactory control achieved by 'convenient' subdivisions can hardly be forgotten. Every archive series or subseries has its own characteristics which vary according to the character of its originating body, its size and its methods.

Archive Groups
The largest category in this model is that of the archive group. It is conceived as being the totality of the archives created by a self-contained administrative entity, classically a government department. Jenkinson's definition has something like this in mind:

all the Archives resulting from the work of an Administration which was an organic whole, complete in itself, capable of dealing independently, without any added or external authority, with every side of any business which could normally be presented to it.(17)

An extension of this definition, in the case of local government or business administration, would allow the major departments to appear as distinct archive groups, thus helping the archivist to break up the mass of his holdings into hierarchical divisions.

Unfortunately these divisions are proving to be too hierarchical and too rigid to be applied to the records of modern administration, and discussion of the validity of the archive group as understood in central government archives was well under way in the 1960s. Ian Maclean's 1962 essay on Australian practice(18) was followed by an influential article by P. J. Scott in 1966 attacking the concept of the record group.(19)

'Changes have been taking place not only between successive transfers of records in the same series but even during the time which it takes to process a series for transfer,(20) departments of government moved from one ministry to another, or their functions were split between two ministries; or they were closed or radically altered. Composite and 'super-ministries' (in the phrase of the popular press) were created, and in some cases it became difficult to maintain the broad classifications, perhaps bearing the names of obsolete ministries or departments no longer controlling those series of archives. The development of records management meant that regular transfers of records from the same series came into the archives as well as closed whole series, and parts of former series could come in from different sources. Parallel changes were taking place in administration generally.

Archive series

The solution to these problems seemed to be to take a smaller
unit as the main archival subdivision, the series. In the words of
P. J. Scott, archive series are(21)

a group of record items which, being controlled by numbers or other symbols, are
in the same sequence of numbers or symbols, or which, being uncontrolled by
numbers or symbols, result from the same accumulation or filing process and are
of similar physical shape and informational content.

This definition visualises a very cohesive group of records,
perhaps an office or departmental filing system which hangs
together for the purposes of that office or department. Each series
will relate closely to one administrative function, and this of
course is its virtue.

Registration of Series

To operate an archival management system satisfactorily where
the principal controls are at this lower level, it is necessary to have
an arrangement for cross reference and registration of record
series. Each series will have a registration entry explaining its
relationship to other series and to large units and superior
authorities, with the changes in these relationships which have
occurred from time to time. A natural extension of this registration
of series is to include current series so that they can in due time
take their place in the total archival system. In time the register of
record series will become a key to the continuously evolving
administrative history of the creating authority. Figure 6.5(22)
outlines the items of information required in it.

In the Public Record Office a moderate application of the same
principle has been adopted, which depends less upon paper-
based systems of registration and more upon the physical and
historical characteristics of archives series received.(23)

It has . . . been possible to reduce the emphasis on the record group and to
concentrate it on the series (known in the Public Record Office as the 'class'). . . .
Successive transfers of records in a continuing series are now placed in the same
class irrespective of their source; new classes are placed in the most convenient
group, having regard to related classes; new groups are not necessarily created
when a new department is established, if there is a convenient existing
group.

There are dangers in this procedure as soon as it leaves the area
of convenient practical control and enters that of the archival
interpretation of records series. The strangest cases are those
where a series is described under the heading of a ministry which
did not exist at the time of the creation of the records in question,

REGISTRATION OF RECORD SERIES: CODE:
1. Series title   Date range

2. Characteristics of the series:
    nature of its arrangement . . . .
    bulk, rate of growth . . . .
    means of access . . . .

3. Controlling authority at inception of the series . . . .
    Subsequent changes of controlling authority . . . .
    Controlling authority at point of transfer to archives . . . .

4. Related record series:
    prior to inception . . . .
    subsequent to inception . . . .
    parallel series . . . .

5. Archival means of access . . . .

6.5 Specimen record for the registration of series

but which happened to be the transferring authority, or was at one
time the transferring authority of one part of the series.

However, if it is not taken too far, there is much sense in the
method of taking the record series as the basic control group. It is
an approach to classification by function, since cohesive records
series will tend to belong to departments which deal with one
thing; where the record series of such departments have been
broken up in the course of administration and later rearranged, it
is because the function in question has been reorganized.(24)

In local government and business concerns the principle of
arrangement under record series still holds good: administrative
function and departmentalization are likely to be linked. The
archivist will look for functional record series which have archival
continuity. Since the machinery of control and policy-making is
not so directly linked in local government or business to the
departmental structure of the authority as it is in central
government, there may be less complication; the records of

control come under the headings provided by committees/clerks, and the records of executive administration and research under those of departmental offices.(25)

But in recent times there have been many complicated realignments in both these categories. Multi-disciplinary programmes are emerging in place of single departments, each with its committee, clerk and chief officer; and in business organizations the relationship between management accountant and departmental heads has been a cause of change. Nevertheless the functional department, with its own personnel, premises and record system, will often provide a historical and archival link through periods of change. And even if this is not so, it provides a convenient unit of control archivally.

There is no reason, of course, why a particular record series should not end, or a new one begin, at the point where a change comes which makes the old series unrecognizable. The record series linked to administrative function then can often be taken as the basic archival unit of control.

Where the administration being served is a small one not every record can naturally be regarded as belonging to a series, and not every series has the cohesion, continuity and size which would make it suitable as a basis for archival control. In these cases the record series becomes a heading under which a number of disparate sub-series or units are described, and there will be a large number of small subdivisions. The all-important thing is that natural divisions between sections of the archives should be recognized. 'In his choice of arrangement for a list the archivist should aim for the "natural" in preference to the "artificial".'(26)

Within the series arrangement as before follows the administrative structure which brought the records into existence. Where records of an earlier system have been integrated into a later one, they should normally be treated as part of the later one; where these records still form a recognizable and separate (closed) record series, however, they can be treated independently. The relationship of sub-series and items to each other, if this is not dictated by the original system, should be treated logically or upon a convenient arrangement, whether chronological, alphabetical by title; or hierarchically (controlling or main series preceding executive or subordinate series).

Existing means of reference—file lists, file analyses, indexes— should be transferred with the records for use as retrieval instruments, wherever possible.

Storage

The final end of archival arrangement is the orderly placement of
the actual archives within the storage areas, coupled with their
presentation for use in a system of reference instruments.
Although the physical arrangement of the archives on the shelf
may in some cases be determined by reasons of convenient
administration, the arrangement and content of the reference
instruments has the important purpose of ensuring the moral
defence of the archives, that is, the preservation and setting
forth of their natural place and interrelationships within the
systems of the originating authority.

7 Description of Archives

Identification and Retrieval

Coding

The process of arrangement and sorting is undertaken in order to establish a sound archival order, which is in itself an explanation of past administrative structures and practice. It remains to make this arrangement permanent by allocating to the various series and sub-series a system of codes or symbols by which they can be referred to and called for in the search room. These codes will be marked on the containers in which the archives are kept and, in many cases, on the actual documents themselves. The codes must be permanent (if at all possible) since, for one thing, they will be quoted in footnotes and references. It is therefore important that the coding system adopted in the office should be well designed, and that the archival analysis of the actual archive series (on which the codes are based) should be well carried out. Reference codes of course will be keyed to lists, and the process of coding will be done as part of the listing process.

The objectives of a coding system are fourfold:
(i) It must satisfactorily identify the archives both at the level of individual items or pieces, and at the level of series and sub-series.
(ii) Since it is permanent, the code must be used to distinguish the interrelationships between series and their components.
(iii) The code may be so constructed that it can demonstrate to a lay user the nature of the archival relationships, as well as the place occupied by the series in question in relation to other groups

and series and in the administrative structures of the originating authority.

(iv) A subsidiary objective is concerned with security: a document marked with an archival code or reference is less easily stolen or lost.

For practical reasons the three main objectives are rarely entirely compatible. Where they are not, it is the two first which are primary. Archival codes must effectively identify the archives and so enable them to be found and replaced, and they must render the archival order and relationships permanent. It is a bonus if the codes themselves, when quoted, can convey some of these meanings to readers without further explanation.

The accession number allocated when the archive series was first received will serve to achieve the first objective during the early stages of existence of the series within the archives office. It should not normally be used as the permanent code, because it does not achieve the second or third objectives. To establish a permanent archival code demands analysis, and therefore comes after the sorting and arrangement of the group and incorporates the results of the archivist's analysis and research.

An ideal archival coding system will therefore be more than a simple call number. It will identify the group, series or sub-series, and piece, in any given case, and if possible it will do this without extensive reference to guides or key lists. This suggests that a mnemonic, or at least a lettered code, is preferable to a purely numerical system, where the number of groups, series or collections is sufficiently small to allow it. In practice, since the probable intake of related series in the future will be great, it will only be possible to use mnemonics to indicate the principal groups; series and sub-series will inevitably remain numerical in most cases. A further consideration is that ready intelligibility would be improved if there could be more uniformity of practice between different archival institutions in one nation, or even internationally.

It is in the local archives office that coding (with arrangement and description generally) comes nearest to classification. The contents of each archives office are unique, but belong to broad categories that are comparable to those found in all or most such offices. In the early days of the county record office it was found that those who published the first guides in practice established classification schemes which tended to be used in archives offices that were slightly less advanced. Most generally recognized is the

scheme for coding Quarter Sessions archives which is associated
with the Essex Record Office.(1) Another scheme which has been
widely adopted is that for Poor Law Guardians initiated by the
Somerset Record Office.(2) A more recent extension is the
scheme for modern County Council records, set out by the Kent
Archives Office.(3) No doubt there will be further extensions of
familiar classifications as more official archives come to be held
by local archives offices. This would be a process to be
encouraged.

Coding systems for private deposits of non-official papers are
somewhat different. There appear to be three methods in use in
local archives offices:

Arbitrary serial numbers, such as U475, U1000. In this case the
symbol U indicates an 'unofficial' collection. The code U1000
designates a portmanteau group to receive miscellaneous small
deposits, each of which receives a sub-number.(4)

Another example is 132M. In this case the number 132
identifies a single deposited collection. The fact that it is a
numerical and not a letter code distinguishes it from any official
archives. The suffix M denotes a subject/form classification.(5)

Mnemonic codes, such as DSA, DDX. In these cases the prefixed
D indicates a deposited accumulation, and the other two letters
are a mnemonic contraction of the principal name of the deposit
(Stanley of Alderley). The second code (DDX) is the customary
portmanteau for small miscellaneous collections, which are so
often of deeds.(6)

Uncontracted titles. Where accumulations are coded by their full
titles or descriptions, references can be quite lengthy, but, if this is
acceptable, there will be no problem of running out of available
codes or of ambiguity.

Some local archives offices have adopted a coding system to
distinguish features or components of a deposited accumulation.
Thus, to extend an example above, 132M/TY12 refers as
follows:(7)

132   a serial number identifying the deposit. It is keyed to
       a register.

M   identifies a subject/form element in the content of the
       deposit which brings it into an arbitrary category, in
       this case 'manorial'. This is convenient, since
       manorial archives must be reported to a central
       register.

TY   sub-categories of a similar kind, applying to particular parts of the accumulation. T refers to title deeds, and Y is an archival sub-division.

12   item or document number.

Other archives offices have even more elaborate versions of this system. The only essential element in the code given is the series, sub-series and item numbers: 132/Y12 would satisfactorily identify the document. The other elements in the code are therefore flags which may serve as additional means of retrieval.

Reference Instruments

Once the archives have been sorted, arranged and coded, the process continues with their fuller description in a series of finding instruments. The archivist should construct as many and as varied examples of these as are necessary for the full exploitation of the information to be found in his archives, subject only to the limitations which the office's resources and priorities may impose at any particular time.

Basically there are only two kinds of descriptive instruments: the *list* and the *index.* The varied purposes which lists may serve suggest that a complex of lists may be called an expository system, while indexes, in their various forms, remain strictly retrieval auxiliaries. The relationships between the various descriptive instruments can be best illustrated by a model (figure 7.1).

All descriptive activities inevitably begin with a summary description or registration which, as has been seen above, is also a necessary beginning to the establishment of any intellectual control over archives at all. The accessions registration makes the group technically available for use, and as far as possible suggests the form of later listing; but it is essentially summary, and must inevitably be done before extensive study and analysis are given to the archives. It is therefore of short-term value only.

Study and analysis of the series being listed may often reveal misconceptions in the initial summary description, and this, of course, will have to be put right. But further listing will proceed until a full archival analysis of the series has been reached and an adequately full description of each item has been included.

A fully developed list has four elements:

(i) An explanatory introduction, which tells the user where the archives came from, and gives some basic facts about their origin, content, size and physical character.

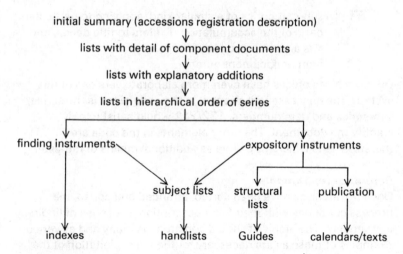

initial summary (accessions registration description)

lists with detail of component documents

lists with explanatory additions

lists in hierarchical order of series

finding instruments   expository instruments

subject lists   structural   publication
                        lists

indexes   handlists   Guides   calendars/texts

7.1 Scheme of reference tools

(ii)   The list proper: an inventory of units, items or pieces
(omitting none) within the series. Each entry will give a
description more or less full, according to the immediate aim of
this particular list, of the character and content of the unit
described.

(iii) A layout which makes the list explanatory, breaking up the
text under headings and subheadings, based upon the original
structure of the archives, and so corresponding to the analysis
presented in the first section.

(iv) A further finding aid based upon the list, typically an index,
with possibly a list of contents or key to the construction of the
series and its components.

   The amount of detail in any particular list should be decided as
a matter of policy within the office. In making a decision the staff
will bear in mind their resources, their priorities of work, and their
immediate aim in constructing the list. They will also have a style
to which this list should conform. But the final goal will be a
complete inventory which gives information on the character and
content of each component or item in all series held.

   Since resources are always limited, and there are always more
archives to be listed, it is unlikely that any particular series will
ever be listed twice. But in its plan the archives office will provide
for a hierarchy of lists, so that, although the overall objective is the
description of every item held, the actual lists fit together into an
explanatory apparatus in which one part depends upon another.

Larger categories of archives will have lists of a rather summary kind giving an over-view of their make-up, and saying what series compose them; these series, for their parts, have rather more detailed lists, explaining how they fit into the group, and giving more detail on their composition and content. At the bottom end of the pyramid, much more detailed lists of sub-series or particular components of the series complete the lists.

The important thing is to see that this family or hierarchy of lists does in fact fit together adequately, and does in fact give, not only keys for the retrieval of particular documents or items of information from them, but also a satisfactory exposition of their archival and administrative relationships. A reader can pass from one list in the hierarchy to another, gaining more information from the lower ones about the content of the sub-series or smaller units he is dealing with, and from the higher ones about the shape and meaning of the archives in their context. Each step in the ladder has a different purpose and value, but no step can really be left out, at least where large and complex archive series are concerned; all these processes are interrelated (figure 7.2).

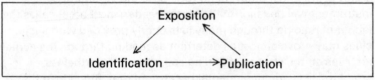

7.2 Relationship of description processes

As the list becomes more detailed, it moves from the exposition pole (where its main purpose is to make the archive group intelligible and to provide some historical authentication) towards the identification pole (where its main purpose is to allow the reader to select which particular document he needs to study). As further detail is added the list moves towards the realm of the calendar (where the main purpose is to publish or disseminate the content of documents) and where there must be some return to exposition in order to make the material comprehensible.

Structural and subject lists
Archival lists or inventories ought to include every component of the accumulation being listed. But it is possible and often useful to make lists on a selective basis. There are in fact two kinds of list available to an archivist: one based upon the structure of the archives, and the other based on the needs of the user. This

central dichotomy separates all types of archive descriptive material: on the one side, there is material with a primarily expository (and authenticating) purpose; on the other, material with a primarily identifying purpose.(8) An archivist must provide both kinds of instrument.

Of the two kinds, structural finding aids are the more fundamental, though they may in many circumstances seem less immediately useful. In practice, most users require only subject-based finding aids. Their enquiries will be conceived in terms of a subject, and when they arrive at the archives office they may present their enquiry in these terms: 'What archives do you hold which bear upon such and such a subject?' To answer this, they will scan the lists and indexes, looking for key words connecting with their subject. Structural lists (though they may give the reader important information which will make him more familiar with the methods used by the office) will only be of direct use for identification of relevant documents to those—obviously relatively few—readers whose purpose is the investigation of the historical growth and operation of the administration whose archives are under study. In this one case the structural instrument will be tailor-made for the reader; in all other cases the labour of reading through many lists poorly provided with subject clues may prove almost as deterrent as reading through the actual archives on the chance of finding something. Nevertheless, structural lists are fundamental because of their function in the moral defence of archives. For this reason they cannot be replaced by descriptive systems which concentrate upon identification or retrieval, and for this reason also a library catalogue method is not a suitable form of control for archives.

A structural system of lists will account for the series, sub-series and items in an accumulation of archives in an order determined by its original administrative structure. Any additional information will tend to be confined to explanations of this structure, the historical circumstances of its creation and of its transfer to archival custody.

On the other hand, the objective of a descriptive system based upon subject will be to bring into one list all significant items or series which bear upon the given subject. The purpose of such a list need not necessarily be strictly confined to identification; it may very well include a large element of exposition. A subject-based list should not ignore or override structural facts about the archives.

There is a range of possible types of subject instrument. At one end, there is the pure subject list, a finding aid like that of a library subject catalogue, bringing together items which have nothing in common archivally, but which give information on the same subject; at the other end, there is a sort of selective guide, which describes the archives structurally, but selects for description those structures which are likely to deal, wholly or in part, with a particular subject area. Since administrative subdivisions and structures are often linked to function, it is very often possible to provide this kind of list quite easily. A good example is provided by some of the handbooks published by the Public Record Office;(9) in another interesting case, subject-chosen structural guides to records held in different archives offices in a region, have been published.(10) It is to be hoped that this kind of finding aid will be multiplied.

Outside the two major categories of descriptive instrument, there are two minor ones to be observed.

(i) It is possible in some cases that a useful finding aid is a list of documents according to form. This list, often called a 'handlist', is typified by some published by county record offices; for example, there are handlists of enclosure records, or of deposited plans. A common extension of this class, which is on the verge of archive work proper, is lists of maps and plans.

(ii) A useful tool within the office is a list based upon the physical order of series of documents. In the form of shelf-lists these can be used for stocktaking (where this is attempted), and for guidance in finding and returning documents; beyond this they can sometimes have a more strictly archival purpose in fixing the original order of a series in their physical locations.

Guides

When an archives office has described most of its holdings in a series of structural lists, it may consider that a general guide is the most appropriate final form of description. In effect this is a collection of structural descriptions put together (usually in summary form) in logical order to provide a more or less general picture of the total holdings of the archive office.

An important prerequisite of a guide is that it should cover virtually every archive series held by the office, or at least every series which falls within a defined category. It is more important that the guide should be comprehensive in this way than that the description accorded in it to any particular series should be complete.

The guide to the Public Record Office is in three parts. The first volume concerns the records of the ancient offices of government, and their direct successors. The second concerns the archives of specialist departments of government, which generally have grown from offices created in the early modern period. The first two sections of the guide are constantly being expanded, the first by the addition of further information which becomes available as parts of the archives are listed, or further listed; the second by the constant addition of new accretions. The third volume is concerned with accessions between 1960 and 1966. In many county record offices, separate guides have appeared for the three main categories of archives held in many of them: official archives of the county, archives of the established Church, and private archives deposited there.

If a guide is not comprehensive, it may not achieve its basic objectives. These are normally twofold:

(i) It should give an explanatory over-view set out to convey essential information about provenance and content to the user. The level at which this explanatory material is given will vary according to the immediate aim. The main purpose may be the education of users completely new to the operations of an archive office; this may often be the case with local archive offices. On the other hand it may be assumed that the user is familiar with these basics, and concentrate only on exposition of the composition and content of the archives; this will usually be the form adopted in national archives or large institutions.

(ii) It should give a co-ordinating over-view also of the finding aids and descriptive systems in use in the archives office. In so far as a guide is for identification, it is to enable the user to identify, not actual archives, but those further or more detailed lists or descriptive instruments which he must use in order to find the archives he needs. There must be a direct link between these further lists and descriptive systems and the guide which serves as a general description of them also.

It has been stated above that a guide should be comprehensive. But is possible to arrange entries on uniform stationery, bind them in some form of loose-leaf folder, and so make up partial guides on a subject or other systematic base.(11) A guide, after all, is a collected series of entries arranged in predetermined order, each describing a particular series of archives, and displayed according to a set pattern. If each description were set out on a separate sheet of uniform stationery, individual users could build up sets of those most appropriate to their needs. Alternatively guides could be issued in sections as the work of description proceeds, or as composite guides to holdings, or parts of holdings, in different archives offices. Figure 7.3 shows two specimens of guide entries.

Indexing
All lists and descriptive instruments should normally be indexed. The index is an instrument which allows users to identify particular documents or pieces of information relevant to their search, and it is therefore the means whereby the arrangement and interpretation of archives in series may be modified to make subject-based inquiries possible. Since searches are mainly subject-based, the successful exploitation of archives depends upon the construction of indexes.

Indexing, however, is a specialized technique which has developed greatly during the present century; at the moment it is developing even more rapidly under the stimulus of information science. It has a large and growing literature, and this should be consulted when an indexing system is to be designed.

It is of course theoretically possible to index original records direct. In some cases (for example, parish registers) this is often done, although usually it is undertaken by associations of users rather than by archivists directly. In fact, this type of indexing is usually regarded as being beyond the resources of the archives office, or low on its scale of priorities. However, only certain kinds of archives are really apt for direct indexing, and indexes in general are keyed to lists. This means that only those names or words which appear in the lists, or only those concepts which are referred to in them, appear in the index; in these circumstances the index will be no more valuable as a means of exploitation than the list itself (though of course it will be a necessary supplement to the list), and the construction of the list will have to be carefully planned so as to include all the words and concepts to be indexed.

Indexes must be planned upon a uniform basis which will allow for their being combined—that is, the indexes relating to different series or kinds of archive or list should be capable of being united in a single series if that is thought desirable. It is probable that thought should be given to the possibility of putting the indexes on to a computer, so that rearrangement of entries and constant

(a) Official Records(12)

LOCAL BOARDS OF HEALTH   LB

Under the Public Health Act, 1848, a General Board of Health was formed with powers to create, by Order in Council, local boards of health as sanitary authorities in towns which lacked borough administration. (In municipal boroughs, the town council was constituted the public health authority). The Local Government Act, 1858, allowed such boards to be formed by resolution of the ratepayers, without the intervention of the General Board. The boards were authorised to appoint officials, including a surveyor, inspector of nuisances, and a qualified medical officer. Their powers were transferred to urban district councils by the Local Government Act, 1894. The Mold Local Board was formed in 1859, that for Holywell in 1862.

HOLYWELL. Minutes, 1869-94; committee minutes, 1864-86; draft minutes, 1872-82, 1892-4; declarations of members (under Public Health Act, 1875), 1876-93; accounts for market hall and assembly hall, 1893-8; specification for new town hall, 1880; general correspondence, 1870-4; circulars concerning Welsh Intermediate Education Act and proposed school, 1890; plans of market and corn exchange, 1864-74, and new baths at St. Winefride's Well, 1869; general district rate books, 1882-92.

MOLD. Minutes, 1859-94; bye-laws, 1891; plans of buildings at Bailey Hill, 1879.

(b) Church records.(13)

RECORDS OF JURISDICTION

6. *Cause Papers* [CP, series E-J]

Files of papers recording the proceedings in cases heard in the archiepiscopal courts. In addition to tithe, matrimonial and testamentary causes, the other main types of case coming before the ecclesiastical courts at York concerned church dues and assessments, defamation, faculties, clerical discipline, dilapidations, disputed presentations to livings and transmitted appeals from other dioceses in the province and from lesser jurisdictions. Obviously the size and content of these files vary considerably and the survival of all or any of the documents produced in the courts—constitutions of proctors, libels, citations, articles, responsions, allegations, interrogatories, depositions, exceptions, exhibits, definitive sentences, taxations and bills of costs—must be a matter of chance. It is hoped eventually to arrange these cause papers by courts but this is very much a long-term project.

early 14th-20th centuries   (653 boxes)

[A summary list of and a partial place index for series E-I are available at the Borthwick Institute.]

7.3 Specimen guide entries

updating in new orders will be possible. This possibility, even if it is not realized, also requires indexes to be written up in accordance with strict instructions regarding layout, vocabulary, punctuation and references. No new index of any importance should now be started without taking specialist advice, or without considering whether existing models, such as that supplied in Britain by the National Register of Archives, should not be adopted as they stand.

Indexes are of names of persons, places or subject words and concepts. Large indexes require a multiplicity of cross-references, whereby relationships between persons, places or subjects can be indicated. Archival indexing encounters particular difficulties in the standardization of spellings of names, and in the identification of names which have changed or which are not certain. Rules of practice exist for the solution of these problems. Subject indexing requires discipline in the use of related concepts, and a permitted vocabulary displaying the principal relationships should be used.

The following extracts from the scheme for subject indexing prepared by the National Register of Archives demonstrate how this discipline can be built up.

The Subject-Index Schema establishes a hierarchical relationship between concepts, in this case using four degrees of ranking (figure 7.4(14)).

(1)	(2)	(3)	(4)
GOVERNMENT, LOCAL:	Finance:	General Rates:	General County Rate Highway Rate Police Rate Poor Rate Sewer Rate
	: Highway Administration	General Finance Street Cleansing, Lighting & Paving	
	: Organisation	General:	Boundaries
		Boroughs:	General Mayoralty Town Halls
		Counties:	General County Councils Shire Halls
		Parish Councils & Parish Meetings Rural District Councils Urban District Councils	

(1)	(2)	(3)	(4)
GOVERNMENT, LOCAL: Poor Relief: (cont.)		General	
		Houses of Industry	
		Overseers of the Poor	
		Public Assistance	
		Settlement	
		Unions and Boards of Guardians	
		Vagrancy	
		Workhouses	
		General	
		Baths & Washhouses	
		Epidemics: General	
			Bubonic Plague
			Cholera
			Smallpox
		Improvement Committees	
		Infestation Control	
		Local Boards of Health & Sanitary Authorities	
		Refuse	
		Sewerage	
		Welfare	
	: Public Order	General	
		Bellmen	
		Constables	
		Coroners	
		High Constables	
		Peace, Commission of	
		Petty Sessions	
		Police	
		Pounds	
		Quarter Sessions	
		Sergeantry of the Peace	
			Shrievalty: General
			A-Z by counties
		Watch & Ward	
	: Public Utilities:	General	
		Cemeteries & Crematoria	
		Water Supply	

7.4 Subject-index schema (extract)

The Subject Index Word-List provides a dictionary of words and concepts which shows how they are arranged in the *Schema*. The cross-references also act as a thesaurus—that is, they suggest developments and related concepts (figure 7.5).

PUBLIC HEALTH	see GOVT., LOCAL: Public Health
	see also MEDICINE
PUBLIC HOUSES	see BREWING: Property
	see also CATERING TRADE: Victuallers, Hotels
	& Innkeepers
PUBLIC ORDER	see GOVT., LOCAL: Public Order
	see also ARMY: Post-1660: Organ. &
	Admin.: Support of Civil Power
	CRIME & PUNISHMENT
	TREASON: Riots
PUBLIC PARKS	see HOUSING & TOWN PLANNING: Parks (Public)
PUBLIC SCHOOLS	see EDUCATION: Schools: Public
PUBLIC UTILITIES	see GOVT., LOCAL: Public Utilities
	see also ELECTRICITY
	GAS
	POSTS & TELEGRAPHS
	TRANSPORT

7.5 Subject index word-list (extract)

Indexes may take one of three forms:
(i) Most commonly they are kept upon cards or slips, which are
arranged in drawers or cabinets. This form is generally most
convenient since new material can be readily inserted at the
appropriate places, and particular sections of the index can be
combined or separated without too much trouble. A variant of this
form is the sheaf index, where the slips are bound into loose-leaf
binders and handled as volumes. There may be one general index
or, more probably, a number of indexes which either relate to
different groups of archives, or which deal with persons, places or
subjects separately.
(ii) The index is written out in alphabetical order upon connected
sheets of paper, like the index at the end of a book. This form of
index is normally most suitable for completed and self-sufficient
units of information such as single volumes (either of original
archives or of information instruments derived from them, such as
calendars).
(iii) Indexes set out in volume form but updated or reproduced

mechanically. An example of this type of index is where cards are photographically reproduced in set sequences. By this means it is possible to publish or disseminate an index. Computer-based indexes are constantly printed out in updated or revised orders, and these too can be distributed outside the searchroom.

Indexes, though essential, are secondary to the various lists produced by the archives office, and therefore the publication of indexes as such will not be a general aim of most archives offices. Published indexes have proved most useful when they deal with specialized forms of record, such as those most used by genealogists. In most other cases, publication of lists will be the primary aim, but it is natural to attempt to publish the index which relates to a list at the same time, and it is in this way that it is most likely that indexes relating to archives held in different offices will be published. However it is important that all archival lists should be indexed, and that these indexes should conform to standards developed and determined on national or international models.

Computers in Archival Description
Computers can be used for archival listing and for the production of the resulting lists, as well as for the retrieval of specific items of information. These two functions can be combined, and, since by using a single set of input information (such as an archival list) a number of different lists and indexes can rapidly be presented, the computer is an instrument which could add considerably to the archivist's power to exploit his material. Archives must in any case be listed, and it is presumably not much more difficult to list them on to forms suitable for computer input than it is to list them on to plain paper. Once it has a list on a suitable medium, the computer will then be able to carry out its characteristic functions, that is, it will be able to arrange or select any of the items of information which it has been given, in any logical order for which it has been programmed, and put out the result rapidly in intelligible form.

The first and most essential point is the selection of an appropriate program from among those in use for archival description and indexing. Normally it will not be feasible or desirable for smaller archives offices to devise their own special programs. Technical advice should be sought to find out what programs are currently available, and what their capabilities are. It will then be necessary to set these capabilities, and the program's corresponding limitations, against the office's needs and resources. At the time of writing, there are some four major programs for archival description by computer in normal operation, together with another five or six programs for indexing or retrieval; but developments in this field are so rapid that a particular description of these would not be useful outside a specialized manual. It is likely that co-operative programs between archives offices, libraries and documentation centres will emerge at national level, in association with the development of planned national information systems (NATIS).

From the point of view of the archivist who is using a computer program, the main factors are these.(15) The program, which is an analysis of the job to be done and a set of rules for setting out the material, will determine the form in which the input information, that is, the archival lists, must be arranged. The archivist will be obliged to follow the rules set out in his program manual exactly, and these will often involve writing out his lists on special stationery, employing technical symbols. Since computers are not capable of independent thought or choice, it is vital to the success of any program that all the identifiers and code marks specified in the instructions are written in with every piece of information fed in, and that they are in the right place and order. The instructions to the staff must be accurate and clear, and the checking of lists must be thorough. The greatest likelihood of a program being abortive occurs at this earliest stage, when basic information is being prepared by the ordinary staff of the archives office.

Some of the earliest archival computer programs used special stationery which involved the archivists in writing on cards or sheets within indicated squares and spaces; these spaces also limit the amount of descriptive material which could be written in. Later programs are much more flexible in their use of input descriptions, and the archivists using them can use either plain paper or, more usually, forms printed so as to guide them in the order of information to be given. In any case, completed input material must be processed into a form readable by the computer. This will normally be by passing it to a keyboard operator, who will type it out on to punched cards or tape or on to magnetic tape, using special machines. The finished list, in its machine-readable form, should also be checked for errors; some programs have an in-built system for verifying and amending input material.

It is in its output that the computer best demonstrates its remarkable versatility and its ability to rearrange items of information rapidly. An archival program will pay particular attention to exploiting all the possibilities when it comes to printing out the information which has been carefully prepared and fed in.

So far there are six forms or uses to which computer print-outs of archival lists have been adapted:

(i) A primary or basic list printed out in order of archival codes, that is, in archival order. Equipped with introductory material explaining the administrative history of the originating department, this list satisfies all the requirements of archival description and the moral defence of archives. It is suitable for lists at all levels from the initial summaries, through guide entries, to detailed calendars.

(ii) Lists of documents chosen from the input material on the basis of particular items in the code or in the subject tags. Thus it would be possible to extract lists in serial, alphabetical or chronological order of all material belonging to a particular department of origin, all material of the same documentary form, or all material belonging to a subject category. Apart from the facility of making up subject lists from archives of widely separated origins, the most interesting possibility here is the ease with which defunct archive groupings could be restored on printed-out lists. Archive series which had become split on transfer to succeeding administrations could thus be reconstructed in list form, provided, of course, that suitable indicators had been included in the input material.

(iii) Computers will extract key words for indexing, and print them out separately, with suitable references, in alphabetical order. To do this there would have to be suitable identifying marks in the input material.

(iv) Print-outs can be on ordinary stationery, or on cards or slips, or, of course, on both. Computer paper can be cut and bound into volumes or binders, and cards can be distributed into index cabinets. Duplicates in either form are easy to arrange.

(v) Print-out can be direct on to microforms. This facility has probably not yet been much used in archives work, since its main advantage would presumably be to provide finding information at a distance. As publishing in microform becomes more established, however, its use in archive work will doubtless grow.

(vi) Any list or index printed out by computer can be readily revised and updated. Corrections, including deletions and new information, can be input in the same way as the original material. When the new input tapes are run through, the computer will produce a corrected version to replace earlier print-outs. This is the most interesting capability of the computer in this connection, and it is this which gives it most significance in the long run. Once the backlog of descriptive material is transcribed as computer input, all future accessions can be fed in direct, and the archives office need never work with seriously outdated or multifarious lists or guides, but will always have one complete system of finding aids constantly updated.

An important feature of computer work, in archives as elsewhere, is that it must be correctly costed. It is well known that computer time is expensive, and that the relevant software is likely to be difficult to design and to be expensive also.

However, there are mitigating factors. Most large institutions, including those which are employing authorities of archive offices, have arrangements for access to computers, and access also to specialist staff. Computer time at slack periods is often cheaper, and it is cheaper to purchase a program which has already been devised, or to co-operate in a joint scheme, than to design a new one. Moreover traditional manual methods of describing archives are also expensive, sometimes enormously so, and it is necessary to make a comparison between these expenses and the cost of a computerized service.

Generally introducing a computer will result in additional costs, since the basic work of arranging and describing the archives will still have to be done manually. What the computer contributes is over and above this, in facilitating the retrieval of information and the exploitation of research material.

The cost of non-documentation is invisible.' It is almost impossible to draw up a satisfactory evaluation of the benefits provided by such improved reference as against the cost of providing it. What is certain is that computers do allow an elaboration of exploitative instruments which would be impossible to carry out manually, and for this reason every archives office or national group of archivists will have to investigate the benefits and possibilities of its use.

Items in the costing of a computer scheme include:
(i) The time of keyboard operators punching the listed information onto tape or cards. This should include verifying and amending.
(ii) Computer time.
(iii) Use of hardware: card or tape readers, printer, magnetic tape for storage of data, and other similar items.

(iv) Output materials.
The resulting cost figures may be used to make a comparison with
the cost of making manual finding aids, which should include
typing and clerical operations. The operations of professional staff
and the general overheads belong to both methods.

Machine-Readable Archives

Records may be created in a form readable only by a machine and
not directly by either the original operator or by subsequent users.
The most typical example of machine-readable records are
magnetic tapes 'read' by a computer, which may then produce its
computations from the data presented to it, either in the form of a
legible print-out, or perhaps in the form of a further machine-
readable record: magnetic tape or disc, or punched tape, or
specialized forms of microfilm. Such records are to be appraised
and disposed of as are other records, but there are particular
difficulties and techniques involved in their description and
control. To a great extent these are the subject of specialist
studies, and it would not be in place here to introduce an
exhaustive discussion of them. Some outline of the subject is
included in order to round out the larger subject of archival
description.

   The first problem is that of control and registration: that is, of
designing a descriptive instrument which will give adequate
information about the form and content of the record. In designing
such an instrument and in filling it up with details of actual
records, the archivist will naturally consult a specialist in the
operation of information machines. It is essential that these
operations should be carried out with the help of expert
knowledge, and not on general principles or by guess work. In
effect, if there is no expert available for consultation, work on the
listing of machine-readable records should be postponed until
there is.

   The national archives of the USA has designed a descriptive
instrument for magnetic tape. The kinds of information recorded
in it include:
(i)   creating department and location, with names of personnel
responsible for the system;
(ii) a brief description of the record content, with title of file,
system, objectives in compiling the data, scope of the data,
arrangement of information, source material and output; date of
original compilation and of any updating;

(iii) physical characteristics of the tape: number of reels, tracks, density ('bits per inch'), and machine system used;
(iv) frequency of use, retention, and security classification.(16)

The appraisal of machine-readable records follows that of statistical records of other kinds, but has certain characteristics of its own. Questions of language and of media are of great importance. Machine-readable records can of course only be read by machines using the same system; there are several mutually incompatible languages, and many different kinds of tape or disc. There is a constant tendency for new generations of machines and systems, and of hardware and software, to be developed.

To read a record of this kind one must have the use of an appropriate machine, and also of an appropriate program or key. Much of the material upon which the information is stored, such as magnetic tape, is expensive but reusable, and any programme for retention of such records must take account of the cost of tying up this reusable material.

Finally, it is difficult to ensure that the complete record is retained: the absence of part of the program, or of some essential part of the information recorded is difficult to detect, and can only be tested by experts.

In a recent article, Meyer H. Fishbein has summarized a set of procedures for the appraisal of machine-readable records:(17)
(i) All files (i.e. components of the record) should be assessed before final completion of the operation in which they are involved. Reuse of material is rapid, and if this is not done there is no likelihood that the total record has been retained, even for a short time.
(ii) All methodological and program documentation must be identified and retained with the records, which, of course, are useless without it.
(iii) Data on tape has been processed, in most cases, from source documentation (survey worksheets or the like). Appraisal of the tape involves comparing the value of the tape itself with its documentary sources.
(iv) Primary, or raw, data tape will often have been further processed onto secondary data tape. This process will have involved the loss of some information, but also the arrangement of the remaining information into a more convenient form. The appraiser will ask himself whether or not the information lost at this point is of value.
(v) Duplicate data may be eliminated.

The operation will result in: (a) a final data tape, in which
information is tabulated in its most usable form; and (b) a plain
language printout or report. Both of these should be appraised.
This should be carried out in association with experts in the
subject area, and probably also with statisticians.
(vi) Files which combine or rework data from two or more
sources may be a special subject for appraisal.
(vii) Tape is frequently updated by replacing items of information
with corrected or updated items. The appraiser will consider
whether to 'freeze' the information at certain periods for historical
purposes.

All machine-readable records can be printed out in some form
which will allow them to be read in plain language. Direct printing
out may not provide an intelligible record in itself, but the
possibility exists of incorporating an element in the controlling
program whereby the data is arranged and printed out in a form
suitable, specifically, for retention as a permanent record. The
dangers in this procedure are the same as the dangers involved in
compiling a planned record from ordinary documents, where the
source records are then destroyed. It is probable that the creation
of deliberate records by modifying programs will become one of
the archivist's tools, but it is not likely that it will be an approach
which will allow the wholesale destruction of source data.

There is at present little experience available to the profession
on this subject, although certain archives offices have now had a
decade's experience or more of working with information
machines. The International Council on Archives is at present
working to develop experience and techniques in the field, and
has founded a technical journal concerned with archives and
automatic data processing.(18) Succeeding years will see a rapid
increase in archivists' interest and practice.

8 Conservation of Archives

Conservational programmes in an archives office provide for custody, a suitable environment for preservation in storage and use, and facilities for repair. In this field there are standards against which the performance of existing or projected archives offices can be measured. The necessary resources to achieve these standards should of course be given by employing authorities. It is surely clear that an archives office cannot accept conservational standards which place archives in danger, or which leave them outside a suitable environment over long periods. If the employer cannot afford to provide what is necessary, it may be that archival functions should be delegated to a larger organization.

Custody

The question of custody is important. An archivist has the custody of his archives, and each archive has a distinctive custodial history which is important to its evaluation as historical evidence. This is equally true whether an archive passes into the archivist's custody by transfer from the creating authority, or by deposit by some external owner; in each case the custody of the archive is being delegated to the archivist. A record of this delegation provides the outline of the documents' custodial history, and allows a strong distinction between the acquisition of archives under a process of delegation and their acquisition by artificial collection.(1)

It is, of course, perfectly legitimate for archives offices to acquire material by collection; for their objective is wide documentation. But the distinction between custody by delegation and ownership by collection remains important. Where custody is delegated, so are other archival functions. It is by delegation that archivists enter the field of appraisal and selection, performing these functions on behalf of the person who by natural descent has responsibility for the records, and equally, by a less formal delegation, on behalf of the research community. Functions to do with access and exploitation are also delegated.

Custody is not breached by sending particular archives out of the office under regulated conditions; it may be necessary or useful to send archives out for such purposes as repair, exhibition, teaching, reprography or reference. Regulations governing this should be flexible enough to allow scope for conservation or exploitation schemes. Precautions against loss may include making photocopies (and, if appropriate, promoting the use of photocopies as an alternative to the originals), registering their issue, approving the person held responsible, and approving the physical conditions under which they will be kept while out of the office. If such reasonable precautions have been taken, there is no reason why external services such as the postal system should not be used,(2) nor why responsible people who are not members of the archives staff should not be used to take charge of documents sent out.

Storage
From time to time the staff of an archives office will have to assess their storage capacity, its use and arrangement, and the amount which remains for current and future accessions.

When the archives office is first set up, it is clearly necessary to calculate the capacity required to house existing accumulations of valuable material, which are the original raw material of the new service. As time continues, accessions of new material increase the original holdings, and the quantity of archives received over any period of time depends on the capacity of the employing authority to create new records which pass the tests of appraisal.

Archives offices are in the unenviable and possibly unique position of having no final control over, and sometimes not even knowledge of, the extent of their intake in the future. Of course, it is possible and usually necessary to regulate intake over particular periods in response to the working of the office's programmes. Thus the acquisition of the backlog accumulations of particular departments of the employing authority can be scheduled to occur in particular years or months, as may suit the programmes

of the office or the operating necessities of the department.
Current accessions cannot be adjusted so easily, but their size can
usually be estimated. Similarly the receipt of large external or non-
official deposits may be regulated within limits to take account of
the authority's building programme and so on.

But it is, of course, with considerable deposits of private
archives that the greatest element of uncertainty comes in,
especially as there is frequently (as with archaeological
investigations) an element of urgency, of rushing in to prevent
wholesale destruction or dispersal, in such cases.

The amount of storage provided should be in direct proportion,
of course, to the demands of the programmes which the office has
adopted. The cost of this storage is therefore justified by reference
to the original policy and statement of objectives.

An archival programme should include means, not only for
ensuring a suitable environment for long-term storage, but also
for constant monitoring of the atmosphere; facilities should
include means for testing environmental conditions at times other
than during working days—at night and during holidays. Records
should be kept over long periods, so that long-term or seasonal
changes can be observed. This means that these records should
also be checked and interpreted; a suggested layout for a record
card is shown in figure 8.1.(3) If possible, atmospheric tests
should cover not only temperature and humidity but also chemical
content.

There are in practice archive buildings which do not enable a
strict control (or even any control) of environmental conditions to
be made. In these cases, it is suggested that measurements
should nevertheless be made since they provide working
information. A professional archivist no doubt will wish to acquire
as much technical information as possible which may affect the
condition of his archives, even though it may not be of any direct
and immediate use.

When planning for improved facilities, it is clearly an advantage
to be able to state the case for allocation of resources in objective
and scientific terms wherever possible. The greatest dangers to
archives from environmental conditions are:

(i) humidity (consistently too high or too low, or extreme
fluctuation);

(ii) temperature (extreme fluctuation, or consistently too high);

(iii) atmospheric pollution (concentration of injurious chemicals);

(iv) atmospheric stagnation (encouragement of moulds);

STORAGE AREA ENVIRONMENTAL CONTROL					
LOCATION					
MONTH:			YEAR:		
DAY	TEMPERATURE READINGS	RELATIVE HUMIDITY	WEATHER	VENTILATION CONTROL	TIME
1					
2					
3					

8.1 Environmental control Record card

(v) animal and insect pests
(vi) in some circumstances, direct sunlight or exposure to light;
(vii) dirt.
The most modern buildings are not immune from any of these dangers.

Shelving, boxing (and packing archives within boxes) and the selection of locations are all aids to controlling environmental conditions. National groups of archivists in many countries are establishing standards for these.

Security
Protection of archives from misuse by intruders follows that adopted by the records centre, where indeed this precaution may be more important than in the archives.

The quality of doors and any other possible entrances or exits will be set by the technical standard of the building. Control measures should not be stricter than the occasion warrants; if they are, they will come to be disregarded. Whether the storeroom doors are kept permanently locked during working hours or not depends on whether they lead directly into the working area of the archives office or into places where there is alternative access. Questions may still arise of the quality and nature of the documents kept inside, and of their secondary packaging and labelling.

Access to keys clearly should be restricted to some extent, but one must always assume that certain people outside the office itself must have them: the security personnel of the whole organization, and those responsible for cleaning and inspection; in many cases it must be much more important that cleaning is carried out regularly than that access should be made difficult. In these circumstances it is surely the duty of the archivist to see that order reigns, and that access by those who are not directly his own staff is given under conditions that do not fundamentally breach his control over the environment in the storage areas. To make access to the store rooms as easy as administrative convenience requires is not to lose control over the conditions in them.

Misuse of archives by intruders will include the possibility of documents being withdrawn and not recorded, or put in the wrong places and so lost. But the relative immunity which archivists have enjoyed in the past from deliberate theft may not continue into the future. There has been a general rise in the saleability of documents, and in many cases theft of archives is difficult or impossible to trace. Therefore in the design of storage areas protection from burglary or unauthorized entry should be considered. There seems also to be greater danger from wilful damage in some places.(4)

Repair
A complete archives service will hope to contain a repair section which may discharge the office's responsibilities, within the terms of its agreed programmes, in the whole area of conservation. The section should have a sufficient budget to allocate it suitable degrees of priority and a share in the allocation of resources.

It is possible for a conservation section to be operated jointly between two or more authorities, even where other archival services remain distinct. Since archive repair requires specialized accommodation and equipment which can most easily be concentrated into one centre, the case for centralization can often be made out without much difficulty. It is also possible for repair and rebinding work to be done by external contract.

There are two branches of document repair, the traditional and the modern, and the differences between them affect the design of repair services and the training and status of technical staff. Traditional repair requires staff of craftsman standard using equipment mainly of the furniture type: benches, sinks, frames and tables. Modern repair methods, which are now established in the larger institutions, are rather different. They require staff with a lower level of personal craft skills, and much larger investment in machines. The main requirement here, apart from conditions in which these machines can safely be run, is adequate management of the repair process.

Where large amounts of documentary material have to be run through continuous processes, including mechanical ones, it is essential that archivists should be able to identify series to be treated, control their progress through the treatment, and incorporate safeguards and finding aids as necessary.

There are methods of repair intermediate between these two, which perhaps combine some of the virtues of both. These include methods of hand lamination, both hot and cold processes, which can be carried out by careful people with little training. Other simple conservational processes, such as deacidification, boxing and packing, can also be undertaken without much investment in equipment or skill, and are popular in some developing countries for this reason. They are also available for the use of smaller archives offices where there are not adequate resources for a fully manned or equipped conservation section.(5)

It is a general principle of archive repair that there should be no attempt to hide the effects of the work.(6) Any conservational treatment which a document may have received in the course of its life becomes a part of its custodial history, and must be borne in mind by anyone who wishes to evaluate its historical authenticity. A second basic principle is that no irreversible operation should be undertaken: this principle is mitigated in practice by the obvious fact that documents once repaired will not normally be unrepaired, and would certainly not be improved by any attempt to remove any repairs. But both traditional and modern repair methods observe the principle, and do not or should not involve totally irreversible changes in the documents they treat.

The specific concern of the archivist in the process of repair is concentrated on matters external to the actual mechanics of it. His first concern is with the repair section's programme. This will involve determining an order of priorities in taking particular archive series or individual documents for repair.

Archives may need repair because they have suffered damage in a particular event in the past; because the material of which they are composed is fragile or unstable; because constant use might endanger their stability; or because their shape and size render either their safe storage or their use (or both) difficult. The archivist must have a means of deciding which series in his care, or which parts of series, fall into these categories.

He may wish to make this decision in terms of a regular programme, proceeding series by series, or he may wish to single out particular series or documents when they come to light, as being in immediate need. In general, it would seem better to have a regular programme, the priorities within which take account of the physical state and constancy of use of the series, but which is not so rigid as to prevent the interpolation of emergency repairs without disturbing the regular flow too much. In either case there should be an orderly means of withdrawing documents from use and transferring them in due order to the repair section, together with suitable comments on their condition.

The system used for this will include a means of controlling the process so that its current state and progress is checked on, and so that the documents repaired duly return to their proper position when work is completed. One way of doing this is by an adaptation of the ordinary requisitioning form (figure 8.2(7)). This type of requisition might be made out initially in triplicate: one copy is sent to the repair section, and is used as a form of accession control there; another is kept on the shelf in place of the original documents; the third copy may be filed centrally as a control on progress.

REQUISITION FOR REPAIR	Job No:
Reference code: Location: Title of document or series:	To repair: From repair: checked: replaced:
Condition of documents; repair required or conservation problem.	
Signature and date	

8.2 Form for requisitioning repairs

The repair section will also keep progress records, which will have the secondary objective of maintaining control over use of

materials, allocation of staff resources and so forth. They may
make use of a repair progress card or work sheet (figure 8.3(8)).

REPAIR SECTION WORK SHEET							
Job No:			Reference code:				
			Title of document or series:				
Received:							
Returned:							
Date		Work done; materials used					time
Analysis of work progress:							
leaves repaired	cleaned	flattened	sized	guarded	numbered	sewn	filed
documents inserted	file boards	covers	cases	volumes bound	seals	total time	

8.3 Repair progress record

The requisition slip (figure 8.2) has as one of its aims the proper
replacement of archives after repair. But documents which have
been repaired inevitably are somewhat different physically from
what they were before, and they may have been given additional
protection and covering. Therefore to repair a series is also often
to cause its removal to another storage order or place. The control
system must of course allow for this without risk of loss by
misplacement.

It is permissible to change the appearance of documents during
the repair process, if this will lead to better management without
damaging their evidential character. Excessively unwieldy rolls or
files may be split and recased, and very large maps may
sometimes be divided. In itself this would be an undesirable
practice, but its undesirability may be easily overridden by
practical considerations. If a proper record is kept of the
dismantling or repair operation, both in the repair section's
records and in the form of a signed and dated note in the
document itself, there will be no objection to the practice in most
cases. The repair and guarding of files or bundles should
perpetuate rather than lose the original order of papers within

the file or bundle. It may be necessary for the repair staff to number or foliate these papers before dismantling the old arrangement, so that it can be reconstituted at the end of the repair process. This is a problem of archival arrangement, but one in which the repair staff naturally participate. Their training should allow for an understanding of the purposes behind archival methods.

Pending the appearance of an advisory service in technical matters, each archives office will need to acquire scientific knowledge sufficient to carry out tests and to recognize the symptoms of deterioration in documents. In Britain, details of at least most of the tests available are obtainable from the technical committee of the Society of Archivists. Current information on developing processes and tests can be got from the Society's *Repairers' Newsletter* and from the technical reports in *The American Archivist*. The International Council on Archives, through its technical committees, offers advice and information to all countries.(9)

Apart from checks on environmental conditions, regular tests, the results of which should be recorded, should be made on the acidity and stability of paper, both of archives in store and those coming in, paper stocks, including stocks of paper for repair, and documents repaired in the past.

9 Searchroom Services in Public Repositories, I

Policy and Attitudes

Archives offices originated in the demand by scholars for access facilities to the archives. From this demand grew the dual duty of these establishments, *conserver et communiquer*.(1)

The basic service under the heading of 'communication' is the provision of a place where the reader can sit in peace, where the archives he wants can be brought to him for consultation, where he can see the various finding aids and perhaps have the assistance of reference books and the advice of staff. The objective of the design of a searchroom will be to facilitate the attendance of readers, to provide a suitable locale for the identification and production of archives for use and for their consultation, and to provide an environment for research activities associated with the archives service.

Readers

Traditionally, readers were thought of as individuals of academic standing who needed to sit consulting records for fairly long periods, using relatively limited classes of archives, studying each for relatively long periods and in considerable detail. But there are now many different kinds of actual or potential readers, and many varieties of reason for their presence in a searchroom.

Firstly, the reader may be an individual, but he may wish to take a rapid glance at a relatively large number of archives in quick succession. He may for instance be tracing reference to particular places through a single long series of archives, or he may be tracing the effects of a particular policy through large

144

series of similar archives in different archives offices. He may be compiling references to a particular type of event, or accumulating items of information so that a statistical or quantifiable result can be reached.

Secondly, the reader may not be an individual but a group. The seriousness and depth of the inquiry made by a team or party which comes to the archives office to develop a common purpose may be great or little, according to circumstances, just as it may with individuals; and collective searchers may study a few archives intensively or many archives lightly, or vice versa, just as may individuals. Collective or team research makes demands on the resources of the search room and its staff different from those made by individual searchers.

Neither the individual nor the collective reader necessarily knows precisely what questions he wishes to answer on the occasion of any visit to a searchroom; nor does he necessarily know precisely which series or documents from among the mass of the archives he may need at that moment. Such readers may take a relatively long time establishing which archives to ask for, and a relatively short time in scanning the document when it comes.

There is need therefore to allow for readers who spend much time and research on the finding aids, giving them the study which others will reserve for original archives; readers who require a good deal of consultation and advice from the searchroom staff; readers, or groups of readers, who need facilities for communicating instructions, findings and advice to each other; and readers who really need, if that were possible, to browse and experiment.

The fact that so many different kinds of user, and so many of them in terms of numbers, come together to make use of the searchroom leads to many complications in the design of the accommodation, and in the planning of the services associated with it.

Access to storage areas
Normally a searchroom should be close to the storage areas, so that documents can be quickly found and easily brought from one to the other. The environmental and security controls appropriate to the storage are carried over into the searchroom. The reader may use the finding systems, either in the searchroom itself or in an adjoining reference room, to order what documents he wishes,

and these are brought to him either at a numbered seat or at a control counter from which he can claim them. Documents required the following day can be kept on convenient shelves near this control counter. It is not likely that in the largest archive institutions and in national institutions arrangements on these lines can really be bettered, except by making the processes more automatic. These can call upon relatively large numbers of lower-grade staff, who carry the burden of issue and return of documents on request. There are ways in which this burden can be minimized, by mechanizing the means of transport from storage to consultation areas, by introducing electronic transmission of order slips, and so forth. The bulk and complexity of the record holdings, as well as restrictions on access which always belong to classes of government papers, all render it necessary to keep the storage areas secluded from the use areas.

Other, non-government, archives offices may however pose radical questions about their arrangements for consultation. For example, greater freedom of access by the user to actual storage areas may be considered. If so there would be three alternative ways of doing this: this freer access might be to all users, to selected users, or through a special section of the archives staff.

There are considerable objections to allowing easier access by all users to the archives storage areas; in most cases these objections will undoubtedly overrule any such possibility. The kind of supervision accorded by the archives staff would have to be radically different from what traditionally it has been. The boxing and labelling of the archives would have to be very clear and universally applied, and in general the storage layout would have to be at least as logical and complete as is customary in a library. The office would require quite a different arrangement of buildings and rooms from that usually found and a high standard of copying and other support equipment. It does not seem self-evident, however, that in no circumstances whatever should the principle of direct access by readers be allowed, provided that the building has been properly designed or adapted, and that the archives are appropriate in form.

To allow access to some parts of the storage by particular individuals is not open to all the above objections. A similar suggestion (providing also for the possibility of certain documents being taken out of the archives office for teaching or display purposes) was made some years ago by Dr Emmison as a policy suitable for county archives offices.(2) The admission of specified individuals as being in a sense honorary members of staff is not quite unknown in various places, and might well be extended to include many who are fairly constant or serious users of the office; these might include lecturers in colleges of education, extra-mural tutors, school teachers, and amateur searchers of experience. To an extent this sort of special relationship does already exist, and there are circumstances not uncommon in the local archives scene which may tend to encourage it. To allow access to storage for even a limited class of user does however depend for its success on the physical layout of the building and the arrangements made in it.

To set up a research section as part of the structure of the archives staff is the third alternative. Research teams develop an intimate relationship with their source material, to which they require free access and the facility to arrange it (within limits) to suit their requirements; they also find it relatively easy to accept on temporary terms colleagues with parallel research interests. In some countries this is already a relatively widespread development. Many of the principal national institutions have a structured publication programme, which in most cases includes both full-time paid staff and external editors who are nevertheless subject to the programmes of the office and to the ethics of its work. In some local archives offices a similar development can also be seen.

The privileged access given to staff members of the research team does not of course do away with the demands made by other users, but it may provide a way of reducing some of the weight of these demands, and at the same time improving the means of access by way of publishing the material.

Something further than this is still needed if the main remaining problems of heavy use are to be overcome. The best approach here would be to concentrate on establishing the maximum flexibility and ease in the physical relationship between searchroom and storage, and between the readers, the staff and the finding system. To put it most negatively, it is simply not reasonable to set up a system where archives can only be obtained through a sort of obstacle course.

Supervision
It is rarely if ever possible for the professional staff of an archives office to remain out of direct contact with the ordinary user. It is not possible in an archives office to provide a completely self-

working finding system. Readers cannot find what they want by
following the shelves round; to master the finding system (even
where it is complete) may require a disproportionately long effort
of learning and comprehension, involving some degree of study of
the administrative history of the employing authority. Indexes may
give useful references, but in an archives system it is unusual to
find presented to readers an index system which covers even a
significantly large part of the total holding; in any case an index is
like a card catalogue in a library: it cannot interpret the records or
give any idea of their meaning and character. Consequently a
large proportion of readers will be forced to consult the archivist in
charge, and it will be a significant part of this archivist's job to give
such consultations. A consequence is that it will always be
necessary to provide professionally trained and experienced
searchroom supervisors.

Equally the reader in an archives office can never really be
anonymous. His purposes and *bona fides* are known to the staff,
as is at least to some extent the progress of his research, and it is
the concern of the office to know what relation this research has
to parallel studies by others, who it is being undertaken for, what
records it involves, and whether it will lead to the publication of
any records.(3)

Subject to the maintenance of necessary standards, which of
course require that enough staff should be on duty to control the
procedures of the searchroom, consultation facilities should be
open for the maximum hours per day. The ideal would be a
searchroom which opens for the full twenty-four hours daily. To
open for normal office hours only is a very poor minimum
alternative, and where it is genuinely only possible to have thirty-
five or so opening hours per week, they should at least be
staggered into the early evening to allow potential readers to
attend after their normal employment. A solution to the problems
of restricted opening may sometimes be sought by sharing
searchroom facilities with an associated library. In large buildings,
or where there is more than one searchroom, closed-circuit
television today offers an effective means of supervision.

Restrictions on access to archives
There have always been restrictions on access to archives. Since
the international discussion of problems of access in 1966,
however, the attitudes of archivists to them have changed in most
countries, and there has been a change also in the legislation

relating to access in many countries. Research demands are bringing in further changes.

It is the professional duty of an archivist to enforce such restrictions regarding access as are in force in relation to his archives; but it is also his professional duty to advise on the modification of these restrictions, both in general and in relation to particular instances where he feels it necessary, and to do this he must be aware of the problems and practices of his colleagues elsewhere. He will be concerned to retain only those access restrictions which are necessary to protect the archives, physically and morally; to protect the interests of persons mentioned in the archives who cannot protect themselves; to observe the conditions specified in contracts for deposit; and to co-operate in the interests of general security. Since access restrictions will be enforced in the searchroom, it will fall to the searchroom supervisor to deal with questions relating to them.

In government, records generally have a security classification which governs access to them during their currency. Normally it should be accepted that archivists should have sufficient access to secret material to carry out the work of appraisal, and there should be a procedure for the declassification of records at a certain point after their retirement. However, under the ordinary rules of administration, records with a restricted classification must remain subject to it until they are formally removed from it.

In other cases, government records will be open to inspection after they come into the archives, after a given period has elapsed. In Britain this period of closure has now been established as thirty years, the date to run from the last date on the record. The minister responsible for archives may however issue instructions which will have the effect either of shortening or of lengthening the period of closure in respect of any record, and there is provision for extending the period where records deal with private information. The relevant section of the Public Records Act, 1958, as amended, is given as appendix E.

Only records which come under the jurisdiction of the Public Records Acts are covered by these rules, though certain important series of records held by local authorities are included in that category. Where other records are concerned, there is no general statutory control, and in Britain there is a great variety of practice.

Archives offices which have non-public records will have to devise an appropriate policy which they can apply to their holdings, and in devising this policy they will consider the practice of comparable archives offices elsewhere. In most countries there is a similar distinction between government or national archives and others.

In drawing up an access policy, the archives office will first consider its holdings of official records. Here it would be hard to argue that arrangements accepted by the national government as suitable for its own archives are too lax for those of lesser organizations. The general access date of thirty years would seem to suggest itself therefore, and to it may be added the provision that the employing authority, through competent officials, may shorten or extend this date in regard to particular series of archives. The archivist should keep these in review, since he must advise his employing authority on such matters, and a more rather than a less liberal policy is always desirable if there are no strong arguments against it.

Archives of non-official origin present a more difficult problem. Here the main distinction will be between those for which the archivist is finally responsible, and those which are in any degree owned or controlled by a depositor. Where documents have been bought, for example, the archivist is responsible. Sales of documents need not necessarily have been public, and where the sale has not led in effect to the opening of the documents for inspection or examination in the sale room there may be special reasons, similar to those set out in section 5, paragraph 2, of the Public Records Act, 1958, which will lead the archivist to establish a period of restriction. There may even be considerations of national security, or of maintaining consistency with national repositories, which apply. The necessary discretion, and the knowledge of practice elsewhere, will be part of the professional skills brought to bear on the problem by the archivist.

Archives held on deposit are naturally held on the conditions laid down in the agreement for deposit. The form of agreement given in appendix C sets out the possible alternatives: (i) access should be granted to all parts of the deposit as a matter of course: (ii) access should be granted after a given period from the creation of each part of the record; (iii) access should be granted at the discretion of the archivist; (iv) access should be granted by referring each case to the depositor; (v) access should not be granted at all pending a new agreement or further instructions. Archivally, the first two are preferable and the third an acceptable alternative. There may be reasons for accepting the fourth, but they will be very strong before the fifth is accepted, though even here, the archivist may feel, a deposit is preferable to destruction or loss, which may be the result if the depositor is excessively sensitive about the possible consequences of granting access.

If an archivist is to assume direct responsibility for deciding on the terms of access, in the case either of official or of non-official documents, he must take into consideration all the possible consequences. Archives are constantly being used as evidence in law or, what is as significant in terms of liability, as information prompting the undertaking of expensive or dangerous enterprises. However, provided certain safeguards are accepted, it is not unreasonable or risky for an archivist to accept the due weight of his professional responsibility in this matter. These safeguards will include statements made in the searchroom regulations of the office; and may be reinforced in certain cases by asking, before access is given, for written assurances by the searcher in a form such as is suggested in figure 9.1.(4) This document serves, sufficiently for legal purposes anyway, to distinguish the purposes a reader may have in seeking access: he has declared himself to have a research interest rather than a legal, commercial or financial one. Alternatively the searchroom staff can put the question of purpose privately where they have cause to suspect the motives of a reader. The danger of unfortunate consequences flowing from incautious granting of access is always there, and it may be that an archives office would be wise to take out insurance against claims based on professional negligence.

It is troublesome to bring about a situation where a reader could be refused access simply because his enquiry was not

---

TO THE DIRECTOR

As my search in the archives held by your office is exclusively for purposes of historical, genealogical, antiquarian or academic research, I apply for permission to inspect them (subject to your normal conditions of access) free of charge.

The subject of my research is:

The university, school, college or society with which I am connected is:

(signed)
(address)

Permission granted/not granted

9.1 Application to inspect records

academic. Restrictions on access may be of two kinds: they may apply to the archives or to the reader. Restrictions on archives are binding on all (subject to provisions in governing statutes); restrictions on readers can vary from one person to another.

In actual practice there are favoured readers who are granted special access; clearly it would be as wrong to forbid access to archives within the closed period to one whose research, duly accredited, was regarded as in the national interest as it would be to open such closed archives to general inspection. Intending readers will be able to obtain privileged access to closed records only if they can show that they belong to a *bona fide* research institution, project or team. Sometimes privileged access is necessarily allowed as part of a contract between the reader and the employing authority, and the terms of this contract can include some provision for restricting the publication of verbatim or other quotations from records. The archives office will also ensure that privileged readers will have the clearance of the creating department before allowing access to records within the closed period. It will be a matter of professional concern, though, to ensure that privileged access is not given except for academic reasons and that information released as a consequence does not give an impossibly biased picture.

Control of the Searchroom
The searchroom is a place of public access where valuable materials are being produced for use. It is a place designed for one principal function, and it should provide an environment in which that function—the consultation of archives—is promoted. There are various ways in which dangers to archives, inconvenience to readers or the spoiling of the environment of study could arise; because of this it is wise to provide regulations for the conduct of visitors in the searchroom, and to take means to inform readers of them and of the means of their enforcement:

Since the aims of the regulations are legal ones, the enforcement of suitable behaviour, the protection of archives, and the limitation of legal liability of the archives office and its staff, it is necessary that the regulations should have some legal standing; normally this means that they should be promulgated by the employing authority under the exercise of recognized powers. Regard must be had to public rights under general laws, and it would be unwise to issue detailed regulations that may affect the rights of individuals without taking legal advice.

A specimen set of regulations is given in appendix D. But all regulations have a repellent look and it may well be the policy of the archives office to reduce the formality of its image and to avoid presenting a forbidding aspect. In this case it may consider whether a much simpler set of rules will serve. If full regulations are decided on, they must be issued freely to every user of the office. An example of a simpler, less official, set of rules is as follows:(5)

SEARCHROOM FACILITIES
The public are asked to co-operate particularly on the following points:
  Please see that you have entered your name and address fully in the register of readers.
  Do not make any mark on documents, or use a pen which may leak or spill.
  Do not disturb the arrangement of documents, or take them out of their folders.
  Please ask the archivist in charge for permission to trace.
  Do not smoke or make a noise in the searchroom.

The archives office reserves the right to withhold documents which are unlisted or fragile, or where there is a restriction on access to them. Documents may not be published in extract or in full without the owner's permission. The staff cannot undertake private researches, nor can they give legal advice.

It is not probable that there has ever been a prosecution or legal action under any such regulations as these, though there have been prosecutions under general laws; an example is for the theft of documents. In view of this, it is worth keeping the searchroom regulations as simple and unforbidding as possible, and to combine them with general instructions or hints on behaviour and procedure.

INITIAL PROCEDURES FOR READERS

Registration

National archives institutions customarily require some preliminary registration of readers. Once a reader's ticket is issued, however, there is no further formality required before attendance. On the other hand, many small archives offices try to ensure that intending visitors come by appointment only, but there is rarely inquiry into the reader's own identity and status; the appointment system is simply to ensure that searchroom staff will be available, or that archival material has been brought in from outside storage.

In virtually all archives offices it is a custom to ask readers to sign a visitors' or attendance book on every occasion. In some cases the practice of signing in is rationalized by including in it an explicit acceptance by the reader of the regulations of the establishment.

There would seem to be three aims in keeping a signing-in book: the identification of the reader, the compilation of information on research demands, and making a count of the numbers of readers attending at different times. The identification of readers is an important objective in the preliminary induction procedure. The other two objectives are not best achieved by this means. Numbers attending can be determined from the searchroom supervisor's records, and their demands on records are best recorded by the requisition slips. Both of these records will be more reliable, since it is difficult and unnatural to enforce the constant signing of a visitor's book on every attendance. If the identification of readers is the main aim of the registration of visitors, it is probably more suitable to do it by filing registration cards than by chronological entries in a signing-in book.

Finding aids

Finding aids are obviously an essential feature of the searchroom equipment; they should be so placed as to be easily accessible to both searchers and staff. Physically, the aids are likely to be of three types: information sheets and pamphlets, volumes, and cards.

Information sheets, brochures and pamphlets are provided in order to explain the office's services and holdings for the benefit of readers generally or for the benefit of specific classes of reader. Their provision and design are an important part of the exploitative system of the office, and they are vital in beginning the education of a skilled group of users.

Format and content should be closely tailored to specific aims, and little generalization is possible. One general principle, however, is that such information sheets should conform to as high a standard of display as possible. Typically, there will be a general introductory sheet, which may give the following types of information:(6) title of the archives office; address, telephone, opening hours; directions for reaching the building, public transport and parking facilities; names of principal staff, with their specific responsibilities; brief history of the office, outline of its holdings; statutory or other basis for the office's work; main facilities for users (such as copying apparatus, photographic, maps, etc.); copyright restrictions; layout and using instructions for searchroom equipment and finding aids; list of publications.

Specialized supplementary information sheets may include advice for specific groups of readers, such as those engaged in genealogical research, or specific subjects of inquiry, for example, parish histories or the history of buildings.

The principal finding aids are likely to be in the form of books. Lists (whether summary or detailed), calendars, selective lists, and guides will all take this form, even though commonly enough the covers will be looseleaf folders of some kind. Volumes are best kept on shelves with open access; their correct use is one of the things the readers will have to master, and the biggest difficulty may be in establishing the relationship of one list to another. There should be a clear system for showing their arrangement, both on the shelves where they belong and on the spine or cover of the volumes. Ideally this system should employ words or titles, and not rely upon codes which have themselves to be learnt by the user; esoteric wording should be avoided. The shelf arrangement should show the hierarchy of lists and inventories: primary (guides, summary lists); secondary (more detailed lists of series); tertiary (calendars, detailed descriptions of individual items). Lists of related records elsewhere might be shelved nearby.

If possible there should be more than one copy of each list, further copies perhaps being shelved elsewhere in the searchroom. One of these copies can be the current working copy, interleaved, used for the insertion of notes and corrections by the staff and perhaps also by the searchers.

Card systems are mainly confined to indexes, since archives do not lend themselves to card catalogues. Card index cabinets should if possible be in integrated masses, with drawers clearly labelled. The first card in each drawer should be a brief description of the content and system in the drawer. If a cabinet which allows for locking bars (to prevent the cards from falling out) is adopted, drawers can be removed elsewhere. If this is not done, then a stool or other seating, with a small working surface, should be supplied at the cabinets. If public use is expected to be heavy, it may be advisable to reduce card indexes to volume form.

Other common forms of index are vertically mounted swinging boards or rotary flaps, which have to be set up on suitable tables or working surfaces to allow room for note-taking.

Indexes, like lists, have a hierarchical relationship one to another, and this should be clear from the titling: this is particularly important where there are primary and secondary indexes relating to the same series, or where original working indexes have been taken over from the originating department and put to use as archival finding aids.

There is no established practice concerning the right of access by readers to finding aids. As a general principle, finding aids should be open to all readers, irrespective of restrictions on access to the archives they deal with, since it is a public right to know of all accumulations of archives that are held, at least in publicly financed repositories, and of restrictions in force relative to them. But this may not always be possible: in the case of government records, there will be series that are particularly sensitive for security reasons, or which are so personal in nature that the finding aids will give too much information to a general searcher. Even where there are considerations of this kind, however, there should surely be an indication of the existence of the group, with a note of the date on which they will be open for inspection.

Directing research

The searchroom supervisor and his assistants are the focal point of the finding aid system. An archives office will naturally try to make its finding aids as far as possible self-explanatory; but this situation is approached in only the most highly developed of archives offices, and even there a good deal of personal guidance is necessary.

In most archives offices it will normally be essential for every new searcher to have at least a short discussion with an experienced member of the staff: he will relate the searcher's needs to the holdings of the office, and suggest the most likely classes of archives for the beginning of the search. It is natural that the searchroom supervisor will come to know when two or more searchers are pursuing related courses of research; in these cases, it will be to the advantage of all concerned that the two searchers concerned should be introduced. In fact the archives office should adopt a positive attitude toward the co-ordination of research, not only arranging meetings between individuals but also, on suitable occasions, conferences and seminars at which findings and technical difficulties can be reported, or providing a centre for informal meetings and discussions of the same kind; a register of principal research projects in progress or a newsletter circulated among regular attenders are also suitable activities; and of course archives offices may also initiate research projects.

But on the other hand, there may be reasons why the work of

individual readers should be kept confidential. The discussion between a reader and the searchroom supervisor in the course of business, like all professional consultations, must be regarded as essentially confidential. To resolve this possible conflict of interests, the supervisor ought to ask as a matter of course if he may use the information gained in informing other searchers for the purpose of furthering research and increasing co-operation. Without an assurance of this sort, no disclosure should be made, and certainly not one which involves names and details. Readers could be asked to sign a simple consent form, and a general statement of the office's policy could be attached to the searchroom regulations.

Enquiries
A large part of the work of any archives office is the answering of enquiries received by post or by telephone; this is complementary to the direction of personal enquiries in the searchroom and should be part of the responsibilities of the searchroom supervisor. Although the volume and nature of the enquiries received will vary from one office to another, some general principles have been generally agreed, and are practised in most places where there are archives. The duty of the archivist is to explain the nature of the archives held and the nature of the finding aids available, and to give what assistance is reasonably possible to enable an enquirer to pursue his research.

This means that there will normally be three kinds of reply given to enquiries: supplying copies of relevant lists, indexes, guide entries, etc., with any necessary explanatory information sheets; copying particular archives; giving information from archives or other sources.

It is clearly right that an archives office should accept some responsibility for the provision of information as well as of facilities for the inspection of archives. This is particularly so where the enquiry comes from the office's employing authority, for it must be assumed that the authority has delegated to its archivists some of its research functions. Moreover, it may well be useful to the operations of the archives office itself to assemble and supply information on points concerning its main subject area.

There are difficulties when it comes to limiting the resources put into the provision of information on demand. One commonly accepted is that of time: the archivist should provide information only when its compilation demands a search of only a few minutes. This means that an external reader could expect an archivist to refer to one or two documents on his behalf, but not more. Beyond this the office's duty is only to make the archival material available. A compromise is available where the enquirer can employ a locally based record searcher, and many archives offices supply the names of such people with the other informational material they send. Some direction on this point must form part of the searchroom supervisor's instructions.

In any case it is useful to maintain a register of enquiries which will form an index of subjects dealt with. The purpose of this index is to prevent duplication of research in response to enquiry, to co-ordinate research in some cases, and to assist in determining the latent demand for extensions to the archives service. The resulting index of enquiries may often be combined with enquiries made personally by readers in the searchroom, where it has been

ENQUIRY FORM				
Name of enquirer		Address (telephone)		
Date of enquiry	Date information required	How received	Related correspondence (file ref)	Received by
Date of action	Information & action taken (References of documents quoted should be given)			

9.2 Enquiry record form

necessary for the archivists to undertake similar researches themselves.

Figure 9.2 is a sample form for recording such researches.(7) For purposes of retrieval these sheets will be stored in a predetermined order, perhaps that of the names of the enquirers. In this case, a subject index of the content of the enquiry and its answer can be added separately. Otherwise the sheet itself may be used as an index by filing it under a suitable subject key word; but in this case there will have to be provision for cross references, and for retrieval of the names of enquirers or enquiring departments and any filed correspondence. Alternatively subject enquiries can be given a serial number keyed to a register.

10 Searchroom Services in Public Repositories, II

Issue of documents

After consulting the finding aids, a reader should be in a position to ask the office to produce items which he wishes to see. The basic requirements for a production system are to identify accurately the archives required, and to provide a control over the documents during the whole period during which they are out of their regular storage place. Accurate identification will allow for rapid finding in the storage area, and accurate replacement later. A secondary aim of the production system may be to record the transaction, to provide information about the demand for certain classes of archive and the amount of use they receive, and so on.

If all these aims are to be achieved, it will be necessary to formalize the requisitioning of archives, and to design a requisition slip. An example is given in figure 10.1. The top slip (a) is completed by or on behalf of the reader.(1) A second slip (b), on tinted paper, forms a 'clean' carbon below the top slip, so that the words written on the top will emerge in the right places on the second. The space at the bottom of the tinted slip may be completed in pen by the archives staff who issue the document. A third slip may be required as an identification ticket attached to the document requested while it is out of place. Readers will be making out many of these slips, and will be reluctant to repeat information, and this therefore must be kept to a minimum. Thus it is unwise to ask for the reader's address on the requisition slip: this information can be obtained from the initial registration of readers. Similarly, the archives staff will be reluctant to write in constantly repeated information when they issue and return the documents. Consequently it should be considered whether even the initials and date of issue and return can be deleted from the working details required.

The reader will hand the completed slips to the searchroom staff or place them in a box for collection. The two parts will be separated: the top slip will remain in the searchroom as a control at that point: any slip held there will represent a document out of place in storage. The second slip will go to the storage area, where it will be placed in the shelf space occupied by the document removed. If this document is kept in a box, the slip can be clipped to the outside of the box, or in a conspicuous place at the end of the shelving bay. Every slip so displayed represents a document removed, and records its reference and location. The document is then brought to the searchroom, and either taken to the reader at his table or taken to the issue desk so that it can be collected. It should be made clear to readers how long this process takes, and how often collections of slips are made; the archives office must be prepared to help readers to plan their time.

When the documents are returned, the process continues in reverse. In some institutions the top requisition slip is handed back to the reader as a form of receipt, and handing it back to him indicates that the archives office has relieved him of his temporary responsibility for the document. If an archives office wishes to adopt this practice, some statement to this effect should appear on the top slip and there should be space on it for his signature. However, the difficulty is that the top slip would have to be returned at the same moment that the document is handed in, whereas in practice it is more convenient to retain the top slip until the document has been replaced. In that case the second slip can be removed from the shelf, brought back to the issue desk to replace the top slip to record that the process is completed.

There is then never a moment when documents removed from their storage place are not controlled by a record at the issue desk. Filed second slips can be retained for a period, to form the record of documents issued which may be needed for statistical returns or the like; if a document has been misplaced, they can sometimes help in the search by recording similar transactions at the same date or in the same part of the storage area.

Readers often do not finish with a particular document on the day of its requisition. In this case the documents can be retained in a convenient storage area near the searchroom and reclaimed the following day. In a large archives office some control will be

(a)

*Searchroom: REQUISITION FOR DOCUMENTS	Name Table No Date
Series or title of document	
Reference No:	
Only one document to be requisitioned on each slip. Documents must be returned to the issue desk every evening.	

*where more than one searchroom is served.

(b)

DOCUMENT REMOVED	Name Table No Date
Series or title	
Reference No:	
Issued by Returned by	date date

10.1 A requisition slip

needed for this also; this may take the form of a coloured card
bearing the name of the reader and placed with the 'kept-out'
documents. Otherwise the same control instruments will serve,
the top requisition slip remaining at the issue desk until the
document has been finally replaced.

Reviewing Needs of Readers
If the archives office wishes to use the requisition slips for
secondary information, it may make triplicates, the third slip
containing further information to be filled in either by the reader or

by the searchroom supervisor. The information asked for may include:

in relation to the documents requisitioned: official or non-official; dealing with one or more subject categories specified; the archive series; shape, size and condition of documents (e.g. maps, microfilm, fragile).

in relation to the use to which they were put: an official inquiry; academic research; private genealogical inquiry; educational uses.

The more elaborate the breakdown employed for this inquiry, the less likely it is that a third slip in the requisition process will be appropriate. An alternative is a questionnaire card which can be completed by the reader once, at the beginning of his period of work in the archives office, and associated with the initial registration procedures.

Recent Developments

The largest archives offices, like the Public Record Office in its new building at Kew, will employ a call and production system which is highly mechanized. To call for a document, a reader will use the equipment—probably in the form of a keyboard linked to a computer—to record details of himself (reader's number, seat and table, date), of the document required (archival and location codes), and 'third copy' details. A computer can determine much about a reader's purposes by collating information filed under his readership number. It can also rapidly check if the document is available, and not either in use for another purpose, or subject to some access restriction.

Production of the document may then also be by some mechanical channel.(2) Documents need not be taken to readers' desks, but can be put in numbered pigeonholes appropriate to each place.

The public archives of Canada uses a variation of this procedure in order to allow twenty-four hour use of the searchroom. Each reader is given a key to a numbered locker, into which are put the documents he is using. The reader can then attend at any hour of the day or night to use them. 'Security is safeguarded by the preliminary screening interview, discreet continuous surveillance by the staff, the use of individual lockers that are accessible to authorized staff at all times, and the maintenance of an exact record of the use each researcher makes of archive facilities.'(3)

Layout and Design

The design of a searchroom is more important in one sense than the design of any other part of an archives office. It is the place of public access, and public recognition of the value of the service provided will depend in great part on the atmosphere and appearance of the searchroom. Since a searchroom is a place of public access, it must possess an adequate entrance. Nearby there should be some point where a reader can make his presence known, and discover how to proceed with his enquiry.

The term 'searchroom' is used as a general word to cover all areas of public access and consultation. The range of functions discharged by the searchroom is quite wide, however, and the needs of some of them are mutually incompatible. It is in this area that intending readers are registered, encounter the finding aids, and have consultations with the archives staff about their sources. The searchroom is therefore a place for talking and moving about.(4) On the other hand, it is where readers sit to consult documents, which involves close and sustained study. The searchroom is therefore a place for silence and absence of disturbance. To reconcile such opposed functions presents a challenge to the designer, and it is probable that the result will not be a room, but a complex of areas, linked by natural and easy access routes:

Induction area: first registration, issue of information sheets, display, notices, access to cloakroom facilities; telephone.

Reference area: control of readers, consultation between staff and readers, finding systems, library, requisition systems, issue, return and reserve storage arrangements.

Study area: tables for study of documents, facilities for study of large documents or items in large containers.

Special study areas: group use of archives, lecture-seminar, typewriter, tape-recorder facilities.

Technical facilities: microfilm readers, copying equipment, ultra-violet or special lighting.

Supervision and issue areas.

Transit: passage for readers and staff from one area to another; passage to and from storage areas (trolleys); passage to: display/exhibition, seminar, common-room, refreshments, cloakrooms, emergency exits, office areas.

Even the smallest and simplest archives office carries out these
functions, although a small office using adapted accommodation
will have to make do with two rooms, perhaps arranged as in
figure 10.2. But where purpose-built buildings are available,
specialized functions may be provided through careful planning,
as for example at the new Lancashire Record Office (figure
10.3(5)).

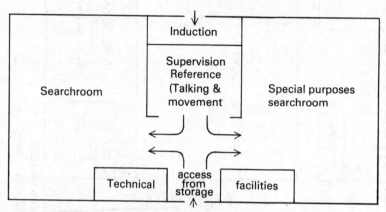

10.2 Arrangement of searchroom accommodation in a small
archives office

An important question in the planning of searchroom facilities
is that of capacity. As in the case of storage, it is important to be
able to judge the likely intake over a given number of years. There
will be variables, but it will be possible to make some calculations
which will assist in projection. The graph of searchroom
attendances in figure 10.4(6) is typical of the experience of local
archives offices during the 1960s. For the late 1970s it is clear
that we have to plan for a continued and possibly intensified
increase in public demand for access to archives, but with the
possibility of setbacks. Much of the demand will be for group
access.

A flexible design, of course, is best; an over-large
searchroom, with regular empty space, is depressing as well as
uneconomical—though not as depressing or uneconomical as a
searchroom which is too small or too undifferentiated in its
functional areas. Crowding and confusion are counter-productive
on all counts. The happy mean will be a searchroom which is
extensible, perhaps by a planned expansion into further rooms, or
by the adjustment of partition walls.

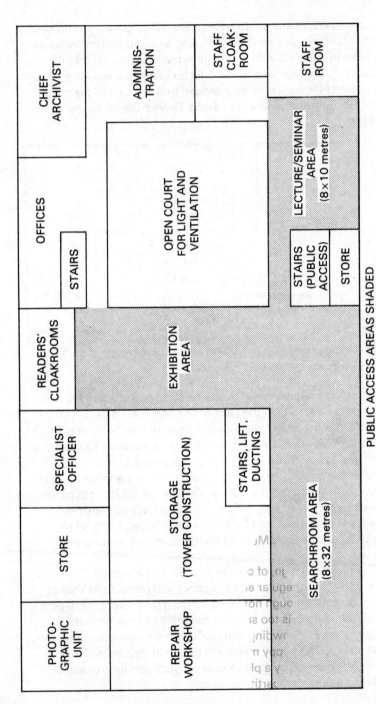

PUBLIC ACCESS AREAS SHADED

10.3 Simplified ground plan of the new Lancashire record office (first floor)

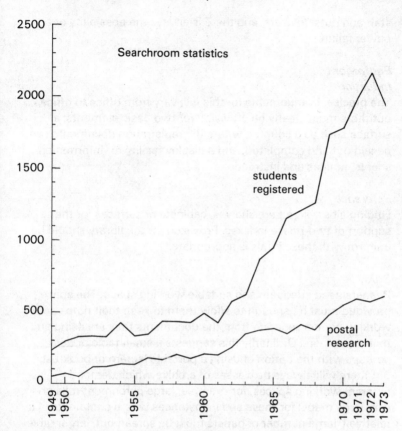

10.4 Enquiries at the Gloucestershire record office, 1949-73

Equipment and Facilities in the Searchroom

There should be as strict a control of the physical conditions in the searchroom as in the main storage; even in a temperate climate this will involve air conditioning. Where a less strict control is the rule, as in older buildings, the environmental standards of the searchroom will not be as good, but they should be related to those of the storage area.

An important consideration is the comfort of readers, who may have to sit long at a document and keep alert. In modern buildings especially the tendency will be towards too much heat and too little humidity. Good illumination also is demanded for readers; nowadays this need not be from natural lighting, but light sources should be well designed technically. In practice a good provision of natural light is highly desirable; windows add interest for both

staff and outside users, and there is always the possibility of a
power failure.

Equipment
Induction
The precise arrangements for this will vary from office to office,
but there must clearly be provision for two basic elements: a
surface such as a counter, where the registration documents can
be laid out and completed; and a display facility for information
sheets, notices and instructions.

Reference
Finding aids will require shelves, cabinets or surfaces for the
support of two-phase indexes. Provision for the library should be
uniform with these if this is appropriate.

Study
Readers need adequate and suitable working space. The space
provided must be enough to allow them to keep their notes and
working papers separate from the documents they are using and
their containers. Ordinarily this suggests a small table or desk,
perhaps with the option of using a portable lectern or bookrest.
But there will always be classes of archive which demand
different working spaces, for example, large parchment rolls or
very large maps: for these and in instances where containers of a
relatively large number of papers must be spread out, larger table
surfaces are needed. It is common practice for a number of small
tables of uniform shape and height to be provided; these can be
pushed together to form larger units when required.
    Table equipment should include covered weights, calibrated
clear plastic rulers, and access to individual angled lamps.

Special study facilities
Group study or seminar facilities need educational aids. These are
discussed in chapter 12. Technical advice should be taken on the
requirements for typewriters and tape recorders and possibly
calculating machines to be used by readers.

Technical
Equipment for using microforms and for providing rapid copies
will be standard. Microfilm readers of a modern design do not
require special building or facilities, but if the screen type is being

used care should be taken to reduce the reflection of extraneous light on the screen. Film readers may occupy the standard tables at one end of the room, where electricity supply may be brought to the tables without trailing flex. A microfilm reader-printer should be provided wherever possible, though for administrative reasons this machine may be kept under staff control. Rapid copying facilities must surely be provided everywhere today; near the searchroom itself a rapid copier of an electrostatic type is appropriate. These may be operated directly by readers, by inserting coins, or by staff.

Non-standard but desirable in some offices where there are substantial holdings of faded and damaged parchments will be an ultra-violet lamp. For best results this lamp will need considerable protection from direct white light; some models provide this by including a box or cover in their design. In other cases the lamp will have to be screened.

Supervision

The searchroom supervisor's desk will be sited with a view of the whole searchroom area and with suitable space for consultations with readers. He will also need to be near the exits and entrances to the storage area and to the archives office administration, if possible. The need for consultation, which will necessarily always have an element of the private and personal, would suggest a separate office, with a window or glass partition. It is in any case a necessity for any professional person to have his own workplace, and a searchroom supervisor will have his own work in hand.

Transit

Apart from adequate space for movement, the main consideration will be soundproofing. Acoustic material can be used on ceilings, exposed walls and floors.

Searchroom library

The searchroom library is a tool for the use of every person using the archives office, both staff and readers, and its stock and layout should be carefully considered. It should be the specific responsibility of one member of staff, after suitable training, with a budget for the purchase of new items and the maintenance of the collection.

It is hard to exaggerate the importance to the staff (apart from its importance to the user) of a searchroom library. They are expected to command a body of professional knowledge, and exercise judgement on a wide range of matters, which need current information. The acquisition of material, including periodicals, for the library is a matter which demands specialist knowledge and should be systematic. On the other hand it would be unreasonable, in most cases, to try to make the archives library self-sufficient. Archivists ought to be familiar users of outside resources available to them, including of course university library and inter-library loan services. Nevertheless the archives library is a technical tool of great value.

Size and character will depend on the function determined for it in relation to the office's overall programmes. The archives staff will need specifically books and periodicals for their professional work, in the following fields:

General Reference Works

Archival techniques and knowledge: archive theory, standards in archive practice, periodicals providing discussion on points of professional practice, domestic and international, and those devoted to the content of archives and related work in English.

Archive work programmes elsewhere: guides, catalogues, lists, reports.

Interpretative sciences: palaeography, genealogy, historical method, information work, data processing.

Exploitation of archive and record sources: in particular those in the same subject area, operating within similar geographical units, using parallel or complementary records, or demonstrating comparable or parallel techniques of interpretation.

Progress of research subjects, financing and personnel: university calendars, research bulletins, abstracts of theses.

Texts or extracts from the archives in the office, or from related archives. Official editions of archival texts. This section may include published secondary works based to any extent on the archives, but the extent to which the office library will extend itself into secondary works will have to be carefully defined. If a book has direct references to archives held in the office, it has a good claim to inclusion.

Printed matter which is primary evidence in research allied to that carried on in the archives. Thus in a local archives office printed material of local relevance might be included. This part of the office library would then resemble the 'local collection' in a public library. The information contained in the archives is often closely linked to, or is complementary to, the information contained in printed matter. Some printed material is itself archival.

11 Developmental Services

Archives offices usually undertake positive exploitation of their holdings; that is, they operate by their own initiative to exploit the information in the archives directly. Positive exploitation usually begins at an early stage in the existence of the office. It is undertaken because the personal and professional satisfaction of the archivists demands it, and because before one can rely on negative services to discharge the function of exploitation there must be a pool of trained users ready to put them to use.

Among the main positive purposes of such activities must then be to form such a pool of users, and to stimulate demand for access. It is not possible for a totally untrained person to use archives effectively, or even at all; this is a difficulty which has frequently brought to nothing schemes for the educational development of archives, where these schemes have depended upon the abilities as searchers of teachers or lecturers. Normally no archive can be asked for, let alone interpreted, unless the enquirer has some knowledge of the administrative structures which called it into being. Archives offices have to take part in the teaching of administrative and institutional history, and in the training of its users. To do this, they must take an active interest in recruiting users, their stimulation to work, and in the appropriate body of knowledge. All this implies a continuing relationship between the staff of the archives office and the students of related subjects in the locality.

There are three points at which the training of readers, individually or collectively, could be considered.

Individual readers seeking advice in the searchroom. Each searcher needs to know two things: which aspects of the creating administration he should examine, and their methods of work; and how to go about identifying and ordering the items that he needs. This level of instruction represents a basic provision, part of the searchroom services.

Collective instruction of potential searchers. The difficulty is to identify a section of the public which constitutes a potential source of users, and to stimulate and instruct it accordingly. Specific instruction in isolation of particular documents is not required here, but rather the development of certain components in the general education of people: a broad knowledge of institutional history, rather more explicit knowledge of the nature of source material in either history or other relevant studies, interpretative techniques, familiarity with the institutions in which the resources of research are administered (libraries, museums, or archives offices). In addition, there is the general dissemination of knowledge on the subject area served by the archives office: either a specific subject (such as history of science, agriculture, labour relations), or a specific locality (county, province, region). The former group of subjects belongs to the realm of general education; the latter is the area where the archives office is a specialist teaching institution. Here the need is to stimulate and develop the field of studies. In the case of a local archives office, this will be in local studies.

Education of institutions. The third level of communication arises from the second. The archives office should have a link of some kind with the teaching institutions it depends on for users (university, polytechnic, college of education). It should know what is being taught that touches on its subject area, and should influence the direction in which this teaching is developed. The office will of course be able to provide teaching material as part of this activity.

Educational Requirements
A local archives office in a rural area itself may be the only establishment actually teaching the higher studies (local or technological) associated with its holdings. But the development of these higher studies and the infrastructure of general educational knowledge would both be necessary to the development of archive work in the area. It is not necessary that

the actual development of these studies should be by the archives office itself; but the office must take an integral part in their development and it must itself have staff who understand these studies and are accepted on both an official and a personal level by the majority of those concerned with them.

Somebody must provide a structure for teaching, research and development, and in some cases it may be appropriate that this should be the archives office itself. Whoever does it must do it effectively, using methods which are educationally acceptable, and deploying appropriate resources. Whether or not the archives office itself undertakes direct teaching in the development of local or specific studies, it must at least accept responsibility for the training of its own staff and for seeing that they do take a suitable place among the students in their field.

A programme for teaching, whether internal or external or both, will demand the apparatus of teaching: staff, time, equipment and administration.

Archives staff should have a good knowledge of the contents of the archives with which they are concerned, and of progress in the body of knowledge for which their archives are a resource. Some instruction in teaching techniques is required for members of staff to be involved in teaching duties: in general this should include all professional archives staff.

Those who are asked to teach should be allowed or required to undertake specific responsibilities for the running and completion of courses which are publicly recognized or validated.

The preparation and follow-up of courses of lectures, seminars or any other teaching method demands time, and the scope of the teaching programme should be tailored to the time available. Opportunity must be allowed for preparation, general reading in the subject area, attendance at libraries, choice and construction of teaching material, including audio-visual aids, and, of course, time for the actual teaching. Ideally the teaching programme should include or lead up to a structured course, which may or may not be associated with the programmes of bodies such as university extension departments.

There is also the possibility of fostering useful intercourse both on techniques and on subjects in an informal way. Some advanced archives offices have provided common rooms for their readers with this in mind. The facilities could include provision for simple refreshments, and it might be customary for the archives staff to use these facilities also.

Archives offices have fostered the development of higher studies and research in their subject areas by both voluntary and official agencies. Voluntary agencies are chiefly societies which, basing their activities on subscriptions from the members, arrange to publish (in print or by lecture) the results of research, and to promote discussion of the subject; there may be many societies within the area of an archives office, or only one. The distinction between societies may be geographical or by topic. In any case, a familiar development in the 1970s is the appearance of federations of societies within a geographical area such as a county or region, or within a subject area nationally.

It is not suggested that archivists should necessarily, as a matter of their office's programme, take a leading part organizationally in such movements, for it is often better to allow voluntary workers to take the lead; but they should, of course, be involved, and allow as much support officially as possible.

Display

The proper and effective display of its material or of aspects of its work is important to the success of any archives office's programmes. The standard and nature of the display should be carefully considered and designed, and suitable resources should be allocated to the realization of the resulting programme. Unfortunately the resources required will not be small, and it is necessary to acquire an expertise in the field (which is, of course, an educational one), and to devote a good deal of energy to planning its proper use.

The purpose will influence decisions on the main points: locale, date, duration, selection of material, manner of display, character of informative material, publicity, supporting services (events, lectures, recorded commentary). All the techniques used in display are the subject of the professional expertise of others, and, though every archives office should develop the capacity to deploy the techniques and expertise of the display industry, it will not necessarily be managed by the use of its own resources alone; the initiative must come from the archives, but the realization may sometimes be achieved by calling on outside consultants, such as museum advisory services as well as private firms.

It is a useful general principle that archives should rarely be the sole material in a display; they are notoriously difficult to show interestingly, except to those who are already expert and involved, as they are essentially two-dimensional pieces of paper covered with writing and, however vivid the information in them is, the writing must be read before there can be any impact on a casual observer. In contrast, an object may make an immediate visual impression, both as the conveyer of information and as a stimulus to a response such as nostalgia, recollection, aesthetic appreciation.

Display should often be planned in conjunction with parallel services, such as museum services, deploying resources external to the archives but with the same general objectives.

The principle of taking closely defined objectives and tailoring all display methods to these militates against committing large resources to one type of display area or equipment. No one type of display equipment—show case, screen, table, block—can do more than fulfil a few specific purposes. Display areas and opportunities should be as adaptable as possible. Great attention should be paid to lighting and the use of support services such as photography, automatic projection and sound. Since location, duration and timing are as important as any other feature to the exact objective, it is likely that a fixed exhibition room and display equipment will not prove adaptable enough for economical and effective use. Facilities for using for display areas of the archives office such as the searchroom, teaching areas, entrance hall might however be provided; these should certainly allow space along walls for equipment, and have electricity supply points for lighting.

Providing exhibition material outside the archives office should certainly be part of the office's routine. But this raises the question of security, against both environmental damage and loss by theft or accident. Each form of display carries its own dangers: caretakers, duty staff, electronic detectors, burglar alarms, fire alarms, insurance are all matters which will have to be decided on in relation to any given locale.

However, there are many resources which are available to the display artist. He may use facsimiles in preference to originals. High-quality photographic facsimiles can be treated, as originals could not, to make them fit the plan of the display—they can be enlarged, for example, to make handwriting more striking or more legible. The original will always have one quality which no reproduction can have, that of direct association with time, place or persons that are in the public's imagination. But reproductions can nearly always adequately convey the information contained both in the wording and in the appearance of the archive, and can often improve upon it as a display item.

Publications

Publication of lists, texts of documents or abstracts of their contents is a natural extension of both display and descriptive work. There have been many imaginative and useful publications arising from archives in recent years, and the range of techniques now possible has made it much easier to duplicate and disseminate both text and facsimile material.

Much recent archival publication has fallen under the heading of display rather than under the traditional categories of lists and indexes, calendars and edited texts. A monograph on what has been and could be accomplished by publication programmes is very much needed.(1)

Microreprography in Archives

In this important field, archivists are fortunate to have an established international standard, and in what follows there is as yet nothing to add to A. H. Leisinger's manual, *Microphotography for Archives*.(2)

Microphotography is the photographic reproduction of documents on film, which may be either in continuous reels or in individual mounts of some kind, and which are much smaller in size than the originals. They must be read on magnifying equipment, and can be used to make prints and enlargements. The various forms which either the reels or the individual frames can take are subject to constant development, and, before any programme of microreprographics is undertaken, information on the current state of the art should be collected.

All microforms require that the documents they deal with should be prepared, and put through the process of being filmed; the film must be processed to appropriate standards, finding aids constructed for it, and equipment for reading provided.

All this means that microreprography is expensive, and the costing of a programme is likely to be of critical importance. Cost can only be considered in relation to purpose, so that the careful choice of appropriate objectives is particularly important.

Aims

There are eight possible aims which an archives office might have in mind for its microreprographic programmes:

Reference. Copying long series of archives for the convenience of users is best done on microfilm, and this is now common where the numbers of documents to be copied are greater than a certain critical quantity, or where heavy postage or transport costs are involved.

Publication. Whole archive series may be published in microform. Smaller numbers of documents or particular files may be reproduced in one of the individual forms such as microfiche or microcard. Material published in this way requires printed or duplicated publicity material, titling and explanatory text. A large number of copies can be taken from a microfilm, whether positive or negative, and this form of publication is now common in many countries.

Acquisition. It is possible for archives offices to acquire complementary material, both primary and secondary, by filming it. In this way, an office can obtain a copy of archive series held by other institutions, perhaps in other countries, or it can get the use of archive series held by private owners who do not wish to part with the originals.

Security. Filmed copies of records and archives can be kept away from the originals, in different buildings or even towns, to guard against loss by any catastrophe. In some countries this has been a main objective for major filming programmes.

Preservation. Film may be used by readers instead of the original in cases where the original is fragile or subject to excessive use. It is now common in many cases for microfilm copies to be automatically produced to readers instead of originals.

Conservation. To microfilm documents may be one of the resources of the conservation section, where the originals are on unstable material, and where the cost of lamination or other direct repair work may be too difficult or expensive. Microfilm is not cheap, but it can be of a quality better consistent with permanent preservation than poor-quality paper.

Space-saving. Preserving documents in microform does result in very considerable saving of space, though at the cost of an expensive and exacting filming programme. It is probable that the cost of such a programme will render it uneconomical where space-saving is the only aim in view. However it is often possible to combine two or more objectives in a filming programme, and even without this condition, there are circumstances in which an archives service may have to accept the cost: this would be likely where the storage accommodation was limited and where there was no possibility of extension. It is only under this heading and the next that it is assumed that the original documents will be automatically destroyed after filming.

Administration. There are several possible administrative advantages for a filming programme: for example, access can be provided to filmed documents at several different points; or finding aids or other reference material can be provided on film for use in departments. It is possible also that executive departments could have a microfilming programme as part of their ordinary administration, and where this is the case, the archives service might share the programme by adapting it to one or more of their own purposes. A very common example of this is where plan-producing departments, such as engineers', architects' or surveyors', opt to keep their plans on 70 mm. or 35 mm. film in the form of aperture cards. These cards, of course, are the record produced and kept by the departments, and eventually become the archive. An easy extension of the filming programme will send suitably selected cards direct into the archives. In other cases, the administrative operations may be recorded directly on film, as where computer output is in microform.

Practical Considerations
Selection of Archives for Filming

Fundamental to the success of any programme is the selection of the archives to be filmed. They should first of all have suitable physical characteristics: ideal might be a long series of archives already in rational or final order, especially if they already have a simple descriptive system and associated indexes. They should be flat and of the same size and colour, easily legible, and preferably in good condition; to film archives which do not conform to these ideals will cost more, since there will have to be special handling, and such additional costs would have to be justified in terms of their value and of the value of the objectives to be achieved by the programme. There are additional considerations of a more purely archival kind in selecting series for filming and in dealing with them. It is a better practice to film entire series rather than selections. This is because (as with the originals, if there were ever a question of selecting them) the integrity of the series is a valuable quality in an archive, a quality which archivists hold it their duty to protect. Selections can never be entirely impartial, or

entirely successful for more than one immediate purpose. In any
case, the cost of filming a series of archives is likely to be
increased, rather than decreased, by the extra process involved in
selection.

Quality of Materials

From the archival point of view, a vital factor in any microreprographic programme is the physical standard of the film.
Microfilm is not necessarily any less stable than most grades of
paper in common use, and is indeed more stable than some of the
cheaper grades. The life of a microfilm, too, can always be
extended by making another copy of it. But the optimum
conditions for the storage of microfilm are more exacting than
those for paper, and blemishes which may develop on the film
through chemical action or poor processing are more serious than
they would be on paper. A very small blemish on a piece of film is
likely to obscure much of the writing, and it is also much more
difficult to detect its appearance at an early stage. Archivists need
to give a good deal of attention to the quality of the film at the
time when it is produced, and to the conditions of its storage and
retrieval. Normal standards of administrative filming are not
expected to conform to archival requirements.

The additional considerations to which an archivist will subject
a filming programme so that it meets his standards concern both
the composition and use of the film and the way the original
material is selected and put together in it. As regards the chemical
composition of the film, he must be assured that the master copy,
which is to be used only to produce the second and further
working copies, conforms to the highest physical standards; these
may be laid down by the national standards institution. At present
these are likely to specify that the film should be of the silver-
halide emulsion type of a certain purity and resolution, and its
chemical composition after processing should be checked to
ensure conformity with this standard. Working copies of the film
may be made by one of the cheaper processes such as Diazo, but
it is imperative that at least one master copy should be retained
and not used except for making further copies of the film. The film,
in reels of about thirty metres and suitably boxed, or in cards,
fiches or jackets, as the system may require, should then be stored
in fireproof areas and cupboards with a controlled environment,
using filtered air conditioning, at a temperature between 18 and
20 degrees Centigrade and an average 40 per cent relative
humidity.

Methods of Identification

Important too is the titling and coding system which the film
series carries. The material on the film cannot, of course, be used
unless it can be recognized; this is doubly important since it
cannot be read by eye, and it may have to conform to international
standards if the film is to be despatched to a user outside the
archives office.

Before filming, the material to be filmed must be properly (that
is, archivally) arranged, since it is exceedingly difficult to rearrange
material on film. Indexes and direct finding aids should be filmed
before the documents to which they relate. Since normally roll
film in thirty-metre lengths is used, the length of the roll and the
amount of material on each roll should be adjusted by deciding on
a reduction ratio to give an appropriate number of exposures per
reel; this ratio should be indicated on the film. Each roll should
contain a title card or page identifying the roll number, the archive
series concerned, the particular documents upon that roll, and
details of when and where filmed.

Since some hundreds of images will appear on any roll of film,
it may be necessary to identify particular frames along its length.
This can be done either by including in the frame a serial number
(an automatic counter can be used) or by inserting flash-cards or
flags at regular intervals along the reel, say at every twenty-fifth
exposure in a continuous series or where a volume or file ends.
Additional flags can be used to explain breaks in the series, or to
give any other identifications or instructions for the benefit of the
reader.

Each roll will also be identified by number and code on its box
and on the leader of blank film which it has at its outer end, and to
find the necessary roll or box, normal lists or indexes will be
maintained. Full descriptions of microfilmed archives will include a
note of the contents as well as a key to the rolls or other film units
used. In the case of published microfilm, additional explanatory
material in print form will be needed.

Forms of Microreprography

Most traditional archival filming programmes have resulted in
series of 35 mm. or 16 mm. rolls of film; this is because archives
are usually by their nature arranged in long continuous series, and
this format is the most suitable. However, it is possible that in
some cases filming in small discrete units, such as microfiche or
jackets made up from 16 mm. film, can be made more useful than

reel film. For example, individual files can be reproduced in fiche form, which can be used for reference either in research or administratively. The danger in this is that a file is not an independent self-explanatory unit as is a book, and, once it is dissociated from its fellows in the archive series, it loses some part of its research significance. Of course, a collection of microfiches can be kept together and coded so as to retain an archival order; but they can also be sorted into other orders, or their units can be separated or stray. Subject to these doubts, however, rendering files onto microfiche may well be a most useful resource for the archival microform programmer.

Conclusion

Microreprography can be a flexible and effective tool in archives and records management, and it is hard to conceive of any archives service which could not make use of it for one or more of possible purposes. Although the design of a microform programme calls for careful thought and for careful justification in terms of objectives, an archivist must also defend his decision, if he makes it, not to use microforms. Such a decision will account for the cost of lost or unattainable aims and programmes not attempted.

12 Archives in Education

It is by now fairly widely accepted that it is a legitimate part of an archivist's professional activity to take at least some interest in the development of educational (school) services using archives. These are a specialized extension of the service provided under the general heading of communication; and in the organization of the archives office, educational activities, if they are not so extensive as to command separate staff and resources, may come under the sphere of operation of the searchroom supervisor. But it is very much to be desired that educational services should have their own programmes and resources.

As long ago as 1923, G. H. Fowler indicated that he thought that there was a future in archival educational work, speaking of 'the interests of county education as [well as] . . . of general historical research.'(1) Education work has developed as a function more of local archives services than of national ones, though *pédagogie et archivistique sont intimement liées',*(2) and it is generally agreed that an aim of archive work is essentially educational. Work with schools and colleges is in the same category as with academic institutions, but it is very much a specialized and technical activity, and ought not to be undertaken in any but the most passive way (in providing space in the searchroom) unless there is the possibility of utilizing educational expertise in designing the programmes. However such advice is widely available: there are advisory services for schools everywhere, and it is hard to imagine that there can be an archives office which is quite unable to draw on that resource, or which has not experienced any demand from schools.

In educational work, as in all other work in which learning is a component, it is important to have clearly defined aims, and to devise methods and use resources which are directed narrowly at these aims; this directness of purpose may not be so necessary with some of the exploitative services, since in the searchroom it is possible—and even laudable—to shift the burden of defining aims on to the user, who may attend at his convenience, and make what he can of it all. With schoolchildren, undergraduates, student teachers, and teachers who are not themselves experts in the use of archives, this is not the case; here the archives service must define the aims and refine the methods, and undertake the training of non-specialists (who will almost always remain non-specialists) in the use of something which has traditionally been a specialist medium. It is important that in every project there should be a specific *educational* objective, which will take into account the means and methods available.

The general aim of an archival education service will be to marshal the archival resources of the service in such a way as to allow for and encourage their use in teaching-learning situations. Such an aim assumes that there has been prior agreement on the value of the operation, and that it is in fact desirable that archival material should be used in teaching. This is not the place for a full discussion of this point, since there is a considerable literature on it, but there is widespread agreement (with some reservations) that archives do constitute an educational resource appropriate for use in normal school situations and may be used for the teaching of skills such as the evaluation of evidence or the identification and collation of information.

Services Inside the Office

It may be possible to arrange for the pupils and teachers concerned in a scheme to come to the office in order to use specially designed facilities. This provides access to the archives for a specialized group, and in this case the archivist may have more responsibility than in other cases for the selection, presentation and explanation of the material. But there are important caveats: 'the worst solution is that in which the public searchroom must be used.'(3)

Finding aids and guides

Educational finding aids have one special characteristic, apart from the simplicity of their language and presentation: the element of selection which has gone into them. Normally a finding aid will include in its scope all documents which fall within the defined archives series, and further selection, to sift the useful from the irrelevant, is the task of the reader, who takes as his criterion the relevance of any document to his inquiry. In the course of this he may find himself in some blind alleys, inspecting documents which turn out to be uninteresting in themselves or for his purpose. Though this experience may be far from valueless in other circumstances, it is out of place in an educational exercise, where the fruitful use of time is of great importance, and a frustrating experience may be counter-productive.

In contrast, a finding aid devised for educational purposes will contain a large element of selection. The compiler of these educational guides will have borne in mind both the subject he was dealing with and the specific educational objectives with which he was concerned at that moment. The result will be a short list of documents which not only bear upon the subject (from any suitable source), but also comply with certain fairly strict criteria of their suitability in that context. These will include secondary characteristics such as their legibility and intelligibility, as well as primary characteristics such as relevance and interest. Similarly the amount and nature of detail to be included in the list will be determined by the precise aims of the list itself: Is it strictly a finding aid—that is, a means whereby a user (teacher or pupil) can order and receive a particular document in the archives? Or is it in effect a publication, something calling the attention of a potential user (a teacher) to something which the archivist thinks will be attractive and useful? Or is it an aid which will allow the user to determine whether any particular document will suit a range of requirements, for example, if it contains vivid personal or social detail, or whether it is interesting mainly because it forms part of a series of happenings which in total, but not individually, show an interesting development; or simply whether it is easily legible, suitable for reproduction and perhaps enlargement and display? Educational guides may therefore contain a good deal of quotation or detail on content and form of the documents with which they are concerned, and in some cases may merge into wider types of publication, though still meeting specific educational needs, being aware of age-range suitability and the capacity to convey concepts, skills or important information.

Thus there should be a large number of educational guides, as there are a large number of educational needs, projects or possible goals. Each guide should have a limited aim in terms of supplying material for specific ages and abilities, to match the complexity or scope of teaching projects, the use of other linked educational auxiliary services such as a museums service, relevance to examination syllabuses, and whether they are for use in team teaching, whole classes or group projects, or individual work. There will inevitably be educational guides covering the same subject areas with different educational objectives, but their content and layout will not be entirely similar. It seems better to have a large number of similar, but not identical, educational guides, each fulfilling a particular job, than to have a small number of generalized guides which do not fulfil particular educational roles. It is possible that the day may come when teachers will be able to undertake their own selection and presentation of archive (and other) material for use in class, but the structure of the teaching profession and the nature of the teacher's relationship with his school really militate against his undertaking such large tasks himself.

There is, of course, a good deal of professional responsibility involved in the selection of material for inclusion in an educational guide, even if it can be shared by taking the advice of experts. This advice can determine the definition of the educational aims applying to particular guides. But in the actual selection of material such advice will be helpful and not decisive; only an archivist will know what the contents and appearance of certain appropriate series are, or where suitable documents may be found, or even the nature of functional organizations whose archives would prove interesting.

In one sense the archivist's responsibility is limited: his selection can only be from what is available; historical accident has accomplished some of the selection. On the other hand, his responsibility is increased by the need to know the whole of the surviving evidence: he can include not only cases which might run through several series of archives, but he must make some effort to complete defective historical presentation by seeking additional material from elsewhere, perhaps from archive holdings in other institutions, in national or private collections, or from museum or other parallel historical accumulations. There is also the possibility of obscuring the truth of an historical situation by inadequate presentation in terms of the capacity of the children who are to use the material. One must try to match the vividness and ease of interpretation of the documents to the capacity of the children, their age, and even the amount of time allocated to the project. No doubt this is the hardest of all the tasks of a selector.

Documents selected in this way may be used in the original, but they also may be reproduced, either as photocopies or in the form of slides or overhead transparencies. A finding aid system to these could be constructed to be usable by children, who could then inspect and work on the document of their choice (from the selected range) by projection or by using copies.

Display

Like all displays, those for school work should as before be tailored to particular objectives. Ideally a different display should be designed for every teaching occasion and each visit from a class. No doubt this is impractical, but an overhaul of a display in the light of the needs of a present objective can bring about significant modifications which will make the display more effective.

Display is a matter familiar both to teachers and to children, particularly junior children, and they are severe critics of amateurish methods. On the other hand, they are not accustomed to expensive materials or finish as are the public at large; home-made display is not out of place in school, provided that it is properly presented in its content and arrangement and that there is some possibility of including displays of the children's own discoveries and comment.

Displays for use in teaching should not usually be static; they should be adapted during the course of the children's project, and be capable of being amended by the children's own work; and there should be provision of some kind for the addition to the display of the children's own contributions. This cannot be done if the display is a fixed and generalized one, or where the children's visit is a formal occasion; but work with facsimiles and display need not be so restricted, nor of course need it be confined to the archives building.

Study and research

Educational projects involve the discovery of facts and documents by children individually or in small groups, using the searchroom services either alone or under supervision. Projects of this kind, at least for older children, have been going on for many years in some places, and there is no doubt that for a small group of older children they can be most successful.

The organizer of a schools service will not neglect to consider
this side of his activities, which from one point of view are nearest
to what has been regarded as the archives office's fundamental
activity, the support of research. But in educational work as a
whole the concern is less with research than with illustration; the
aim is to illuminate and explain historical situations by using the
method of discovery. This is not an ignoble work, and not one
incompatible in any sense with the aims of a research institution.
The dissemination and general understanding of history is a task
which society is engaged upon, and in which the appearance of
archives offices is one stage.

Services Outside the Office

Schools services may be mounted outside the premises of the
archives office, and there are many archives offices which have
long undertaken such services. If the children cannot be brought
in to the archives, the documents should be taken to them—the
choice between the two methods may depend on the nature of
the project rather than on transport difficulties—and the work
outside may be in schools, in colleges of education, in teachers'
centres or in specially arranged places. This may be done using
originals or reproductions of various kinds. Again, the material
sent out can be used directly or in display.

Before designing an external service, the archivist will no doubt
satisfy his professional conscience on questions of conservation
and security from loss. It is clear that no activity which will
damage unique documents ought to be undertaken. In practice,
however, means will be found to overcome most such difficulties.
Many of the documents, at local level at least, will not be in
danger from a moderate degree of handling. It is assumed that in
practice most external use of archives will be by the use of
facsimiles in some form. Still there are advantages in allowing
children both to see and in many cases to handle originals
(particularly where the original is a volume or file or a series of
volumes or files, from which they have to extract information over
a period). Conservation in these cases must generally be by
supervision rather than by protection in display cases. Whether
this supervision has to be by archives office staff in all cases or
sometimes delegated is a matter for the archives office and the
school to decide.

Both in schools and in colleges of education the question will
arise of project or team work which has to be fitted into a

crowded timetable. In most cases it is necessary to visualize an extended contact with the archives which may not be possible inside the archives office, and which may require access to many more than one item in the archives selected. This will involve copying programmes, which may require either Xerox, stencil or litho duplication, or microfilm. The archives office in any case, as a matter of routine, will probably be filming archives which are sent out on display or for some other purpose.

Outside work will be either in schools, where the work will be done either through an individual teacher or with a team, or in colleges of education, where the contact will be with the lecturing staff or with groups of students. Work in colleges will be structured in accordance with syllabus requirements, such as the requirements of the Bachelor of Education degree. Activities may also be associated with teachers' centres, resources centres or voluntary or temporary associations of teachers. Many of these are listed in the Historical Association's periodical *Teaching History*.

Publications programme
Like the rest of the education service, a publications programme will be designed separately from the general programmes.

Individual documents. It is possible to publish individual documents for educational uses, provided that the document is legible and reasonably self-explanatory, and contains in itself at least one distinct and important teaching point that can be discovered by reading the document, and which will remain in the student's mind, with illuminating conclusions, because of its vividness or of the interest which discovery brings, or because of its intrinsic importance.(4)

Here, too, it is necessary to bear in mind specific educational aims. It is not enough simply to reproduce and issue such documents, at least not in an educational context. For one thing, ends determine the means of presentation. The documents should be accompanied by notes containing as a minimum the information required to put the document into its context, and to render it intelligible to the point where students may use it for discovery in their own way.

An individual document need not be confined to one page or to one particular format, unless practical reasons of reproduction determine this. Small booklets of up to a dozen pages often make

very satisfactory subjects for reproduction, and offer a good
opportunity for adding explanatory information on the back pages.
Many commercial publishers have found this and have reproduced
either newspapers or guide books and directories for their general
public appeal.

Select documents and readings. There are several useful
publications of this type, pioneered by the Essex Record Office and
particularly developed there and in the Kent Archives Office.(5)
The problem here is that the educational aims are getting rather
general, which means that they are merging into general public
interest. The tendency in this direction is reinforced, of course, by
the cost of letterpress printing. But there are also specifically
educational versions which do not belong to particular archives
offices, which do retain an educational status, albeit directed
towards the upper age ranges.(6)

Film strips, loops, and sets of slides. Essentially these are merely
alternative forms of publication, although they are necessarily for
use in active instruction rather than for project or discovery work.
The written explanatory material must accompany it, just as with
facsimiles; but it will naturally take the form of instructions or
information for the teacher. One must include as an extra
possibility sets of transparencies for overhead projection, though
it may be felt that this medium is more suitable for documents
personally selected by teachers.

Bound volumes of reproductions, with notes and supporting
material. This has been found a satisfactory medium, but there are
two reservations. Firstly, the volume will probably be very large,
perhaps as much as thirty by forty centimetres; any smaller size
will probably involve the reduction of at least some of the
material, and, while this is technically possible in many cases, it
tends to reduce the legibility and general appeal of the
documents. The second reservation is that the form of a bound
volume is really adopted for the purposes of distribution and
identification, and not for the use of the archives as such. Such
volumes are not read through, as are ordinary books, or even the
anthologies of readings mentioned above. Essentially they are
collections of facsimiles. Therefore it will be necessary to allow for
the binding to be removed for use in class, and probably it will be
a light binding (or staples) from the beginning. Once separated,
there are difficulties in storing and controlling the material.(7)

Archive Teaching Units

Most educational work in archives is done through the
construction of archive teaching units. These were first devised in
the late 1950s by Mr G. R. Batho in the Institute of Education of
Sheffield. The earliest units were bulky and were not produced for
general distribution; they were for use, within the ambit of the
Sheffield institute, by student teachers or by schools who would
borrow the units for relatively extended periods, or who would
acquire a copy and store it. The unit contained facsimiles of
documents, enlarged illustrations of pictures and maps for
hanging on the classroom wall, and explanatory material for
teachers and for children.

Soon afterwards commercially published units appeared called
Jackdaws,(8) a name which has become to some extent generic.
Although these quickly became established as a popularly
accepted form of publication, and bookshops were providing
special racks for them by about 1970, Jackdaws have never
attained technical effectiveness as teaching aids; their objectives
were too general, and the limitations imposed by their commercial
status and by the wide-ranging topics chosen, were too obtusive.

The Jackdaw is a wallet, measuring about twenty-three by
thirty-eight centimetres, containing a number of reproductions of
documents on a theme accompanied by explanatory material and
some illustrations. None of the reproductions inside the envelope
may be too large to fit into it after folding. Their primary purpose
was therefore individual or group study and investigation rather
than classroom display. Another important feature of the Jackdaw
is that the reproductions, within broad limits, were produced in
shape, size and colouration to resemble the original from which
they were taken. Consequently, the contents of any one unit are of
different shapes and sizes.

The idea was taken up with some enthusiasm by bodies such
as the Department of Education at the University of Newcastle
upon Tyne and the Liverpool Education Authority; a large number
of non-commercial units were published in the late 1960s and
early 1970s, and an even larger number were distributed locally.
Many archives offices developed teaching units similar in
intention but different in detail. The Public Record Office of
Northern Ireland has developed sets of about twenty facsimiles
uniform in size:(9) each reproduced document is self-explanatory,
with glossary and notes on the back. The drawback to this, as to
many forms of facsimile, is that the document selected must

occupy only one page. The Essex Record Office has also produced units which consist of reproductions in plastic folders reduced to the same size, supplemented by editorial additions such as diagrammatic plans and other material which goes beyond simple explanation.(10)

To prepare a document for the use of teachers or children demands that unfamiliar words and phrases, common forms and the context, both in general administration and in the particular case, should be brought out and explained. The Essex units go beyond this to give examples of the assembly of evidence in documents to provide an historical interpretation, particularly where this can be done (as in urban history) by composing plans. In this they resemble edited texts published by a record society, and may be linked to the scholarly rather than solely to the educational publications of the office. Educational publications will no doubt gain from this additional quality, provided that the educational apparatus is adequate and the educational objectives are clear.

Other archives offices have developed teaching units which are not formally published. Commercial exploitation requires a great deal of preparation and some capital investment: facsimiles must be produced by a process which allows for production of relatively large numbers of relatively high quality; design and editorial processes must be elaborate; and there are problems of distribution, the issue of copyright and review copies, and financing which will daunt a small organization without facilities to deal with these matters.

Moreover, where the publication is explicitly educational, there may well be better ways of arranging distribution and finance than through commercial distribution and sale. Less formal methods of reproduction can be used, and the composition of the unit can be made more flexible and therefore apt for a wider range of educational objectives. These less formal units range in complexity from what is virtually a publishable unit, but perhaps using office-quality methods of reproduction, which are distributed to schools through the education committee's organization, to a simple arrangement for providing schools on request with combinations of facsimiles, again produced by office methods, chosen by the school from a prepared list. At this end of the scale the service merges into that offered to the public generally, and might well offend against the principle that all educational work must be designed with specific educational objectives in view.

Whether or not it is formally published, an archive teaching unit ought usually to include the following:

(i) A cover or wallet with check-list which will allow for its use by the teacher, in avoiding loss of constituent parts and in allowing for their distribution in a class when work is allocated on a project. It is highly desirable that the wallet and the list should be well designed.

(ii) Explanatory material for the teacher, containing a statement of the educational objectives in mind, and instructions or advice on how the unit may be used in accordance with these objectives. Examples of basic objectives are:(11) to *find* information through reading, listening, observing; to *understand* and *interpret* pictures, charts, maps, graphs, etc.; to *organize* information through concepts and generalizations; to *communicate* findings through an appropriate medium; to *evaluate* information; to *test* hypotheses and generalizations and to *question* the adequacy of classifications. All these may be attained through work on a teaching unit, and the instructions and special applications of the unit will include a clear indication of the unit's use in the classroom. It will be aimed at a particular age group, for use over a particular length of time, and there must be a practical ratio of items in the unit to the number of children participating. If a unit is to be split up among a group, the information required to answer questions or to allow a child to make up his mind on a problem must be available from documents within the child's reach at the appropriate time. One consequence of the adoption of such varied and socially valuable skills as are among the educational objectives is that archive teaching units should often (perhaps always) be multi-disciplinary, and should contain relevant material of a non-archival character.

(iii) Explanatory material addressed to children of the appropriate age and capacity. This will include: an explanation of the source of the documents used, and the administrative structures which gave rise to them; the particular circumstances behind the actual documents used, if these are not self-evident; a discussion of the wider implications of the subject chosen, including some statement of the outcome historically; explanations of technical or difficult words or phrases, or forms of document; suggestions for reading, again at an appropriate level of comprehension or attainment.

(iv) Material for putting the documents to use—that is, an apparatus whereby the child can be directed to investigate the sources provided, criticize them, and manipulate the information he finds there to come to conclusions. This may be in the form of worksheets containing sets of questions which require the student to discover and marshal items of information obtained by studying the documents or supporting material or both. In theory most units (as the name implies) try to be self-contained, in that they contain every item of information required for a rounded picture of the subject concerned and its implications.

(v) Material for developing the knowledge and skills gained by additional activities, such as simulations or games, outings to a site, construction (such as model-making), or other suggestions involving other teaching staff or other disciplines.

(vi) Documents or source material in facsimile. The choice of these will be in accordance with the aims of the unit as they concern depth of understanding, width of subject approach, degree of detail and ease of reading and interpretation. It is of course desirable to include a proportion of visually effective material, drawings or pictures, plans or attractively laid out printed material. Not all items in the unit need to be originals in the archival sense, nor do they have to come from one archival source; the historical picture and the method of interpretation are the principal concern.

Finally, it is possible to issue a teacher's kit to supplement the unit itself. This kind of supporting material might include film strips or loops, slides or overhead projection transparencies, large illustrations or diagrams for display. Where co-operative museum loan or schools services exist, objects may be made available either in the original or in facsimile.

Joint Educational Services
Museums and Libraries
Many of the services of an archives office are best developed in association with similar or parallel services, such as those of libraries and museums. In the educational field above all, there is ground for a special approach, particularly since educational technology, resource services and curriculum development are rapidly expanding.

Museums have developed specialized educational services. Entrants to the museums service are generally required to have undergone some training in this field, and the larger museums have specialist departments staffed by teachers and backed by the technical services of the museum. The museums education services have developed the techniques of structuring children's discovery by the means of guided search, usually by workbooks or trails. Museums usually also include at least some archive materials in their displays, thereby improving these materials in visual appeal and content, and associating them with related objects, pictures and explanation. Effective and honest liaison between museums and archives services is more necessary in the educational sector than in any other, and should always be developed wherever possible.

Teachers' Centres

It is also important that an archives office should develop a close working relationship with the appropriate sections of the education service. The most important educational institutions for the development of archives work are the teachers' centres and teachers' resources centres. The latter are as yet new institutions; but already there are many of them, and they appear to be a rapidly developing educational facility whose role is becoming more important. However, there are many places which do not have them yet, and there is a wide variation in the services they offer and in the resources available.

At their best, teachers' resources centres perform several functions: they devise and carry out schemes for curriculum development in their area, store and issue the resources so created, reproduce further material and instruct teachers in their use and development. Teachers may also use their equipment to reproduce their own teaching material. A resources centre may contain not only the equipment (offset litho, electronic stencil-cutter, transparency maker) required to carry out an archival programme using reproductions, but also the resources in production, use and design for teaching which are needed to devise teaching units and kits. Such units will be much more interdisciplinary than those devised purely in an archives office, and will draw upon all types of evidential material—newspapers, statistics, printed books, objects, photographic views, plans and maps, archives, and taped reminiscences. In fact the best teacher's resources centres may be expected to command all the expertise required in the production of archival educational material except knowledge of the actual contents of archives locally available. Co-operative programmes with teachers'

resources centres will no doubt grow rapidly, and ought to be
fostered.

Schools

Liaison with schools ought also to be structured, and in most
cases this will be through the local education authority's advisory
service; in other cases teachers' voluntary associations may be
used; but in either case there ought to be a formal arrangement
for regular meetings to devise a programme, which will have at
least a minimal budget for operations mounted either directly or
through the teachers' centres. Provision for special access or use
of the educational service within the archives office should be
made.

Staffing

It is clearly not reasonable for all the operations involved in an
educational programme to be carried out by one person. An
archivist's professional responsibility covers all matters connected
with the provision of access to the archives, including selection of
suitable material and finding aids, and making these available in a
convenient form. It may also include the provision of direct
teaching at least to some limited extent. But teaching inside
schools in the context of normal curricula is naturally the
professional province of the teacher, as it is also to have a
knowledge of his subject field and the principal sources of
evidence, archival and other, within it, and the means of access to
them. Clearly the spheres of interest for each profession overlap
here, and into this area comes the new profession, the specialisms
of the wardens or directors of teachers' centres, teacher tutors
and directors of probationary or in-service training. Clearly any
planned and structured operations in this field must include co-
operation from several people, and cannot be expected to be
developed from the normal resources of either archives offices or
schools.

To develop an educational service, then, staff with specialist
qualifications should be appointed or trained. They may be
recruited from four categories:

Archivists.

Teachers on secondment. Many education authorities have
adopted schemes for the release of teachers for a period of
training or study. Attachment of a teacher to the archives office

for a period has the merit of training him in the resources of that particular office. During his period of attachment he belongs to the archives staff, shares in their duties and privileges, and gains an insight into their problems and outlook.

A local education authority adviser. A specialist adviser is able to see that usable archives resources can be brought into schools throughout his area. He is able to co-ordinate work in different schools and relate it to examination syllabuses better than individual teachers.

Specialists, to be trained specifically in educational or archival studies.

Arrangement of an Educational Service

However excellent the work of an educational service may be in selecting and predigesting suitable archives and promoting their use in schools, its long-term aim must be the education of people who can come to the archives office and decide for themselves what documents they wish to see.

Preselection is a necessary and useful technique inseparable from work with schools; it is proper for archivists aiming at promoting potential abilities and skills. But the necessity for it should one day disappear. Then the products of a national educational system will feel able to use the archival facilities provided for them, will wish to use these facilities, and will do so with pleasure and understanding. Meanwhile, the archives office must be prepared to participate in the formative stages of this development, and should have suitable accommodation to offer its specialist staff and their pupils. Like the main searchroom, it should have a means of easy access, through controls, to the storage areas. It should have a battery of finding aids compiled on educational principles, a library and display facilities which take cognizance of materials held in other institutions and of developments in classroom techniques. It will have a range of teaching equipment: projectors, blackboard and screen, and, if there is to be any work in integrated or environmental studies, additional equipment such as tape recorders will be needed also. It should have access to reproduction facilities, particularly for immediate reproduction: with perhaps an electronic stencil-cutter with stencil duplicator. Its seating arrangement and tables will allow both for simultaneous teaching (that is, where the teacher addresses the whole group as in a lecture) and for group and individual discovery work. It will in short be designed and equipped as a history room with the additional facilities of reprographics and of access to original archive materials.(12) It should have sufficient adaptability for a whole class to work in it as a whole or in groups. The atmosphere in the teaching areas should be like that in the best schools—cheerful and informal, with plenty of scope for movement, display and discussion.

At least one British local archives office does at present have such a room, though it is not so splendidly equipped as is suggested here. But these facilities should be designed with the actual situation of the archives office and its area in mind. Much depends on such factors as the distance between the office and the outlying users, the availability of alternative centres or parallel educational services, and the relationship between these and the archives office; and also on the scope of the archives held in the office and the state of development of the promotional services there. Archives offices should be able to participate wholeheartedly in co-operative or joint ventures in this and other specialist fields; if they do this, they may avoid the necessity of duplicating facilities within themselves.

A standard for the educational services to be provided by smaller archives offices in Britain is under discussion at present by the Society of Archivists.(13)

13 Local Archives Services

The full range of activities involved in a public archives service demands an investment in staff, accommodation, equipment and resources which makes it uneconomic for a small organization. Yet it is equally uneconomic to cut down the staff and resources to suit the scale of smaller employing authorities, for the result of this is to curtail the services provided to an unacceptable level. A solution to this problem is suggested by an analysis of the various functions of a full archives service. It can be planned co-operatively on two levels: the higher deploys a number of professional staff, and concentrates on management, supervision and advice; the lower uses more limited resources, and provides local services.

The basic functions may be rapidly surveyed as follows:

Records management. Each organization needs to manage its own records, and local authorities are required by law to make 'proper arrangements' for them. Only the largest authorities will be able to employ professionals for this job, but they may use their greater manpower and organization to provide management and advisory services for the smaller ones, and also some central facilities such as records centres.

Collection of non-official archives. The survey of private archives (including the archives of churches and other semi-official bodies) and, in appropriate cases, their acceptance on deposit has always been one of the most important functions of local archives services. This function depends on an intimate knowledge of the locality and its principal institutions, and it is best carried out on the most localized basis possible. However, greater centralization is usually necessary in rural areas, and there is an essential place for the higher authority in acquiring and registering information about surveys and accumulations of archives.

Storage and access are closely linked. The case for centralizing storage may be that it can keep archives away from the high-cost and most congested areas, especially since these will be the most polluted. Additionally, central accumulations of archives which are very rich in content attract users from a wide area. But central storage may be an excessive burden financially, and is not necessary to the success of the service overall. Provided that the problems of handling records—transferring them from active use, retrieving them for information, producing them for consultation—can be solved, archives may be stored where space or local demand suggests. The problem is one that is most likely to be solved on an *ad hoc* basis.

Access. The demand will be most clearly experienced at local level, and facilities ought to be as near the centres of population as possible, particularly as the cultural institutions, especially libraries, are sited there. There is scope for co-ordinating the public user services with these.

Conservation and repair. This is a central function, and it can only be properly undertaken by an authority able to provide a workshop which conforms to national standards and trained specialists to man it. A conservation service run jointly by two or more local authorities or a unit run by one larger authority for use, on agreed terms, by other smaller authorities are both practical possibilities. The workshop can be situated in a low-cost area convenient for transport but away from the congestion, expense and pollution of city centres.

Overall control and planning of the service is a function more appropriate to the larger authority, which may take a regional viewpoint and where the completeness of the documentation held by local authorities and the adequacy of the services offered may be judged. Effective co-ordination is the key to the success of the whole service. Here the archivist is likely to exercise his professional skills to the best advantage, and he should have a management structure which adequately supports him.

A model for a regional archives service may divide these functions, sending some to local centres, concentrating some at the regional centre, and providing overall a well-managed service which is adequate for the region as a whole and for the local communities within it.

Archives services are only one of the information services of a nation. Parallel with them are many others: libraries, museums, documentation centres, research institutes. In the past, these different organizations have developed independently, or, where they have been linked, it has often happened that one has been subordinated to the other in the partnership; but in the future it is likely that national information services will become a much more integrated network of increasingly specialized units. From the point of view of the user, this will be an almost wholly beneficial development. For after all, the most desirable thing would be a structure of information and research services where an enquirer could go to work out the answers to his questions, irrespective of the kinds of source material to be used. Archives services of today, both national and local, should be designed with co-operative development in view.

It is not likely that any archives service will ever quite conform to a theoretical model. Like other public services, both cultural and managerial, it will have to be tailored to suit the circumstances of every employing authority. It should still conform to professional standards and practices, and should take part in the co-ordinating facilities which exist for its nation or region.

This book has attempted, very briefly, to suggest what are properly professional practices. They are of value to society, and this value will increasingly be recognized in the establishment and refining of appropriate institutions.

Appendix A

Recommendations for British Local Government Archive Services

The following outline standards were issued by the Society of Archivists in March 1971.

Functions

The terms of reference under which a local government archives service is required to operate should be clearly defined as to minimum standards.

The fundamental and primary responsibility of the archive service should be to the administration which it serves and of which it forms a part. This should include responsibility for the preservation and safe custody of the archives of all departments, sections and other sub-divisions within the administration, and ultimate control over the destruction of records.

The archivist will normally have in his custody (by virtue of the powers conferred on local authorities by the Local Government (Records) Act 1962) gifts and deposits of archives other than those of the administration he serves, including the records of other local authorities and private records of a local nature. Public records of a local nature will normally be accepted under the terms of the Public Records Acts, 1958 and 1967.

In addition to the provision of information and the production of records to the officers of the administration, the archivist also has responsibility for maintaining a service to the public through the provision of a properly equipped searchroom, with an adequate reference library and lists, indexes and other finding aids. Rules for the use of the searchroom should be clearly displayed, and a member of the staff should be present at all times when the search room is open to the public to supervise and advise searchers.

There should be a definite though flexible policy governing the amount of research that may be done by the staff in response to enquiries by post or by telephone.

It should be part of the policy of the archive service to furnish photocopies at reasonable cost, where this does not contravene copyright or conditions of deposit or prejudice the interests of the owners of the documents.

It should be part of the archivist's responsibility to develop such educational and schools services as may be regarded as appropriate. He may also be associated with photographic or archaeological surveys.

The archivist should participate in records management, either by accepting full responsibility or by co-operating closely with the department responsible for it. Records management is the administration of current and semi-current records prior to their appraisal and designation for permanent preservation, or for immediate or ultimate destruction, or for microfilming prior to destruction.

The archivist may have advisory responsibilities over current filing, in order that
(a) disposal may be systematically and easily carried out;
(b) the files selected for preservation may be transferred to him in a systematic order;
(c) he may assist in the formulation of any programme for microphotography.

Organization
The effectiveness of the archive service will depend on the standing of the archivist. He should therefore be accorded a position in the structure of the administration he serves that will enable him to deal independently with all departments.

In addition to his responsibility for evolving and implementing policies within his own office under the general direction of the committee to which he reports, the archivist should be entitled to represent his department in its relations with members and officers of the administration, with institutions of higher learning, the Public Record Office, the Society of Archivists, other learned and professional societies, and the general public.

The annual estimates should be drawn up by the archivist and, where the overall policy of the authority permits, submitted by him.

In order to guarantee a service of a uniformly high standard of competence, professional standards must be maintained, and staff adequate in qualifications, training and numbers should be provided in the following categories:

Professional (archivists). For professional posts, professional as well as academic qualifications are required. The duties of professional staff should include:

A Negotiations with officers of the administration about the transfer of documents from departments to the archive service and their subsequent disposition.
B Negotiations with owners and custodians about the care, accessibility and custody of their documents, especially in respect of gifts to or deposits in the repository.
C The arrangement and listing of holdings.
D The preparation of guides and other finding aids to enable the searcher to discover for himself the documents relevant to his research or enquiry.
E The preparation of calendars, edited texts, and other appropriate publications as part of an office publications policy.
F Relations with the public, especially correspondence, lectures, advice to students, supervision of the searchroom and the provision of exhibitions.
G Supervision of all tasks undertaken by non-professional and technical staff, e.g. records management, repair, photography, storage.
H Representation of the office and attendance at meetings of learned and professional societies as part of their professional and official duties.

Professional staff should not normally be employed on activities that could be carried out under supervision by less highly qualified staff. The salary structure for professional staff should be commensurate with their academic and professional qualifications. Service as an officer of a learned or professional society should constitute an acceptable part of the official duties of a professional archivist.

Non-professional (archives or records assistants, records clerks). For non-professional posts a satisfactory standard of secondary education should be required. Non-professional staff may be employed:

A In the routine work involved in records management, although final appraisal of records for destruction or preservation is the responsibility of the archivist.
B In the production of documents requisitioned by officers of the administration or members of the public.
C In the numbering, boxing and storage of new accessions, and general maintenance of the repository.
D In assisting in the preparation of exhibitions.
E In simple listing under supervision.
F In simple searches in connection with postal enquiries.

Technical (document repairers and binders, photographers). No specific training is yet available, but training through 'apprenticeship' to an experienced person, often in another repository, should be arranged where possible, and staff should be released for instructional and training courses.

General (clerical and other maintenance staff): typists, porters, cleaners, etc.

Other professional staff. If ancillary services are to be developed, due provision should be made for the employment of teachers and other specialist staff on a permanent or a temporary basis.

Accommodation and Equipment
Recommendations for the storage of documents are shortly to be issued by the British Standards Institution. These have been drawn up by experts, with advice from a wide range of specialist interests. They should be adhered to as closely as possible, and the archivist should be consulted at every stage in the planning of a new repository or in adapting an existing building.

Equipment for the provision of copies by photography, microphotography or other reprographic methods should be available.

General
The resources provided by a local government archive service should be capable of expansion and development to meet the changing needs and demands of research, and also to take advantage of new technological developments.
March 1971

Appendix B

Criteria for Selection of Public Records for Permanent Preservation
(extracted from the Public Record Office *Guide for Departmental Record Officers* (1962), pp. 29-31.)

This note is intended to suggest a general standard for the appraisal of papers at the second or final review, which should take place about twenty-five years after the papers were created, and when the perspective of time should give a clearer picture of the papers likely to have a continuing administrative significance. Those whose administrative significance is exhausted, or will be exhausted after a known lapse, and whose historical value seems minimal, will then be destroyed or earmarked for destruction at a given future date.

Circumstances vary in each Department and between Departments; no universal rule of thumb is applicable. The sort of material which should be considered for permanent preservation is what may be valued for (i) the Department's purposes, (ii) research purposes, and (iii) other purposes. Such values may coincide wholly or partially.

Value for the Department's Purposes
Papers of the following categories will normally be among those required to be kept indefinitely for the use of the Department:
(i) Evidence of rights or obligations of or against the Crown, e.g. title to property, claims for compensation not subject to a time limit, formal instruments such as awards, schemes, orders, sanctions, etc.

(ii) Major policy decisions, including papers relating to the preparation of legislation.

(iii) Set of minutes and papers of the Department's more important committees, working parties, etc.

(iv) Precedents for procedure, e.g. administrative memoranda, historical reports and summaries, legal opinions, etc.

(v) Standard set of all headquarters guides or instructions of general application to out-stations, regional or local offices, or bodies with which the Department is in regular contact.

(vi) Some evidence of organization and staffing of the Department.

(vii) Papers relating to important litigation or *causes célèbres* in which the Department was involved.

Value for Research Purposes
Much of the material likely to be preserved for departmental purposes will be of interest for research purposes; but papers of the following categories should be specially examined for value to historians:

(i) Papers relating to the origins of the Department; how it was organized; how it functioned; and (if defunct) how it was dissolved. In this connection, office notices, organization charts and directories may be of value.

(ii) Data about what the Department accomplished. Samples by way of illustration may be enough, but the need for such samples may be reduced where a published annual report is available.

(iii) Papers relating to a change of policy. The quality is not always easy to recognize, but watch should be kept for

(a) a reasoned submission to a Minister or senior official;

(b) the appointment of a departmental or inter-departmental committee or working party;

(c) a paper to the Cabinet or to a Cabinet Committee.
Generally there should be a conscious effort to preserve such papers, including earlier drafts of memoranda and of the report, which will often show conflicting points of view. In the case of inter-departmental committees it is important that a set of papers should be kept by the department mainly concerned— usually the one which provided the secretary. If the change of policy resulted in legislation (whether by Act or Statutory instrument), the relevant papers should be kept.

(iv) Papers relating to the implementation of a change of policy.
These will often be embodied in an instruction of general
application to outstations, regional or local offices, local
authorities, etc., and a complete set of these instructions, together
with any relevant forms, should be preserved.

(v) Papers relating to a well-known public or international event
or *cause célèbre*, or to other events which gave rise to interest or
controversy on the national plane.

(vi) Papers containing direct reference to trends or developments
in political, social, economic or other fields, particularly if they
contain unpublished statistical or financial data covering a long
period or a wide area.

(vii) Papers cited in, or noted as consulted in connection with,
official histories.

(viii) Papers relating to the more important aspects of scientific or
technical research and development.

(ix) Papers containing matters of local interest of which it is
unreasonable to expect that evidence will be available locally, or
comprising synopses of such information covering the whole
country or a wide area.

(x) Papers relating to obsolete activities or investigations, or to
abortive schemes of the Department, should be carefully noted for
the historian, as they are unlikely to be valued for departmental
purposes.

Value for Purposes other than the Department's or Research Requirements

Papers valuable for other purposes are unlikely to occur
frequently, but possibilities of usefulness should be borne in mind,
e.g. to:

(i) The Government as a whole or to Departments other than that
responsible for the records (this will generally occur where a
function has passed from one Department to another, but related
records have not passed with it).

(ii) Local authorities and the like, e.g. establishing a boundary.

(iii) Individuals in the isolated cases establishing some right.

Qualifying factors which should be taken into consideration
include:

(i) The status of the Department or Office and the general
importance of its work. Papers not of obvious interest have a
stronger claim to preservation if found among the records of
certain senior Departments, or in the private offices of Ministers or

senior officials. *Per contra*, many papers are submitted by a Department to a Minister or senior official for noting or for formal approval, which would justify preservation only if significant comment has been made.

(ii) The bulk of the papers. If the files in a particular series are numerous, it may be worth while considering whether the needs of research would be met adequately by the preservation of a representative selection similar to the arrangements made in the case of certain 'particular instance paper' classes.

(iii) The length of time for which papers have been retained. Deliberate withholding of a document from destruction for a period unexpectedly long, having regard to its subject matter, may indicate a former administrative importance justifying preservation on historical grounds.

(iv) Genealogical and local research. A good deal of material useful to genealogists and biographers will be preserved as a by-product of the criteria mentioned above, and it is unneccessary for any special steps to be taken for the preservation of material whose primary interest would be to these researchers. Similarly, it is unnecessary to take special steps in respect of material of which it is reasonable to expect that copies or counterparts will be preserved by local authorities or other responsible local bodies.

Appendix C

A Schedule of General Conditions for Deposit of Archives
(adapted from the form used by Liverpool University.)

1 The archives office accepts archives of public interest for care and preservation and for the benefit of research, either as a gift or on deposit or indefinite loan. Where records are on deposit or loan, the depositor or owner retains the right to withdraw all or part of the collections deposited or loaned by them upon reasonable notice and at their own charge, subject to the conditions following, or to any special conditions agreed upon at the time of the deposit or loan.

2 Archives accepted by the office will be produced for study by any bona fide researcher under conditions of supervision similar to those provided for the office's own archives. Special conditions may be agreed between the office and the depositor or owner at the time of the deposit or loan. Such conditions may include provision for restriction of access to all or part of the collections deposited or loaned.

3 All reasonable care is taken of records placed in the custody of the office, but no liability for loss or damage to documents on deposit or loan is accepted.*

4 The office may take such measures for the administration of deposited or loaned archives as are professionally acceptable. This includes stamping, marking or numbering documents, arranging, packing or sorting them, and their disposition in storage areas as may be suitable or convenient.

5 Repairs to archives are undertaken where practicable. Where archives are withdrawn by owners or depositors, the office

reserves the right to claim reimbursement of expenses incurred in repairs, conservation, listing or administration of the records.

6 Archives produced to searchers are so produced in accordance with the office's rules for the public use of records and archives.

7 Archives may be reproduced for purposes of study; but for any other purpose, including publication, the consent of the owner or depositor is necessary. Where archives are reproduced by mechanical or photographic means, the office will decide what means are appropriate and permissible. Photographic or other reproductions of documents will be marked with the conditions laid down for reproduction.

8 Records may be removed from the office by

(i) the owner or depositor, under the conditions laid down here or in any special agreement made at the time of the deposit or loan.

(ii) staff of the archives office for any of the following purposes:

    (a) for repair;

    (b) for the purpose of exhibition or lecture arranged by the office, the archives remaining in the custody of a member of staff or in the custody of some body or person appointed for this purpose by the office;

    (c) for deposit in another recognized archives repository for purposes of study or exhibition, subject to the consent of the owner or depositor.

    (d) for production in a court of law, subject to the consent of the owner or depositor.

* An additional clause for insertion after item 3, if the policy of the archives office or its employing authority permits:

All archives on deposit or loan are covered by insurance against damage or loss from fire, flood, aircraft or theft, in so far as repair or replacement are possible; and where the owner or depositor so requests, such archives are further covered by an 'all risks' policy for specific sums at valuation to be agreed between the office and the owner.

Appendix D

Regulations for Readers
(adapted from the regulations of the Kent Archives Office.)

1   The Archives Office is normally open to readers for the inspection of documents on Mondays to Fridays (except on advertised public holidays) from 9.30 a.m. to 6.00 p.m.

2   A person desiring to inspect documents shall write his full name and address in the register of readers, and complete requisition forms in the manner indicated in the searchroom. Signing the register of readers shall imply an agreement to observe these regulations, and their infringement shall render the reader liable to exclusion.

3   Readers may not smoke, eat or drink inside the searchroom.

4   Documents must not be taken out of the searchroom, but should be handed back to the officer in charge or his staff before a reader leaves.

5   The conditions of access relating to documents are set out in appropriate places in the searchroom. Archives staff have the authority to enforce these restrictions.

6   The officer in charge of the searchroom has the authority to decide

   (a) the quantity of documents issued at any one time to a reader. Where a reader is allowed a number of documents at one time, he must take all possible means to ensure that the arrangement of these documents is retained, that they are in proper order, and that they are returned to their proper container.

(b) whether or not a document or group of documents is sufficiently robust to be handled. Where documents are too fragile for consultation, the officer in charge may withhold them.

(c) whether a microfilm or other copy should be used rather than the original.

7 Readers should not use writing materials which in the opinion of the officer in charge might damage the documents he is consulting. No mark shall be made on a document, and no person shall lean upon any document or place on it the paper which he is writing. Any defect in or accident to a document must be reported at once to the officer in charge. The greatest care must be exercised in handling documents.

8 Tracings may only be made by permission of the officer in charge, who may specify the way in which they must be made.

9 The staff of the archives office may not give legal advice to readers.

[10 Fees are payable for certain services. Details of these services and the conditions of payment are given on request. (*If appropriate.*)]

11 Reproductions of photographs, photostats or photocopies supplied by the office may be made only with the permission of the director. Application for permission shall be made in writing, stating the object of the reproduction. The archives office reserves the right to make a charge.

12 The director of the archives office or the officer in charge of the searchroom may exclude or cause to be removed from the archives office any person who contravenes these regulations, or whose exclusion from the archives office is . otherwise necessary for its proper use and regulation.

Appendix E

Access to Public Records in Britain
(extracted from the Public Records Act, 1958, as amended by
subsequent legislation.)

5. Access to public records

(1) Public records in the Public Record Office, other than those to
which members of the public had access before their transfer
to the Public Record Office,(1) shall not be available for public
inspection until the expiration of the period of thirty years
beginning with the first day of January in the year next after
that in which they are created, or of such other period, either
longer or shorter, as the Lord Chancellor may, with the
approval, or at the request, of the Minister or other person, if
any, who appears to him to be primarily concerned, for the
time being prescribe as respects any particular class of public
records.(2)

(2) Without prejudice to the generality of the foregoing
subsection, if it appears to the person responsible for any
public records which have been selected by him under section
three of this Act for permanent preservation that they contain
information which was obtained from members of the public
under such conditions that the opening of those records to
the public after the period determined under the foregoing
sub-section would or might constitute a breach of good faith
on the part of the Government or on the part of the persons
who obtained the information, he shall inform the Lord

Chancellor accordingly and those records shall not be available in the Public Record Office for public inspection even after the expiration of the said period except in such circumstances and subject to such conditions, if any, as the Lord Chancellor and that person may approve, or, if the Lord Chancellor and that person think fit, after the expiration of such further period as they may approve.(3)

(3) Subject to the foregoing provisions of this section, subject to the enactments set out in the Second Schedule to this Act (which prohibit the disclosure of certain information obtained from the public except for certain limited purposes) and subject to any other Act or instrument whether passed or made before or after this Act which contains a similar prohibition, it shall be the duty of the Keeper of Public Records to arrange that reasonable facilities are available to the public for inspecting and obtaining copies of public records in the Public Record Office.(4)

(4) Subsection (1) of this section shall not make it unlawful for the Keeper of Public Records to permit a person to inspect any records if he has obtained special authority in that behalf given by an officer of a government department or other body, being an officer accepted by the Lord Chancellor as qualified to give such an authority.(5)

(5) The Lord Chancellor shall as respects all public records in places of deposit appointed by him under this Act outside the Public Record Office require arrangement to be made for their inspection by the public comparable to those made for public records in the Public Record Office, and subject to restrictions corresponding with those contained in the foregoing provisions of this section.

Notes on the above extract

(1) There are certain classes of record, in government, local government and in some cases in business, to which there is a statutory right of access. Examples of such records are registers of companies, or of births, marriages and deaths, minutes of county councils, electoral rolls, transfers of shares.

(2) The most considerable order made under this section was the opening, in January 1973, of the records of the Cabinet for the whole of the period of the Second World War, that is, when twenty-eight years out of currency.

(3) A usual restriction adopted for records under this subsection is one hundred years. The best-known example of such records is the

returns of information under the decennial census, where the forms filled in by heads of households are specifically restricted to certain uses. Other sensitive records have varying periods of closure.

(4) It is to be noted that the provision of copies and copying facilities is statutory, not only within the Public Record Office but in 'places of deposit'.

(5) Provided that the requisite permissions have been obtained, this subsection allows access without any general restriction to any record. Thus the special treatment of particular researchers has a statutory backing.

Abbreviations

The following abbreviations have been used throughout in references and in the bibliography.

AA *The American Archivist,* The Society of American Archivists. Quarterly.

Jenkinson, Essays   A. E. J. Hollaender (ed.), *Essays in Memory of Sir Hilary Jenkinson* (London, Society of Archivists, 1962).

Jenkinson, Manual   H. Jenkinson. *A Manual of Archive Administration* (1922). Second edition revised with introduction and bibliography by R. H. Ellis (London, 1965).

JSA   *Journal of the Society of Archivists* (1955–   ). Two issues a year.

Manuel   Ministére des Affaires Culturelles, Association des Archivistes Français. *Manual d'Archivistique* (Paris, 1970).

Munden, Archives.   K. Munden (ed.) *Archives and the Public Interest: selected essays by Ernst Posner* (Washington, 1967).

Roy. Comm.   Royal Commission.

Schellenberg, Modern Archives   T. R. Schellenberg, *Modern Archives: Principles and Techniques.* (1956; Chicago, 1971).

References

Chapter 1

(1) Schellenberg, *Modern Archives,* pp. 11–16; M. Cook, L. J. MacDonald and E. Welch, 'The Management of Records', *JSA,* III, viii (1968), p. 418.
(2) *Report of the Committee on Privacy* (the Younger report). Cmd 5012 (London, HMSO, 1972). The discussion has gone further in the USA.
(3) Jenkinson, *Manual,* pp. 83–121.
(4) E. Posner's introduction to American archival legislation (*Archivum,* XXI (1971), pp. 83–5).
(5) An example is the archival law of Indonesia (*Archivum, sub loco*).
(6) For example, the State of New South Wales (Australia) (*Archivum,* XXI (1971), pp. 179–80).
(7) For example, the Province of New Brunswick (Canada) (*Archivum,* XXI (1971), p. 51).
(8) For example, the Republic of South Africa (*Archivum,* XX (1970), pp. 17–26).
(9) *Archivum,* XIX (1969), pp. 123–46.
(10) F. Ranger, in *Archivum,* XVII (1967), pp. 173–208. The summary in fact covers material up to 1971.
(11) 6 & 7 Eliz. II, c. 51; 1967 Eliz. II, c. 44.
(12) See below, chapter 4, and appendix E.
(13) Public Records Act, 1958, s. 10, and first schedule.
(14) J. H. Collingridge, 'Liaison between Local Record Offices and the Public Record Office in the Light of the Public Records Act, 1958', *JSA,* II, x (1964), p. 451.
(15) Public Records Act, 1958, s. 2.
(16) Manorial Documents Rules, 1926 (revised in 1959 and amended in 1963 and 1967). These rules are poorly enforced. 'Concern has

again been expressed at the number of manorial documents that appear still to remain unrecorded in solicitors' offices among clients' papers' (Royal Commission on Historical Manuscripts, *Secretary's Report to the Commissioners, 1972–3*, p. 7).

(17) Tithe (Copies of Instruments of Apportionment) Rules, 1960 (amended 1963).

(18) 19 & 20 Geo V, no. 1.

(19) D. M. Owen, *The Records of the Established Church in England excluding Parochial Records* (London, British Records Association, 1970). A supplement to the list which this contains (pp. 58–60) appears in *Archives*, X (1971). pp. 53–6.

(20) 45 & 46 Vict, c. 50; 23 & 24 Geo V, c. 51.

(21) Local Government Act, 1972, ss 224–9.

(22) 10 & 11 Eliz. II, c. 56. Six authorities were granted powers under this act by order of the Secretary of State. Schedule 30 of the Local Government Act, 1972, has amended the 1962 Act so that only the county councils (metropolitan and non-metropolitan) are, outside London, 'archive authorities' (Department of the Environment consultation paper, *Local Government Records* (LG1/43/1 of 14 May 1973), s. 5).

(23) 1963 Eliz. II, c. 33; I. Darlington, 'Record Offices in Greater London', *JSA*, III, v (1967), p. 248.

(24) Ministry of Housing and Local Government, Circular 44/62 (3 Sept. 1962).

(25) 13 & 14 Geo. V, c. 20 (Northern Ireland).

(26) Public Registers and Records (Scotland) Act 1948 (11 & 12 Geo. VI, c. 57); Public Records (Scotland) Act 1937 (1 Edw. VIII & 1 Geo. VI, c. 43); Local Government (Scotland) Act 1947 (10 & 11 Geo. VI, c. 43).

(27) Scottish Home and Health Department. *Local Authority Records* (the McBoyle report) (London, HMSO, 1967).

(28) Royal warrant dated 5 Dec. 1959; R. H. Ellis. 'The Royal Commission on Historical Manuscripts: a Short History and Explanation', *Manuscripts and Men* (London, HMSO, 1969).

(29) Finance Acts, 1930, 1956, 1973; Treasury Note, *Private Owners and Public Collections* (Oct., 1973). The fund is administered through the Victoria and Albert Museum purchase grant fund. In 1973 it amounted to £30,000. It is 'to assist, on a pound-for-pound basis, the purchase of manuscripts and documents, including photographs, by local, university and other record offices in England and Wales, in order to divert these from export' (Royal Commission on Historical Manuscripts, *Secretary's Report, 1972–3*, p. 9).

(30) F. Ranger, 'Export Control of Archives', *JSA*, III, x (1969), pp. 570–1. I am also indebted to Miss Ranger (now Mrs Strong) for information.

(31) *Archivum,* XVII (1967); XIX–XXI (1969–71).

(32) For an agreed recommendation on these points, see 'Archive Policy for French-speaking African Countries', *UNESCO Bulletin for Libraries,* XXVI, ii (1972), pp. 84–7.

(33) *The New Local Authorities: Management and Structure* (the Bains report) (London, HMSO, 1972), p. 101.

(34) S. Carbone and R. Gueze, *Draft Model Law on Archives* (Paris, UNESCO, 1972), p. 59.

(35) E. Posner, 'Archival Administration in the United States'. *Archives and the Public Interest* (Washington, 1967), p. 124.

(36) East Sussex County Council, County Record Office. *Staff Manual* (duplicated typescript, 1970). I am indebted to Mr S. C. Newton, formerly County Archivist.

(37) In this discussion I have drawn on material sent by many colleagues, but particularly by the Director of the National Archives of Malaysia, Mrs Zakiah Hanum Nor, and by her staff; and by the former Head Archivist of the Greater London Record Office, Miss E. D. Mercer, and her successor, Mr W. J. Smith.

(38) *Recommendations for Local Government Archives Services* (1971); see appendix A.

(39) E. Posner, *American State Archives* (Chicago, 1964), p. 353.

(40) J. H. d'Olier and B. Delmas. *La Planification des infrastructures nationales de documentation, de bibliothèques et d'archives; esquisse d'une politique générale.* (Paris, UNESCO, 1974), p. 310.

(41) W. R. Serjeant. 'The Survey of Local Archive Services, 1968'. *JSA,* IV, iv (1971), 300–26.

Chapter 2

(1) *Manuel,* p. 697 (author's translation); See also p. 709.

(2) The material in this section is based on M. Cook, 'Surveying Current Records', *JSA,* IV (1972), pp. 413–22, where further acknowledgements are made.

(3) E. J. Leahy and C. A. Cameron, *Modern Records Management* (New York, 1965); W. Benedon, *Records Management* (New Jersey, 1969).

(4) Jenkinson, *Manual,* p. 111. E. Posner (*American State Archives,* p. 371) defines a series as 'a sequence of records classified and filed in accordance with a filing system'.

(5) As for example in an Australian manual by the training section of the Commonwealth Public Service Board (*Handbook for Departmental Registrars* (Canberra, n.d.), pp. 16–20).

Chapter 3

(1) Jenkinson's suggestion of 'probationary archives' (*Manual,* p. 184) has not found favour.

(2) W. Benedon, *Records Management* (New Jersey, 1969), p. 65. This however adopts a much more restricted view.

(3) E. G. Campbell, 'Buildings and Equipment of Federal Records Centers in the United States', in V. Gondos (ed.), *Reader for Archives and Records Center Buildings* (Society of American Archivists, 1970), p. 89.

(4) Cf. British Steel Corporation, *Regional Records Centres* (1974).

(5) *Thirteenth Annual Report of the Keeper of Public Records* (1971), s. 42.

(6) *Manuel,* pp. 69–71.

(7) M. Cook, 'Regional Archives Offices: some Reflections', *JSA,* III, vi (1967), p. 274.

(8) M. Duchein, *Les Bâtiments et équipements d'archives* (Paris, 1966), p. 204.

(9) W. Benedon, 'Features of new Records Center Buildings', in Gondos, pp. 77–87.

(10) *Thirteenth Annual Report of the Keeper,* s. 42.

(11) F. R. J. Verhoeven. *The Role of Archives in the Public Administration . . . of Developing Countries* (UNESCO, 1972), p. 16.

(12) I am indebted to the director of national archives, Singapore, Mrs H. Anuar, and to her staff, especially Mrs L. Tan.

(13) From British Steel Corporation's brochure on records centre services at Irthlingborough (1973).

(14) Grigg report, p. 6.

(15) *Manuel,* p. 711 (author's translation).

(16) Information from Mr D. Charman, who suggests that this is a rule-of-thumb calculation in the USA, but that a minimum of two staff, excluding professional grades, are needed to man a records centre.

(17) Based primarily upon the records centre handbook of the British Steel Corporation. I am indebted to the Corporation and to its archivist, Mr D. Charman, for permission to use it and for additional information. Readers will appreciate that this handbook represents one particular scheme; it is not suggested that the solutions adopted here will be appropriate for all problems.

(18) Adapted from British Steel Corporation form RM1/C and D.

(19) Adapted from British Steel Corporation form RM2.

(20) Adapted from a label used by the University Archives, Liverpool.

(21) Adapted from British Steel Corporation form RM3. See also pp. 160 ff.

(22) University Archives, Liverpool.

Chapter 4

(1) Jenkinson, *Manual,* pp. 149–150.

(2) Schellenberg, *Modern Archives,* pp. 30–1.

(3) Jenkinson, *Manual,* p. 152.

(4) *Care of County Muniments* (1923), p. 11.
(5) For example, F. I. Dolgikh. *Interconnexion and continuity of the work of State and Agency Archives* (Moscow, 1972).
(6) For example, F. Hull (ed.), 'Report on the Records of the Children's Department in Local Government: their Retention and Disposal'. Society of Archivists, *Symposium on Records Management* (1968).
(7) A. W. Mabbs, 'The Public Record Office and the Second Review', *Archives,* VIII, xl (1967–8), p. 183.
(8) Cmd. 9163 (London, HMSO, 1954).
(9) Ibid., s. 78.
(10) Ibid. ss. 59–60.
(11) Ibid., ss. 77, 83.
(12) Ibid., s. 67.
(13) Ibid., ss. 200–5.
(14) Ibid., s. 87 (author's italics).
(15) Ibid., s. 136.
(16) Ibid., ss. 137, 226. The phrase quoted occurs in s. 52, where the committee actually comments that the Public Record Office, for historical reasons, has *not* developed as a national archives 'in the true sense'—that is, that there are important groups of records which are separately administered, and some which were never transferred.
(17) Ibid., ss. 137, 108.
(18) Public Record Office, *A Guide for Departmental Record Officers* (1st edn. (provisional), 1958; 2nd edn. (revised), 1962; 3rd edn., 1971).
(19) *Guide* (1962), appendix A, pp. 29–31.
(20) *Guide* (1971), appendix A, pp. 24–5.
(21) *The Appraisal of Modern Public Records* (National Archives Bulletins, no. 8 (Washington (DC), 1956).
(22) Schellenberg, *Modern Archives,* p. 139.
(23) Ibid., pp. 140–8.
(24) *Guide for Departmental Record Officers,* 1958, p. 31.
(25) Grigg report, ss. 105, 108.
(26) Grigg report, ss. 88–110.
(27) The point is made obliquely in Grigg report, s. 104.
(28) Grigg report, s. 97; Keeper of the Public Records, *Annual Reports;* D. Alexander, 'A Description of Indexing Procedures for the "Agreement on Account of Crew"', *Archives,* XI, (1973), pp. 86–93.
(29) Grigg report, s. 45.

Chapter 5
(1) *Guide for Departmental Record Officers* (1971), p. 6.
(2) British Steel Corporation, *Corporation Retention Schedule,* p. 2.

(3) F. Hull (ed.), *Handlist of Kent County Council Records, 1889–1945* (Maidstone, 1972), p. 11.

(4) Adapted from Kent Archives Office record card. I am indebted to Dr Hull and Miss M. Scally.

(5) Grigg report, s. 77.

(6) J. B. Rhoads, *New Archival Techniques* (Moscow, 1972), pp. 41–2.

(7) Ibid., p. 33; *Manuel,* pp. 173–4.

(8) Schellenberg, *Modern Archives,* p. 158.

(9) 'Problems of Sampling as related to Records Preservation', *Archives,* IX (1970), pp. 155–7.

(10) M. Cook. 'Regional Archives Offices: some Reflections', *JSA,* III, vi (1967), 271–4.

(11) See also below, pp. 177 ff.

(12) *Microfilming.* Report of the O & M Work Study Panel of LAMSAC. (London, 1971).

Chapter 6

(1) Adapted from the general conditions of deposit of the University of Liverpool, themselves derived from those of the Cheshire Record Office.

(2) Based upon a form used by the Public Record Office of Northern Ireland.

(3) Adapted from a form used by the East Sussex Record Office.

(4) See above, pp. 14–15.

(5) Adapted from a form used by the Ipswich and East Suffolk Record Office.

(6) Cf Schellenberg, *Modern Archives,* p. 168.

(7) F. G. Emmison, *Guide to the Essex Record Office* (Chelmsford, 1946), Part I introduction (pp. viii–x). See also the second edn. (1969), p. vii.

(8) Jenkinson, *Manual,* p. 104.

(9) Schellenberg, *Modern Archives,* p. 118. In his refusal of the term 'provenance' as a description of the central archival principle, Jenkinson was led astray by a narrow dictionary definition (*Manual,* p. 97).

(10) *Manuel,* p. 545.

(11) Jenkinson, *Manual,* p. 97.

(12) Jenkinson, *Manual,* p. 85.

(13) J. C. Lancaster, *A Guide to Lists and Catalogues of the India Office Records* (London, 1966). See also Jenkinson, *Manual,* p. 122n.

(14) Jenkinson himself was significantly misled (*Manual,* p. 106).

(15) Jenkinson, *Manual,* p. 84, and elsewhere.

(16) I. Maclean, 'An Analysis of Jenkinson's *Manual* . . . in the Light of Australian Experience', in *Jenkinson Essays,* p. 144.

(17) *Manual,* p. 101.

(18) *Jenkinson Essays,* pp. 128–52.

(19) 'The Record Group Concept: a Case for Abandonment', *AA,* XXIX, iv (1966), pp. 493–504. See also his article, 'Facing the Reality of Administrative Change: some Further Remarks on the Record Group Concept', *JSA,* V, ii (1974), pp. 94–100.

(20) M. Roper, 'Modern Departmental Records and the Record Office'. *JSA,* IV, v (1972), p. 403.

(21) Art. cit., p. 498.

(22) Adapted from Scott, p. 499. The example is from the Commonwealth Archives Office, Canberra.

(23) Roper, p. 403.

(24) See also *Manuel,* p. 192.

(25) Hull, *Handlist.* This instrument recognizes three archive groups: (a) proceedings of County Council and its committees; (b) archives of the office of the Clerk of the Council; (c) archives of county departments. But these groups will presumably fail after 1972.

(26) Roper, p. 405.

Chapter 7

(1) F. G. Emmison (ed.), *Guide to the Essex Record Office* (Chelmsford, 1946).

(2) Somerset County Council, *A Handlist of the Records of the Boards of Guardians in the County of Somerset* (Taunton, 1949).

(3) Hull, *Handlist.* A departure from tradition, however, is that this handlist does not set out the coding scheme in any way that could be directly copied by other archives offices. It includes provision for coding series arising from the work of the reorganized county councils after April 1974. I am indebted to Dr. Hull for particular information.

(4) Kent Archives Office.

(5) Devon Record Office.

(6) Cheshire Record Office.

(7) Devon Record Office.

(8) F. Biljan, *Information Instruments in the Service of Science* (Moscow, 1972), pp. 14–17.

(9) For example, B. Swann and M. Turnbull (eds.), *Records of Interest to Social Scientists, 1919–1939,* Public Record Office Handbooks, no. 14 (London, 1971).

(10) Hampshire Archivists Group, *Poor Law in Hampshire through the Centuries: a Guide to the Records* (1970).

(11) As practised in the Cheshire Record Office.

(12) A. G. Veysey (ed.), *Guide to the Flintshire Record Office* (Flintshire County Council, 1974), p. 37.

(13) D. M. Smith (ed.), *A Guide to the Archive Collections in the Borthwick Institute of Historical Research* (York, 1973), p. 57.
(14) National Register of Archives, *Subject Index Schema and Word-List.* (London, 1969). Since the publication of these there has been continuous revision.
(15) The following is based principally upon the practice of the Public Record Office and the East Sussex Record Office, with regard to the National Register of Archives indexing program. I am particularly indebted to Mr S. C. Newton and Mr R. A. Storey for information. F. McCall, *PROSPEC Manual,* Public Record Office, n.d. L. Bell and M. Roper (eds.), *Proceedings of an International Seminar on Automatic Data Processing in Archives* (London, HMSO, 1975).
(16) E. O. Alldredge, 'Inventorying Magnetic Media Records', *AA,* XXXV, iii–iv (1972), pp. 337–46.
(17) Adapted from 'Appraising Information in Machine Language Form', *AA,* XXXV, i (1972), pp. 35–44.
(18) *ADPA, Archives and Automation/Informatique* (1972–   ).

Chapter 8

(1) Continuous custodial history has been a major principle at the Public Record Office; see Jenkinson, *Manual,* pp. 11–15, and Grigg report, s. 224 and note, quoting V. H. Galbraith, *An Introduction to the Use of the Public Records* (Oxford, 1934). p. 12.
(2) The national archives service of France regularly transfers archives for consultation elsewhere than in their place of deposit, using the postal service (*Manuel,* pp. 309–11).
(3) Adapted from a form used by the Ipswich and East Suffolk Record Office.
(4) For further discussion of problems of security, see the *Society of American Archivists Newsletter,* which includes an 'Archival Security Newsletter' from Sept., 1975.
(5) Y. P. Kathpalia, 'Restoration of Documents', in Y. Perotin, *A Manual of Tropical Archivology* (Paris, 1966), pp. 121–49. But see the reservations of J. R. Ede in 'Archives in the Tropics', *JSA,* III, vii (1968), pp. 364–6.
(6) Jenkinson, *Manual,* p. 68. In this respect archives may be subject to different rules from those which govern the restoration of books.
(7) Adapted from a form used by the Public Record Office of Northern Ireland.
(8) Adapted from a form used by the Ipswich and East Suffolk Record Office.
(9) The *Bulletin* of the International Council on Archives commenced publication in 1975, and contains current details.

Chapter 9

(1) *Manuel,* p. 464.
(2) F. G. Emmison, in a discussion following his paper, 'Repatriation of "Foreign" Estate and Family Archives', *Archives,* II (1956), pp. 467–76.
(3) These observations are given weight by the findings of the commission of enquiry into the Roosevelt Library affair (H. Kahn, 'The Long-Range Implications for Historians and Archivists of the Charges against the Franklin D. Roosevelt Library', *AA* XXXIV, iii (1971), pp. 265–76.
(4) Formula employed by the Public Record Office of Northern Ireland.
(5) Based upon the rules used in the Cumbria Record Office.
(6) This summary is based upon publicity material compiled in the Greater London Record Office.
(7) Based upon a form used by the Ipswich and East Suffolk Record Office.

Chapter 10

(1) See also pp. 56 ff.
(2) Rhoads, *New Archival Techniques,* pp. 44–45. I am indebted to Mr A. W. Mabbs, for information on the Public Record Office. See also L. Bell, 'The New Public Record Office at Kew', *JSA,* V, i (1974), pp. 4–6.
(3) Rhoads, p. 85.
(4) I am indebted to Miss Mary Waddell for this observation.
(5) Simplified first-floor plan of the new Lancashire Record Office. I am indebted to Mr R. Sharpe France and Mr D. Smith.
(6) *Reports of the Gloucestershire Records Office, 1970–1,* supplemented by information from the County Archivist, Mr B. S. Smith.

Chapter 11

(1) On this subject, see R. H. C. Davis, 'Record Societies in England: a Review Article', *History,* LX (1975), pp. 239–46.
(2) (International Council on Archives, Washington, 1968). I am also much indebted to Mr Leisinger for additional information, and for helping to compile the bibliography to this section. See also pp. 93–94.

Chapter 12

(1) *Care of County Muniments* (1923), p. 48.
(2) *Manuel,* p. 672.
(3) *Manuel,* p. 677 (author's translation).

(4) *Manuel*, pp. 684–5.
(5) For example, E. Melling (ed.), *Kentish Sources* (Maidstone, 1959). In progress.
(6) For example, D. Read (ed.), *Documents from Edwardian England, 1901–15* (London, Harrap, 1973).
(7) For example, the series edited by J. M. Thomas, *History at Source* (London, Evans, 1970–).
(8) Published by Jackdaw Publications, Ltd (a subsidiary of Jonathan Cape, Ltd).
(9) *Education Facsimiles,* 1–160.
(10) Essex Record Office, SEAX series of teaching portfolios, 1–6.
(11) Schools Council, 'History, Geography and Social Science, 8–13', *Project Report* (September 1973). I am indebted to Professor W. A. L. Blyth and his research team for this material.
(12) W. H. Burston and C. W. Green (eds.), *Handbook for History Teachers,* 2nd edn. (London, Methuen, 1972).
(13) Work on this began with M. Cook. 'Educational Methods and Theory for Record Offices', a discussion paper at in-service course (University of Liverpool, 1972), and was continued by Society of Archivists, South-eastern Region, in 'Draft Recommendations for Educational Work in Local Government Archives Services' (1974). Further work is in progress.

Bibliography

The bibliography includes only items that are reasonably accessible. It is arranged as follows:
General bibliographies; Archival practice and theory; Legislation, control and management of archives; Local archives services; Archives and libraries; Archives and universities; Business archives services; Records management, including appraisal and disposal; Arrangement and description of archives; Information systems and retrieval as applied to archives; Indexing in archives work; Access policy; Publication; Microreprography; Buildings; Conservation; Archives and education; Professional education.

International Directory of Archives (as of January, 1975) (Paris, Presses Universitaires de France, 1975). Issued as *Archivum*, XXII–XXIII (1972–3).

General Bibliographies
International Council on Archives, *Bibliographie analytique internationale des publications relatives a l'archivistique et aux archives, Archivum,* special fascicule (1964). (Publications prior to 1959.)

F. B. Evans (ed.), *The Administration of Modern Archives: a Select Bibliographic Guide* (Washington, 1970). *Modern Archives and Manuscripts, a select bibliographic guide* (Washington, 1975).

Annual bibliographies are contained in *The American Archivist;* the latest is: I. V. Clarke and others, 'Bibliography: Writings on Archives, Current Records and Historical Manuscripts during 1973; XXXVIII, iii (1975), pp. 339–74.

R. H. Ellis and W. Kellaway, 'A Bibliography of the Writings of Sir H. Jenkinson'; *Archives*, II (1955), pp. 329–43. 'Select Bibliography of Archive Administration', *JSA,* II, ii (1960), pp. 67–72.

Archival Practice and Theory

Association des Archivistes Français, *Manuel d'archivistique* (Paris, 1970).

R.Claus, 'The Proposal for a United Nations Archival Agency', *AA,* XXXIII, (1970).

M. Duchein, 'The Archival Revolution: the Challenge of Modern Archives to the Archivist', *Southeast Asian Archives,* V (1972), pp. 4–14.

G. Duboscq, 'La Profession d'archiviste et son avenir', *Manuel,* pp. 86–9.

J. R. Ede, 'Archives in France', *Archives,* X (1972), pp. 86–93.

—— 'The Public Record Office and its Users'. *Archives,* VIII (1968), pp. 185–92.

R. H. Ellis, 'The Archivist as Technician', *JSA* I, v (1957), pp. 146–7.

—— 'The British Archivist and his Society', *JSA,* III (1965), pp. 43–7.

—— 'The British Archivist and History'. *JSA,* III, iv (1966), pp. 155–9.

F. B. Evans, 'Modern Concepts of Archives Administration and Records Management', *UNESCO Bulletin for Libraries,* XXIV (1970), pp. 242–7.

—— D. F. Harrison, E. A. Thompson and W. L. Rofes, 'A Basic Glossary for Archivists, Manuscript Curators and Records Managers', *AA,* XXXVII, iii (1974), pp. 415–34.

V. H. Galbraith. *Studies in the Public Records* (London, Nelson, 1948).

A. E. J. Hollaender (ed.) *Essays in Memory of Sir Hilary Jenkinson* (Society of Archivists, London, 1962).

F. Hull, 'Limits', *JSA,* II, iv (1961), pp. 138–9.

R. C. Jarvis, 'Jenkinson Reissued', *JSA,* III, v (1967), pp. 254–5.

H. Jenkinson, *A Manual of Archive Administration* (London, 1922; 3rd edn. 1965).

—— *The English Archivist: a New Profession* (London, H. K. Lewis, 1948).

—— 'Archive Developments in England, 1925–50', in *Miscellanea Archivistica Angelo Mercati* (1952).

—— 'The Future of Archives in England', *JSA,* I, iii (1956), pp. 57–61.

—— 'Modern Archives: some Reflexions on T. R. Schellenberg'. *JSA,* I, v (1957), pp. 147–8.

—— 'Roots', *JSA,* II, ii (1961), pp. 131–7.

H. G. Jones. *The Records of a Nation: their Management, Preservation and Use* (New York, 1969).

H. Kahn, 'The Presidential Library: a new Institution', *Special Libraries,* L (1959), pp. 106–13.

C. Kecskeméti, 'Les Activités et les Problèmes du Conseil International des Archives', *Archivum,* XVI (1966), pp. 197–206.

D. S. Macmillan, 'Archival Reform in Australia', *JSA,* I, viii (1958), pp. 210–12.

M. Marquant, 'Les Archives et les Recherches modernes économiques et sociales', *Archivum,* X (1960), pp. 127–64.

S. Muller, J. A. Feith and R. Fruin, *Manual for the Arrangement and Description of Archives* (1898 in Dutch. Trans. A. H. Leavitt, New York, 1968).

K. Munden (ed.), *Archives and the Public Interest: Selected Essays by Ernst Posner* (Washington, 1967).

H. G. Nicholas, 'The Public Records, the Historian, the National Interest and Official Policy', *JSA*, III, i (1965), pp. 1–6.

J. E. O'Neill, 'Will Success Spoil the Presidential Libraries?' *AA*, XXXVI, iii (1973), pp. 339–52.

A. E. B. Owen, 'The Image of the Archivist', *Archives*, VII (1966), pp. 189–90.

Y. Pérotin (ed.), *A Manual of Tropical Archivology* (Mouton et Cie, Paris, 1966).

H. J. Pinkett, 'A Glossary of Records Terminology: Scope and Definitions', *AA*, XXXIII, i (1970), pp. 53–6.

E. Posner, *Archives in the Ancient World* (Harvard, 1972).

—— *American State Archives* (Chicago, 1964).

—— 'Archivists and International Awareness', in Munden *Archives* pp. 198–9.

M. Rieger, 'The Function of Archives in Public Administration', *UNESCO Bulletin for Libraries*, XXVII (1973), pp. 40–2.

J. B. Rhoads, *New Archival Techniques* (Seventh International Congress on Archives, Moscow, 1972).

C. Samaran, 'Problèmes archivistiques d'aujourdhui et de demain', in *Miscellanea Archivistica Angelo Mercati.* (1952).

T. R. Schellenberg, *Modern Archives, Principles and Techniques.* (1956; Chicago 1971).

—— *The Management of Archives* (Columbia University, 1965).

—— 'The Nature of an Archival Program', in Y. Pérotin (ed.). *Manual of Tropical Archivology* (1966), pp. 19–32.

P. J. Taylor, 'Two Indian Record Offices; the National Archives of India and the Nehru Memorial Museum and Library', *JSA*, IV (1970), pp. 60–1.

E. K. Timings, 'The Archivist and the Public'. *JSA*, II (1962) pp. 179–82; (1963), pp. 366–7.

J. J. Valette, *Le Rôle des archives dans l'administration et dans la politique de planification dans les pays en voie de développement.* (Paris, UNESCO, 1972).

F. R. J. Verhoeven, *The Role of Archives in the Public Administration and the National Planning Policy of Developing Countries* (Paris, UNESCO, 1972).

—— *Singapore: the National Archives and Records Management* (UNESCO, 1967).

B. Weilbrenner, *Haute-Volta: réorganisation et développement des archives.* (UNESCO, 1972).

Legislation, Control and Management
The International Council on Archives has published the text of
substantive archival legislation in *Archivum:* 'Part I. Europe', XVII (1967),
XIX (1969); 'Part II. Africa and Asia', XX (1970), 'Part III. America,
Oceania', XXI (1971).
'Archive Policy for French'speaking African Countries', *UNESCO Bulletin
for Libraries*, XXVI, ii (1972), pp. 84–7.
R. H. Bautier, 'Définitions Générales et Problèmes juridiques des
Archives', in *Manuel*, pp. 21–45.
—— 'Principles of Archival Legislation and Regulation', in Y. Pérotin
(ed.), *Manual of Tropical Archivology'* (1966), pp. 33–58.
E. E. Burke, 'Some Archival Legislation of the British Commonwealth'.
AA, XXII, iii (1959), pp. 275–96.
S. Carbone and R. Guêze, *Draft Model Law on Archives: Description and
Text.* (Paris, UNESCO, 1972).
Department of the Environment, *Local Government Act 1972: Local
Authority Records in England,* Circular 17/74 (29 January 1974).
J. H. d'Olier & B. Delmas, *Planning National Infrastructures for
Documentation, Libraries and Archives* (Paris, UNESCO, 1975).
G. Duboscq, 'Les Archives françaises: organisation, législation,
évolution', in *Manuel*, pp. 46–103.
H. Finch, 'Administrative Relationships in a Large Manuscript
Repository', *AA*, XXXIV, i (1971), pp. 21–6.
H. Kahn, 'The Long-range Implications for Historians and Archivists of
the Charges against the Franklin D. Roosevelt Library', *AA*, XXXIV, iii
(1971), pp. 265–76.
Ministry of Housing and Local Government, *Local Government (Records)
Act 1962,* Circular 44/62 (3 September 1962).
The New Local Authorities, Management and Structure (the Bains
report) (London, HMSO, 1972).
S. C. Newton. 'The Archivist as Legislator'. *JSA*, IV, (1973), pp. 654–9.
HM Treasury, *Private Owners and Public Collections,* note (October,
1973).
F. Ranger, 'Export Control of Archives', *JSA*, III, (1969), pp. 570–1.
R. A. Storey, 'Sales and Deposits of Non-Governmental Records', *Library
Association Record*, LXXI (1969), p. 81.

Local Archives Serivces in Britain
A chronicle of archival activities was provided in a regular series of
reports, issued quinquennially: 'Work in Archives, 1948–55' and
'1956–60' reprinted by the British Records Association from the Library
Association's *Five Years Work in Librarianship, 1951–5* and *1956–60*
respectively.

'Work in Archives 1961–5', *Archives*, VIII (1968), pp. 193–203.

Archives, published twice yearly by the British Records Association, carries a series of descriptions of the history, working and contents of local (and some other) record offices, beginning with: J. Godber, 'The County Record Office at Bedford', *Archives* I (1949), pp. 11–20.

T. G. Barnes, 'The Local Record Office and the Historian's Apprenticeship', *JSA,* II, i (1960), pp. 25–32.

L. Bell, 'An Archivists' Co-operative?', *JSA,* V (1975), pp. 149–57.

M. F. Bond, 'The British Records Association and the Modern Archives Movement', in *Jenkinson Essays,* pp. 71ff.

D. Charman, 'On the Need for a new Local Archives Service for England', *JSA,* III, vii (1968), pp. 341–6.

M. Cook, 'Regional Archives Offices: some Reflections', *JSA,* III, vi (1967) pp. 271–4.

I. Darlington. 'The London Government Act, 1963, and its Effect on Local Records in the Greater London Area', *JSA,* III, vi (1967), pp. 291–5.

—— 'Record Offices in Greater London', *JSA,* III, v (1967), pp. 248–9.

K. Darwin, 'The Irish Record Situation', *JSA,* II, viii (1963), pp. 361–5.

J. R. Ede, 'The Record Office, Central and Local: Evolution of a Relationship', *JSA,* V, iv (1975), pp. 207–14.

R. H. Ellis, 'The Historical Manuscripts Commission, 1869–1969', *JSA,* III, ix (1969), pp. 441ff.

G. H. Fowler, *The Care of County Muniments* (County Councils Association, 1923).

H. Hall. *A Repertory of British Archives.* Part I: England (London, Royal Historical Society, 1920).

Historical Manuscripts Commission. *Record Repositories in Great Britain,* 5th edn. (London, HMSO, 1973).

—— *Manuscripts and Men* (London, HMSO, 1969).

J. H. Hodson, *The Administration of Archives* (Oxford, Pergamon Press, 1972).

F. Hull, 'The Local Authority Record Office—Whither?', *JSA,* III, vii (1968), pp. 357–8.

Local Authority Archive and Records Management Services in Metropolitan Areas (London, Society of Archivists, 1972).

R. H. McCall and others, 'Archives Services and the Smaller Repositories', *Archives,* IV (1960), pp. 189–203.

A. E. B. Owen, 'Local Records in Scotland: the McBoyle Report', *Archives,* VIII (1968), pp. 119–22.

—— 'Too many Repositories?'. *Archives,* VII (1966), pp. 133–4.

E. Posner, 'European Experiences in Protecting and Preserving Local Records', *Archives,* pp. 107–13.

E. Ralph, 'The Development of Local Archive Service in England', in *Jenkinson Essays,* pp. 57–70.

F. Ranger (ed.), *Prisca Munimenta: Studies in Archival and Administrative History* (London, 1973).

L. J. Redstone and F. W. Steer (eds.), *Local Records: their Nature and Care* (London, Bell, 1953).

W. R. Serjeant, 'The Survey of Local Archives Services, 1968', *JSA*, IV, iv (1971), pp. 300–26.

Society of Archivists, *Recommendations for Local Government Archives Services* (London, 1971).

J. M. Thomson, *The Public Records of Scotland* (Glasgow, 1922).

Archives and Libraries

A. Aziz, 'Archives-Library Relationships and their Educational Implications', *Southeast Asian Archives*, IV (1971), pp. 44–55.

R. L. Brubaker, 'Archival Principles and the Curator of Manuscripts', *AA*, XXIX, iv (1966), 505–14.

P. Hepworth, *Archives and Manuscripts in Libraries* (Library Association Pamphlet no. 18) (London, 1958; 2nd edn., 1964).

—— 'Manuscript and Non-Book Materials in Libraries', *Archives*, IX (1969), pp. 90–7.

J. L. Hobbs, *Local History and the Library* (London, 1962).

Library of Congress, *Rules for Descriptive Cataloging in the Library of Congress. Manuscripts* (Washington, 1954).

L. Q. Mumford, 'Archivists and Librarians. Time for a new Look', *AA*, XXXIII, iii (1970), pp. 269–74.

'The Place of Archives and Manuscripts in the Field of Librarianship', *Archives* IX (1969), pp. 40–1.

F. Ranger, 'The Common Pursuit', *Archives,* IX (1970), pp. 121–9.

Archives and Universities

M. J. Brichford, 'University Archives: Relationships with Faculty', *AA*, XXXIV, ii (1971), pp. 173–82.

—— *Scientific and Technological Documentation: Archival Evaluation and Processing of University Records relating to Science and Technology* (University of Illinois, 1969).

—— T. Cassady and others. *Proceedings of the Conference on Archival Administration for Small Universities, Colleges and Junior Colleges.* (Urbana, University of Illinois Graduate School of Library Science, 1967).

British Records Association. *The Preservation and Use of Records: the Universities' Contribution* (London, 1967).

College and University Archives Committee of the Society of American Archivists, *Forms Manual* (1973). 'A Select Bibliography', *AA*, XXXVI (1974), pp. 67–72.

'College and University Archives', *AA*, XXXI, iii (1968).

F. G. Emmison, 'Local Record Offices and the Universities, *History*, no. 181 (1969), pp. 229–32.

J. H. Hodson, 'A University Archive Repository: the University of
Nottingham Department of Manuscripts', *Archives,* v (1962), pp.
145–50.

C. A. McLaren, 'Record Repositories in British Universities', *AA*, XXXVIII
(1975), pp. 181–190.

E. Posner, 'College and University Archives in the United States', in
Miscellanea Archivistica Angelo Mercati (1952); and *Archives*, pp.
148–58.

M. A. Renshaw, 'A University Archive Repository', *Library Association
Record,* LVI (1954), pp. 75–80.

A. D. Ridge, 'The McGill University Archives', *Archives*, VIII (1967), pp.
16–23.

R. Stevens (ed.), *University Archives* (Ann Arbor (Michigan), 1965).

University of London, *Report of the Study Group on the Archives of the
University* (1973).

Business Archives Services

J. H. Archer, 'Business Records: the Canadian Scene', *AA*, XXXII (1969),
pp. 251–60.

G. Clark, 'British Business Archives, 1935–48', *Business Archives,* no. 34
(1971), pp. 7–9.

H. M. B. Cushman, 'The Modern Business Archivist', *AA*, XXXIII (1970),
pp. 19–24.

R. W. Ferrier, 'The Archivist in Business', *Business Archives,* no. 37
(1972), pp. 17–22.

R. W. Lovett, 'The Status of Business Archives', *AA*, XXXII, iii (1969), pp.
247–50.

D. S. Macmillan, 'Business Archives: a Survey of Developments in Great
Britain, USA and in Australia', in *Jenkinson Essays,* pp. 108–27.

P. L. Payne, 'Business Archives and Economic History: the Case for
Regional Studies', *Archives,* VI (1963), pp. 21–9.

J. E. Thexton, 'Archival Potential of Machine-Readable Records in
Business', *AA*, XXXVII, i (1974), pp. 37–42.

A. Zechel. 'The Development and Present State of Business Archives in
the Federal Republic of Germany', *Archivum*, XVIII (1968), pp.
196–204.

Records Management
Bibliography

'Writings on Records Management: a Select List', *AA,* XXXVI, iii (1973),
367–72.

F. B. Evans (ed.), *The Administration of Modern Archives: a Select
Bibliographic Guide* (Washington, 1970, 1975).

See also the bibliographies in the books listed below.

General
A. Alsberg-Alssur, 'The Academic Archivist and Current Records', *Archivum,* XVIII (1968), p. 177.
H. E. Angel, 'Archival Janus: the Records Center', *AA,* XXXI, i (1968), pp. 5–12.
W. Benedon, *Records Management* (New Jersey, 1969).
H. Blaquière, R. Favreau, Y. Pérotin, 'Les Archives en formation et le pré-archivage', *Manuel,* pp. 104–26.
D. R. Bodem, 'The Use of Forms in the Control of Archives at the Accessioning and Processing Level', *AA,* XXXI, iv (1968), pp. 365–70.
British Steel Corporation, *Regional Records Centres* (1974).
E. G. Campbell, 'Buildings and Equipment of Federal Records Centers in the US', *Archivum,* VII (1957), pp. 21–5.
H. Charnier, 'Les Archives et la Documentation Administrative', in *Manuel,* pp. 695–716.
J. H. Collingridge, 'Implementing the Grigg Report', *JSA,* I, vii (1958), pp. 179–84.
——— 'Records Management in England since the Grigg Report', *JSA,* II, vi (1962), pp. 242–6.
'Contrôle des archives en formation', *Archivum,* I (1951).
M. Cook, 'Surveying Current Records', *JSA,* IV, v (1972), pp. 413–22.
——— L. J. McDonald and E. Welch, 'The Management of Records', *JSA,* III, viii (1968), pp. 417–23.
F. I. Dolgikh, *Interconnection and Continuity of the Work of State and Agency Archives* (Seventh International Congress on Archives, Moscow, 1972).
I. Darlington, 'Methods adopted by the LCC for the Preservation or Disposal of Modern Records', *JSA,* I, v (1957), pp. 140–5.
R. H. Ellis and J. C. Ellis, 'Archivist and Architect: an ideal Design for a Limbo Repository', *Archives,* I (1952), pp. 2–9.
V. Gondos (ed.), *Reader for Archives and Records Center Buildings* (Society of American Archivists, 1970).
F. Hull, 'The Destruction of Administrative Records: the County Repository and the Grigg Report', *JSA,* I, ii (1955), pp. 41–2.
——— 'The Management of Modern Records', *JSA,* IV, i (1970), pp. 45–50.
——— 'Modern Records then and now', *JSA,* IV, v (1972), pp. 395–9.
E. N. Johnson, 'Trends in County Records Management', *AA,* XXIV (1961). pp. 297–301.
L. C. Johnson, 'Administration of the Archives of the British Transport Commission', in *Jenkinson Essays,* pp. 91–107.
P. E. Jones, 'Departmental Records', *JSA,* I, i (1955), pp. 7–9.
Kent County Council, *Guide for Officers in Charge of Modern County Council Records* (1972).
E. J. Leahy and C. A. Cameron, *Modern Records Management* (New York, 1965).

O. McCool, 'The Metes and Bounds of Records Management', *AA,* XXVII (1964), pp. 87–93.

A. W. Mabbs and G. Duboscq. *The Organisation of Intermediate Records Storage* (UNESCO, 1974).

J. Mady, R. Marquant, Y. Pérotin and J. Rigault, 'L'Entrée des documents aux archives', in *Manuel,* pp. 127–60.

National Archives of the USA, *Federal Records Centers* (General Services Administration Handbooks) (1967).

S. C. Newton, 'Pre-Archival Records Control in East Sussex', *JSA,* IV, vii (1973), pp. 581–7.

I. Place and E. L. Popham, *Filing and Records Management* (New Jersey, 1966).

Public Record Office, *A Guide for Departmental Record Officers* (2nd ed. 1971).

Public Record Office of Northern Ireland, *Modern Departmental Papers, Memorandum on New Review Procedure* (1968).

Report of the Committee on Departmental Records (the Grigg report) (London, HMSO, 1954) (Cmd 9163).

M. Roper, 'Modern Departmental Records and the Record Office', *JSA,* IV, v (1972), pp. 400–12.

D. E. Russell, 'Records Management: an Introduction', *Special Libraries,* LXV, i (1974), pp. 17–21.

D. Shadd, 'Some Problems in Providing Reference Service at a Records Centre', *JSA,* II, ii (1960), pp. 61–6.

Appraisal and Disposal of Records

M. Baudot, 'Les Triages et éliminations', in *Manuel,* pp. 161–86.

Bethlehem Steel Company, *Records Retention Program: Procedure Manual* (Bethlehem, Penn., 1972).

British Steel Corporation, *Corporation Retention Schedule* (1971).

J. H. Collingridge, 'The Selection of Archives for Permanent Preservation', *Archivum,* VI (1956), pp. 25–42.

I. Darlington, 'The Weeding and Disposal of Files', *JSA,* I, ii (1955), pp. 47–9.

M. H. Fishbein. 'A Viewpoint on Appraisal of National Records', *AA,* XXXIII, ii (1970), pp. 175–89.

—— 'Appraising Information in Machine Language Form', *AA,* XXXV, i (1972), pp. 35–44.

F. Hull, 'County of Kent Working Party on Records', *JSA,* III, x (1969), pp. 572–4.

T. W. M. Jaine, *Report on the Records of Urban and District Councils in Northamptonshire* (Northants County Council, 1965).

L. Kaiser, 'Selection of Statistical Primary Material', *Archivum,* VI (1956), pp. 75–82.

W. K. Lamb, 'The Fine Art of Destruction', *Jenkinson Essays,* pp. 50–6.

P. Lewinson, 'Archival Sampling', *AA,* XX (1957), pp. 291–312.

A. W. Mabbs, 'The Public Record Office and the Second Review', *Archives,* VIII (1967–8), pp. 180–4.

T. W. Mitchell, 'New Viewpoints on Establishing Permanent Values of State Archives', *AA*, XXXIII, ii (1970), pp. 163–74.

National Archives of the USA, Applying Retention Schedules (General Services Administration Handbooks) (1961)—*Record Retention Requirements* (General Services Administration Handbooks) (updated annually).

'Problems of Sampling as Related to Records Preservation', *Archives,* IX (1970), pp. 155–7. The British Records Association has issued many recommended retention lists relating to the records of types of institution.

Report of the Committee on Legal Records (the Denning report) (London, HMSO, 1966) (Cmd 3084).

Report on Records of the Children's Department in Local Government; their Retention and Disposal (Maidstone, Society of Archivists, 1968).

V. B. Santen, 'Appraisal of Financial Records', *AA*, XXXII, iv (1969), pp. 357–62.

T. R. Schellenberg, *The Appraisal of Modern Public Records* (Bulletin no. 8) (Washington, National Archives of the USA, 1956).

W. I. Smith, 'Archival Selection: a Canadian View', *JSA*, III, vi (1967), pp. 275–80.

H. M. Walton, 'Some Comments on Destruction Schedules', *Archives,* VI (1964), pp. 147–53.

—— 'Destruction Schedules: Quarter Sessions, Magistrates' Courts, and Coroners' Records', *JSA*, III, ii (1965), pp. 61–74.

Arrangement and Description

E. O. Alldredge, 'Inventorying Magnetic-Media Records', *AA,* XXXV, iii–iv (1972), pp. 337–46.

C. Barratt and C. H. Thompson, 'The Preservation and Classification of Modern Local Government Archives; two Views', *Archives,* I (1952), pp. 1–12.

M. Baudot, 'Les Instruments de Recherche', in *Manuel,* pp. 243–94.

R. C. Berner, 'Manuscript Catalogs and other Finding Aids: what are their Relationships?' *AA,* XXXIV, iv (1971), pp. 367–72.

F. Biljan, *Information Instruments in the Service of Science* (Seventh International Congress on Archives, Moscow, 1972).

D. R. Bodem, 'The Use of Forms in the Control of Archives at the Accessioning and Processing Level', *AA,* XXXI (1968), pp. 365–70.

British Records Association. *The Classification of English Archives.* 1936.

F. G. Emmison, 'Repatriation of "Foreign" Estate and Family Archives', *Archives,* II (1956), pp. 467–76. Linked with this discussion are: R. B. Pugh. 'Quod Dominus Conjunxit Cartophylax non Separet'. *Archives,* III

(1957), pp. 39–42. J. C. Lancaster, 'Some Views on Sanctity', *Archives*, III (1958), pp. 159–71.

F. G. Emmison, 'Lists, Indexes and Inventories', *Archives*, I (1951), pp. 24–7.

J. Finch, 'Some Fundamentals in Arranging Archives and Manuscript Collections', *Library Resources and Technical Services*, no. 8 (1964), pp. 26–34.

G. L. Fischer, 'Letting the Archival Dust Settle: some Remarks on the Record Group Concept', *JSA*, IV, viii (1973), pp. 640–5.

L. J. Gordon, 'Arrangement and Cataloguing of Modern Historical Papers in the British Museum', *Archives*, VIII (1967), pp. 2–7.

P. M. Hamer, *The Control of Records at the Record Group Level* (Staff Information Circular no. 15) (National Archives of the USA, 1950).

O. W. Holmes, 'Archival Arrangement: Five Different Operations at Five Different Levels', *AA*, XXVII (1964), pp. 21–41.

J. C. Lancaster, *A Guide to Lists and Catalogues of the India Office Records* (1966).

I. Maclean, 'An Analysis of Jenkinson's *Manual* in the Light of Australian Experience', in *Jenkinson Essays*, pp. 128–52.

J. Mady, Y. Pérotin and J. Rigault, 'Le Classement et la Cotation', in *Manuel*, pp. 187–242.

K. Munden, 'The Identification and Description of the Series', *AA*, XIII (1950), pp. 213–27.

E. C. Papenfuse, 'The Retreat from Standardisation: a Comment on the Recent History of Finding Aids', *AA*, XXXVI, iv (1973), pp. 367–72.

G. Parker, 'Calendar or "List and Analysis"?' *Archives*, IX (1970), pp. 202–3.

Y. Pérotin, 'Classification Schemes', in idim., *Manual of Tropical Archivology*, pp. 65–76.

E. Posner, 'Max Lehmann and the Principle of Provenance', in Munden, *Archives*, pp. 36–44.

M. Roper, 'Modern Departmental Records and the Record Office', *JSA*, IV, v (1972), pp. 400–12.

T. R. Schellenberg, 'Archival Principles of Arrangement', *AA*, XXIV (1961), pp. 11–24.

A. Scherer, 'Methods of Dealing with Unclassified Record Groups', in Pérotin, *Manual of Tropical Archivology*, pp. 59–64.

P. J. Scott, 'The Record Group Concept: a Case for Abandonment', *AA*, XXIX, iv (1966), pp. 493–504.

A. Szedo, 'Les Méthodes modernes de classement d'archives (documents postérieurs à 1800)', *Archivum*, XIV (1964), pp. 57–68.

Information Systems and Retrieval as Applied to Archives
P. Abrams and W. Corvine, *Basic Data Processing*. 2nd edn. (San Francisco, 1971).

'Archives and Automation', in *Record of Thirteenth International Conference of the Archival Round Table* (Bonn, 1971).

D. Austin and P. Butcher, PRECIS: *a Rotated Subject Index* (London, British National Bibliography, 1969).

L. Bell and M. Roper (eds.), *Proceedings of an International Seminar on Automatic Data Processing in Archives* (London, HMSO, 1975).

F. Biljan, *Information Instruments in the Service of Science* (Seventh International Congress on Archives, Moscow, 1972).

D. Boer, 'Business Archives in Automated Information Retrieval Systems', *Archivum*, XVIII (1968), pp. 191–5.

F. G. Burke, 'The Application of Automated Techniques in the Management and Control of Source Materials', *AA*, XXX (1967), pp. 255–78.

M. E. Califano, 'L'Introduction et l'adaptation des moyens mécanographiques aux archives', *Archivum*, XIV (1964), pp. 147–56.

East Sussex Record Office, *Systems Description: Computer Indexing and Cataloguing for the County Records Office* (1970). *Pre-Archival Records Control Operation Manual* (1973; revised 1975).

M. H. Fishbein, 'ADP and Archives: Selected Publications on Automatic Data Processing', *AA*, XXXVIII, i (1975), pp. 31–42.

J. C. Gardin, 'Document Analysis and Linguistic Theory', *Journal of Documentation*, XXIX, ii (1973). pp. 137ff.

F. McCall, PROSPEC *Manual* (London, Public Record Office, n.d.).

National Archives of the USA, *Information Retrieval Systems,* Records Management Handbook (1970).

D. H. Perman, 'Computers and Bibliography for the Social Sciences', *AA*, XXXII, i (1969), pp. 15–21.

J. B. Rhoads, *New Archival Techniques.* Seventh International Congress on Archives (Moscow, 1972).

C. J. Van Rijsbergen and K. S. Jones, 'A Test for the Separation of Relevant and Non-Relevant Documents in Experimental Retrieval Collections', *Journal of Documentation*, XXIX, iii (1973), pp. 251–7.

J. R. Sharp, *Some Fundamentals of Information Retrieval* (1965).

P. Simmons, L. Bell and M. Roper, 'PROSPEC: a Computer Application for the Public Record Office', *JSA*, IV, v (1972), pp. 423–7.

B. C. Vickery, *Techniques of Information Retrieval* (London, Butterworth, 1970).

—— *Information Systems* (London, Butterworth, 1973).

See also: ADPA: *Automation—Archives—Informatique,* (International Council on Archives, 1973–).

Indexing in Archives Work

D. Alexander, 'A Description of Indexing Procedures for the "Agreement on Accounts of Crew"', *Archives*, XI, (1973), pp. 86–93.

Alphabetical Arrangement, BS 1749 (London, British Standards Institution, 1968).

L. Bell, 'Controlled Vocabulary Subject-Indexing of Archives', *JSA*, IV, iv
    (1971), pp. 285–99.

G. V. Carey, *Making an Index*, Cambridge Authors' and Printers' Guides,
    no. 3, 3rd edn. (London, Cambridge University Press, 1963).

R. L. Collison, *Indexes and Indexing*. 3rd edn. (London, 1969).

N. S. M. Cox and R. S. Davies, *The Indexing of Records in the Public
    Record Office* (1970).

K. Darwin, 'The Use of the Computer in Indexing Records', *JSA*, IV, iii
    (1971), pp. 218–29.

Historical Manuscripts Commission, National Register of Archives,
    Subject-Index Schema and Word-List (1969).

C. G. Holland, 'Indexes, Computers and the Public Service', *JSA*, IV, v
    (1972), pp. 428–31.

R. F. Hunnisett, *Indexing for Editors,* Archives and the User, no. 2
    (London British Records Association, 1972).

E. A. Ingerman, 'A new Method of Indexing Manuscripts', *AA*, XXV
    (1962), pp. 331–40.

B. Josephson, 'Indexing', *AA*, X (1947), pp. 133–50.

Access Policy

C. M. Barker and M. H. Fox, *Classified Files—the Yellowing Pages: a
    Report on Scholars' Access to Government Documents* (New York,
    1972).

P. K. Grimsted, 'Archives in the Soviet Union: their Organisation and the
    Problem of Access', *AA*, XXXIV, i (1971), pp. 27–41.

F. Hull, 'Facilities for Access', *Archives*, I, iii (1950), pp. 20–3.

C. Kecskeméti, 'La Libéralisation en matière d'accès aux archives et de
    politique de microfilmage', *Archivum*, XVIII (1968), p. 25.

W. K. Lamb, 'Liberalization of Restrictions on Access to Archives',
    Archivum, XVI (1966), pp. 35–40.

H. G. Nicholas, 'The Public Records, the Historian the National Interest
    and Official Policy', *JSA*, III, i (1965), pp. 1–6.

*Recommendations for the Preparation of Indexes for Books, Periodicals
    and other Publications*, BS 3700 (London, British Standards
    Institution, 1964).

A. Reitman, 'Freedom of Information and Privacy: the civil libertarian's
    dilemma', *AA*, XXXVIII, iv (1975), pp. 501–8.

V. R. Stewart, 'Problems of Confidentiality in the Administration of
    Personal Case Records', *AA*, XXXVII, iii (1974), pp. 387–98.

A. Wagner, 'The Policy of Access to Archives: from Restriction to
    Liberalization', *UNESCO Bulletin for Libraries*, XXIV, ii (1970), pp. 73–6.

Publication

G. Belov and O. W. Holmes, 'National Documentary Publication
    Programming', *Archivum*, XVI (1966), pp. 67–96.

British National Archives. Sectional List no. 24 (London, HMSO). Updated annually.

P. C. Brooks, *Research in Archives: the Use of Unpublished Primary Sources* (Chicago, 1969).

H. B. Cox, 'Publication of Manuscripts: Devaluation or Enhancement?' *AA,* XXXII, i (1969), pp. 25–33.

C. R. Elrington, *Victoria History of the Counties of England. Handbook for Editors and Authors* (London, Institute of Historical Research, 1970).

P. Gouldesborough and W. D. McNeill, 'Lithographic Printing for Record Publications', *Archives,* VIII (1968), pp. 172–8.

D. Iredale, *Enjoying Archives* (Newton Abbot, David and Charles, 1973).

H. C. Johnson, 'Publication of English Records: the Public Record Office', *Archives,* IV (1960), pp. 214–18.

K. Major, 'Record Publications and the Teaching of Diplomatic', *Archives,* II (1953), pp. 20–5.

G. H. Martin, 'The Publication of Borough Records', *Archives,* VII (1966), pp. 199–206.

Notes for the Guidance of Editors of Record Publications (London, British Records Association, 1946).

E. Offenbacher, 'The Economics of Reprography for Technical Communication', *UNESCO Bulletin for Libraries,* XXIV, i (1970), pp. 23–6.

Publications of the Royal Commission on Historical Manuscripts. Sectional List no. 17 (London, HMSO). Updated annually.

R. B. Pugh, 'The Publication of Modern Records', *Archives,* I (1949), pp. 31–5.

—— 'Publishing the Public Records: a Replication', *Archives,* V (1961), pp. 78–83. Related to next entry.

G. D. Ramsay, 'The Publication of English Records', *Archives,* IV (1960), pp. 138–48.

Specimen Pages for Record Publications (London, British Records Association, 1947).

F. Shelley, 'The Choice of a Medium for Documentary Publication', *AA,* XXXII, iv (1969), pp. 363–8.

J. M. Sims, *London and Middlesex Published Records: a Handlist* (London Record Society, 1970).

Symposium of Editors of Documentation, Library and Archives Journals, report in *UNESCO Bulletin for Libraries,* XXVI, vi (1972), pp. 298–300.

Microreprography

H. W. Ballou, *Guide to Micrographic Equipment (National Microfilm Association (USA). 1975).* Periodically updated.

M. Baudot, 'Perspectives d'Emploi du microfilm dans les dépôts d'archives', *Archivum,* II (1952), pp. 89–92.

Essential Characteristics of 35 mm. Microfilm Reading Apparatus,
   BS4191 (London, British Standards Institution, 1967).

M. B. Gille., 'Esquisse d'un plan de normalisation pour le microfilmage
   des archives', *Archivum,* III (1953), p. 87.

W. R. Hawken, *Copying Methods Manual* (American Library Association,
   1966).

International Council on Archives (Microfilm Committee), *Bulletin*
   (Budapest, 1972–   ).

A. Jantan, 'The Problem of Acquiring Microfilm Copies of Archive
   Materials from Abroad', *Southeast Asian Archives,* IV (1971), pp.
   41–3.

C. G. La Hood, jr, 'Microfilm for the Library of Congress', *College and
   Research Libraries,* XXXIV, iv (1973), pp. 291–4.

A. H. Leisinger, jr, *The Preparation of Records for Publication on
   Microfilm,* National Archives Staff Information Paper no. 19
   (Washington, 1951).

—— *Microphotography for Archives* (Washington, International Council
   on Archives, 1968).

—— *A Study of the Basic Standards for Equipping, Maintaining and
   Operating a Reprographic Laboratory in Archives of Developing
   Countries* (Brussels, International Council on Archives, 1973).

Library of Congress. *Specifications for microfilming newspapers* (1972).

C. S. McCamy, *Inspection of Processed Photographic Record Films for
   Aging Blemishes,* National Bureau of Standards Handbooks, no. 96
   (Washington, 1964).

C. S. McCamy and C. I. Pope, *Summary of Current Research on Archival
   Microfilm,* National Bureau of Standards Technical Note no. 261
   (Washington, 1965).

J. McDonald, 'The Case against Microfilming', *AA,* XX (1957), pp.
   345–56.

Microfilm Spools and Reels, 35 mm. and 16 mm., BS 1371 (London,
   British Standards Institution, 1956).

National Microfilm Association (USA), *Quality Standards* on: computer
   output microfilm (1971, 1976); facsimile transmission of microfilmed
   documents (1972); flowchart symbols in micrographics (1973);
   microfiche of documents (1975); glossary of micrographics (1971);
   inspection and quality control of first generation silver halide
   microfilm (1972); operational procedures for the production of
   microforms (1974); microfilming newspapers (1975).

*Recommendations for the Processing and Storage of Silver-Gelatin-type
   Microfilm,* BS 1153 (London, British Standards Institution, 1975).

M. M. Weis, 'The Case for Microfilming', *AA,* XX (1959), pp. 15–24.

B. J. S. Williams, *Evaluation of Microrecording Techniques* (London,
   1967).

Buildings

L. Bell, 'The new Public Record Office at Kew', *JSA,* V, i (1974), pp. 1–7.

M. Bond, 'The new Record Repository at the Houses of Parliament', *Archives,* VI (1963), pp. 85–94.

R. G. Bonnington, 'The West Register House: a New Annexe for the Scottish Record Office', *Archives,* IX (1969), pp. 64–72.

J. F. Christian and S. Finnegan, 'On Planning an Archives', *AA,* XXXVII, iv (1974), pp. 573–578.

I. P. Collis, 'The Ideal Layout of a Local Record Repository', *Archives,* I (1951), pp. 31–5; (1952), pp. 52–9.

—— 'Notes on Modern Archives Buildings in England, Wales and Northern Ireland', *Archivum,* VI (1956), pp. 100–7.

M. Duchein, *Les Bâtiments et équipements d'archives* (Paris, 1966).

—— 'Les Bâtiments d'archives départementales en France', *Archivum,* VI (1956), pp. 108–76.

—— 'Les Bâtiments et installations des archives', in *Manuel,* pp. 566–606.

—— *Malaysia: Planning and Equipment of the National Archives Building* (UNESCO, 1971).

I. M. Graham, 'A new Archives Building in Central Africa', *JSA,* III, i (1965), pp. 26–8.

L. C. Gwam, 'The Construction of Archive Buildings in Tropical Countries', in *Manual of Tropical Archivology,* pp. 77–92.

R. H. Ellis, 'The Building of the Public Record Office', in *Jenkinson Essays,* pp. 9–30.

V. Gondos (ed.), *Reader for Archives and Records Center Buildings* (Society of American Archivists, 1970).

J. C. Lancaster, 'The India Office Records and the India Office Library: the Move to a New Building', *Archives,* IX (1969), pp. 2–10.

T. R. Schellenberg, 'Modern Archival Buildings', *Archivum,* VI (1956), pp. 88–92.

L. Simon, V. Gondos, jr and W. J. Van Schreeven, *Buildings and Equipment for Archives,* Bulletins of the National Archives of the USA no. 6 (1944).

D. B. Wardle, 'The Public Record Office: the Repository', *Archivum,* VII (1957), pp. 26–8.

Conservation

Australian National Advisory Committee for UNESCO, *Preservation of Documentary Material in the Pacific Area, a practical guide* (Canberra, 1972).

P. N. Banks, 'Environmental Standards for Storage of Books and Manuscripts', Library Journal, XCIX, iii (1974), pp. 339–43.

W. J. Barrow, *Manuscripts and Documents: their Deterioration and Restoration* (University of Virginia, 1955).

V. W. Clapp, 'The Story of Permanent/Durable Book Paper, 1915–1970', *Restaurator,* Supplement no. 3 (1972).

J. K. H. Cunningham, 'The Protection of Records and Documents against Fire', *JSA,* III, viii (1968), pp. 411–16.

J. Davies, *A Study of the Basic Standards and Methods in Preservation and Restoration Workshops applicable to Developing Countries* (Brussels, International Council on Archives, 1973).

Draft Standard Recommendations for Storage and Exhibition of Documents, BS 73/80106 (London, British Standards Institution, 1973).

M. Duchein, 'Le Traitement et la restauration des documents endommagés', in *Manuel,* pp. 607–23.

D. M. Flyate (ed.), *The Preservation of Documents and Papers* (Moscow, Academy of Sciences of USSR, 1968) (Israel Program for Scientific Translation).

L. Hasznos, 'Modern Methods for the Protection of Archival and Library Material: Care and Restoration of badly damaged Documents', *UNESCO Bulletin for Libraries,* XXIV, vi (1970), pp. 302–4.

Y. P. Kathpalia, 'Restoration of Documents', in *Manual of Tropical Archivology,* pp. 121–49.

—— *Conservation and Restoration of Archive Materials.* (Paris, UNESCO, 1973).

S. Kula, 'The Storage of Archive Film', *JSA,* II, vi (1962), pp. 270–1.

W. H. Langwell, *The Conservation of Books and Documents* (London, Pitman, 1957).

—— 'The Permanence of Paper Records'. *Library Association Record,* LV (1973), pp. 212–15.

—— 'The Vapour Phase Deacidification of Books and Documents'. *JSA,* III, ii (1966), pp. 137–8.

National Fire Protection Association (USA), *The Protection of Records.* NFPA Standard No. 232, (Boston, n.d.).

H. J. Plenderleith and A. E. A. Werner, *The Conservation of Antiquities and Works of Art.* (Oxford, 1956; 2nd edn., 1971).

Repair and Allied Processes for the Conservation of Documents. Part I: Treatment of Sheets, Membranes and Seals, BS 4971 (London, British Standards Institution, 1973). *(Part II: Makeup and Binding of Documents* in progress.)

M. Slocombe, 'Storage of Tape Recordings', *JSA,* I, viii (1958), pp. 226–8.

Society of Archivists, *Repairers' Newsheet* (1964–   ).

Standing Commission on Museums and Galleries, *The Preservation of Technological Material: report and recommendations* (London, HMSO, 1971).

Standing Commission on Museums and Galleries, *The Preservation of Technological Material: Report and Recommendations* (London, HMSO. 1971).

H. F. Tottle, 'Strongroom Climate', *Archives,* II (1956), pp. 387–97.
D. B. Wardle, *Document Repair* (London, Society of Archivists, 1971).

Archives and Education
J. P. Babelon, R. Bousquet and R. Sève, 'Les Activités éducatives des
   archives', in *Manuel,* 672–94.
G. R. Batho, 'Sources', in W. H. Burston and C. W. Green (eds.),
   Handbook for History Teachers (London, 2nd edn., Methuen, 1972).
H. J. Behr, 'Archives and School Education: Possibilities, Problems,
   Limits', *UNESCO Bulletin for Libraries,* XXVIII, iii (1974), pp. 131–8.
J. E. Blyth, 'Archives and Source Material in the Junior School'. *Teaching
   History,* I, i (1969), pp. 24–30.
G. A. Chinnery, *Studying Urban History in Schools,* Pamphlet no. TH 33
   (London, Historical Association, 1971).
J. B. Coltham, *The Development of Thinking and the Learning of History,*
   Pamphlet no. TH 34 (London, Historical Association, 1971).
J. B. Coltham and J. Fines, *Educational Objectives for the Study of
   History,* Pamphlet no. TH 35 (London, Historical Association, 1971).
T. Corfe (ed.), *History in the Field* (London, Blond Educational, 1970).
Deaprtment of Education and Science, *Archives and Education,*
   Education Pamphlet no. 54 (London, HMSO, 1968).
Direction des Archives de France. *La Classe d'Histoire aux Archives*
   (1957).
R. Douch and F. W. Steer. *Local History Essays: some Notes for Students*
   (University of Southampton, n.d.)
G. Duboscq, 'The Educational Role of Archives', *UNESCO Bulletin for
   Libraries,* XXIV, iv (1970), pp. 205–10.
R. Dunning, *Local Sources for the Young Historian* (London, Muller,
   1973).
J. Fines and D. J. Steel, 'College of Education Students in the Archives
   Office', *Archives,* IX (1969), pp. 22–8.
J. Hancock and H. Johnson, 'Archive Kits in the Secondary School',
   Teaching History, II, vii (1972), pp. 207–17.
History of Education Society, *Local Studies and the History of Education*
   (London, Methuen, 1972).
G. Jones and D. Watson, 'Archives in History Teaching—Some
   Problems'. *Teaching History,* I, iii (1970), pp. 188–93.
F. P. McGivern, 'An Approach to Archives and Local History', *Teaching
   History,* II, v (1971), pp. 31 ff.
H. Richtering, 'Les Services éducatifs des archives de France', *Der
   Archivar* (1969), 261–70.
Schools Council, *Environmental Studies 5–13: the Use of Historical
   Resources,* Working Paper no. 48. (1973)—*School Resource
   Centres.* Working Paper no. 43 (London, 1973).

J. Standen, 'A new Resource Unit (*Wilsontown, a Resource Unit for
Schools,* by Hamilton College of Education)', *Teaching History,* III, x
(1973), pp. 156ff.

W. B. Stephens, *Sources for English Local History* (Manchester
University Press, 1973).

W. E. Tate, 'The Use of Archives in Education', *Archives,* I (1949), pp.
20–8.

H. A. Taylor, 'Clio in the Raw: Archival Materials and the Teaching of
History', *AA,* XXV, iii–iv (1972), pp. 317–30.

D. Turner, *Historical Demography in Schools,* Pamphlet no. TH 30
(London, Historical Association, 1971).

S. Wheeler, 'Young Children, Documents and the Locality', *Teaching
History,* I, iii (1970), pp. 181–7.

R. G. E. Wood, 'Archive Units for Teaching', *Teaching History,* II, vi
(1971), pp. 158–64; II, vii (1972), pp. 218–27; III, ix (1973), pp. 41–5.

Teaching History (the Historical Association) maintains a register of
teachers' groups working in archives, and also notices all archive
teaching units which achieve publication.

Professional Education

E. O. Alldredge, 'Archival Training in a Records Center', *AA,* XXI (1958),
pp. 401–7.

A. Aziz, 'Archives-Library Relationships and their Educational
Implications', *Southeast Asian Archives,* IV (1971), pp. 44–55.

A. Bein, 'The Training of Archivists in the State of Israel', *Archivum XI
(1961), pp. 179–82.*

L. Bell, 'The Professional Training of Archivists', *UNESCO Bulletin for
Libraries,* XXV, iv (1971), pp. 191–7.

A. Bousso, 'The University of Dakar School for Librarians, Archivists and
Documentalists', *UNESCO Bulletin for Libraries,* XXVII, ii (1973), pp.
72–7.

J. C. Colson, 'On the Education of Archivists and Librarians', *AA,* XXXI, ii
(1968), pp. 167–74.

M. Cook, *Establishment of Regional Training Facilities for Archivists in
Southeast Asia* (Paris, UNESCO, 1973).

——— 'The Planning of an Archives School', *JSA,* V, iv (1975), pp.
232–244.

M. Cook and F. Ranger, 'The Training of Record Office Staff', *JSA,* IV, iii
(1971), 230–3.

R. H. Ellis, 'The British Archivist and his Training', *JSA,* III, vi (1967), pp.
265–70.

F. B. Evans. 'Educational Needs for Work in Archival and Manuscript
Depositories'. *Indian Archives,* XXI, ii (1972), pp. 13–30.

E. Franz, *Liban: formation archivistique* (Paris, UNESCO, 1974).

'Formation des Archivistes'. *Archivum,* III (1953).

R. Irwin, 'The Education of an Archivist', In *Jenkinson Essays,* pp.
178–89.

H. G. Jones, 'Archival Training in American Universities', *AA,* XXXI, ii
(1968), pp. 135–54.

C. Kecskeméti, *La Formation professionalle des archivistes* (Brussels,
1966).

E. Posner, 'Archival Training in the United States', *Archivum,* IV (1954),
pp. 35–48; and in *Archives and the Public Interest,* pp. 58–77.

—— 'European Experiences in Training Archivists', in *Archives and the
Public Interest,* pp. 45–57.

M. Rieger, 'The Regional Training Center Development', *AA,* XXXV, ii
(1972), pp. 163–72.

T. R. Schellenberg, 'Archival Training in Library Schools', *AA,* XXXI, ii
(1968), pp. 155–66.

Society of American Archivists, *Education Directory: Careers and
Courses in Archival Administration* (Ann Arbor, Michigan, 1973).

'The Training of Archivists', *JSA,* II, vii (1963), pp. 330–1.

University of New South Wales, *A Postgraduate Course in Archives
Administration* (1973).

A. Vytterbrouck, 'Le Recrutement et le début de carrière du personnel
scientifique des archives de l'état', *Archivum,* XIV (1964), pp.
185–204.

R. M. Warner, 'Archival Training in the United States and Canada', *AA,*
XXXV, iii–iv (1972), pp. 347–58.

D. E. K. Wijasuriya, 'The Training of Librarians and Archivists', *Southeast
Asian Archives,* IV (1971), pp. 56–9.

Index

Abstracts, 27, 177 *see also* calendars
Academic liaison, 69, 70–173, 86, 156–9, 173–5, 183, 188
Access, to archives, 12, 14, 16, 81, 111, 144, 148, 152, 196, 200 closure, periods of, 156, conditions of, 212, demand for, 172 to deposited archives, 150–1, 210 depositors' control of, 150–1 educational, 165, 196 (*see also* education, group access) to finding aids, 59, 155–6 by groups (*see* group access) by microfilm, 178–9 policy on, 150–1 to public records, 214–16 reasons for, 151–2 to records in records centre, 38, 58–9 restrictions on, 4, 146, 148–53, 156, 163, 215 right of, 215 special provisions for, 152, 214, 216 to storage areas, 55, 139, 145–7
Accession, codes, 100–1, 115 control in repair processes, 141–2 register of, 117
Accessions, of archives, 22, 95, 99–102, 137, 205 temporary 103 *see also* accrual, acquisition
Accountant, management, 112
Accrual, 16, 95–6, 100, 122, 137 from changing administrative structures, 109 rate and measurement of, 73, 136 *see also* accessions, acquisition, transfer of archives
Acidity, tests for, 143
Acknowledgement of transfer, 101
Acoustics in searchroom, 169
Acquisition, limitations on, 5–9 by microfilm, 178 objectives covering,

4–9, 95–7 *see also* accessions, accrual, collection of archives
Administration, microfilm in, 179, 182 modern changes in, 109–10 optimum size of, 112
Administrative, functions, 121 history, 68–9, 110, 120, 130, 148, 172–3, (*see also* institutional history), values, 64, 206 (*see also* appraisal)
ADPA journal, 134
Advertisement, 97
Advisory council, 12, 71
Affidavits, 106
Age range, of users, 185–7, 193 *see also* education
Agency fee, 92 *see also* delegation
Agreement for deposit (q.v.), 97–8, 210–11
Agriculture, archives of, 7, 173
Air conditioning, 167, 180
Alphabetical arrangement (q.v.), 105–7
American Archivist journal, 143
American State archives, 23
Analysis of archives (q.v.), 117
Ancient Correspondence, 106
Antiquarian research, 151
Aperture cards, 94, 179
Application for access (q.v.), 151
Appraisal, 5, 8, 16, 28, 51, 73–4, 95–6, 203, 205 in acquisition programmes, 99, 136–7 administrative and historical values in, 64–8, 75, 84–5, 206 analysis of functions in, 67, 79 box, unit in, 90 bulk as factor in, 5, 33–4, 209, (*see also* cost) chance as factor in, 76 common standards in, 62,

75–6, 79, 82–3 comparative evaluation in, 65 cost as factor in, 66, 71, 76 criteria, general, 60–3, 66–7, 206–9 date, criteria in, 99 of ephemera, 87–9 evidential and informational values in, 68–9, 75–6, 79, 87 in field work, 96–7 file, unit of, 87 local values in, 70, 73–4, 88, 208 of machine-readable records, 132–4 performed by delegation, 136 personal bias in, 82 precedents, factor in, 64, 207 primary and secondary values in, 68–70 in Public Record Office, 63–7, 206–9 reviews in, 84–7 (*see also* reviewing), of secret records, 91, 149 (*see also* security classification) specialist advice in, 76 status of appraiser, 87 validation of system, 74–5 *see also* archives, archives office, archivist, disposal schedules, sampling, selection

Archaeology, 99, 137, 203

Architectural drawings, 6, 94, 179

Archival, objectives (*see* archives office), order, in microfiche, 182 (*see also* arrangement), quality, 5, 7–8, 46–7, 71, 76, 80, 84–5, 88 *see also* appraisal

Archive teaching units, 191–4 *see also* education

Archives, analysis of, 104, 108–10, 114, 117 assistants, 204–5 authorities, 15–17, 219 (22 n) buildings, 147 changes in appearance of, 142 class, 110 (*see also* archives series), cleaning of, 102 coding of, (*see* codes, archival), compensation for withdrawal of 97–8, 210–11 content of, 23 dates of, 6 defined, 1–3, 95 delegation of costs, 74 (*see also* delegation), demand for, 200 discovery of, 99 duty of society to keep, 4, 76 educational publication of, 189 (*see also* education), filming programmes, 181–2 fragile, 140–1, 153, 163, 178, 213 handling by users, 188 identification of, 119 (*see also* description, retrieval), interpretation of, 105, 110 (*see also* moral defence), loan of, 3, 14, 97, 146, 176, 211 loss by misplacement, 139, 142, 161 market value of, 6–8, 98, 139 marking, 153 material of (*see* conservation) measuring demand for, 158, 160 microreproduction of, 177–82 original, in microform, 179 overuse of, 140–1 personal detail in, 156, 214–15 public,

12–14 (*see also* public records) purchase of, 16, 18, 97–8, 150, 219 (29 n) repacking of, 102 reproduction of, 176, 194 (*see also* education) publications, retrieval of, 27, 38, 42, 102, 112, 114–28, 131, 200 selection for publication, 179, 190 subdivisions of, 176, 194 (*see also* education publications) retrieval of, 27, 38, 42, educational uses, 184–5 theft of, 115, 139, 153, 176, 211 uniqueness of, 4, 104 uses of in teaching, 184–5 withdrawal of, 97–8

Archives groups, 21–3, 114–15, 130 defined, 108–9 validity questioned, 109–11

Archives office, access outside, 189 accommodation in, 5, 205 (*see also* storage), acquisition objectives in, 5–8, 96–7 administrative functions of, 19, 121 advises on comparative values, 66 advises on record design, 72 agent for academic research, 158 agreement with creating departments, 97 analysis of services in, 199–201 answers enquiries, 157–9 appraisal objectives of, 61–2 appropriate, for deposits, 5–9 attachment of teachers, 196–7 behaviour in, 152–3 budgeting for, 23–4, 204 building, 24, 40, 137, 164–6, 205 cannot control intake, 136 capacity of, 33–4, 136, 165 centralisation of, 7, 12, 199–201 circulate information, 102 committee governing, 12, 19, 203 common room in, 164–6, 174 computers in, 131–4, 163 conservation standards in, 135 control of doors in, 138–9 control of processes in, 98–102 co-ordinates research, 156–7 defined, 2–3 deposits in other offices, 74 determines reader needs, 162–3 develops higher studies, 174–5 dispersal of public records to, 73 divisions, administrative or research, 20–1 duty to receive archives, 75–7, 136 editors in, 147 educational programmes in, 173–4, 188–9, 192, 195–8 exploitation programmes, 172–3 formality of, 153 functional divisions in, 20–2 joint education services, 186, 198 joint services, 24, 92, 128–9, 139, 194–5, 198, 200–1 legal powers, 11–18 local (*see* local archives offices), mechanises office systems, 163 office areas in, 164, 166 optimum size of, 3,

21–2, 24, 67, 140, 199 programme divisions in, 20–2, 100 public relations in, 101 records centres and, 48, 95 regional, 121 repair services in, 139–43, 200 services by, for payment, 92–3 specialised, 6–7 staff information needs in, 69–71 staffing standards, 24, 204–5 subject-based, 5–9 as teaching institution, 172–3 territorial, 5–7 types of, 2 ff

Archives series, 23, 68, 99, 108–12, 114–15, 117–18, 120, 123, 140, 144–5, 155, 163 access to, 150 defined, 105, 110–12 in education, 185 in microfilm, 178–9, 182 for repair, 140–3

Archives services, defined, 2–3 distinct from libraries, 2–3 planning of, 199–200 public, 3, 197–8 (*see also* archives office),

Archivist, in acquisition, 99–102 as administrator, 60–1 as adviser, 55, 92, 156–7, 164, 203–4 analyses records, 105 as appraiser, 60–1, 65, 67, 79–83, 86–7 arranges archives, 105–7 comparative practices of, 149–50 (*see also* professional standards), controls access, 59, 150–1 controls environment, 136–9 controls issues, 160–2 dependent on administration, 87 duties of, 12, 19–22, 105, 204 as educator, 183, 186, 196–7 exploits archives, 172–3 in field work, 96–7 (*see also* records management) legal liability of, 151–2 as manager, 200–1 personal interests of, 23 predicts research needs, 69–71 qualifications of, 204 recommends. destruction, 81–2 (*see also* appraisal), as records manager, 28–9, 38, 48, 203 in repair programmes, 140–3 in research, 158–9, 172 as reviewer of records, 84–5 salary scale of, 204 as sampler, 87–9 seeks advice, 70–1, 76, 88–9 selects archives for educational use, 184–5 status of, 19–20, 27, 203 supervisor, 147–8, 188 as teacher, 174, 196 as user of libraries, 170

Archivum, 13, 18

Arrangement, archival, 3, 11, 99, 103–7, 113–6, 123, 130–1, 142–3, 204, 210, 212 as conservation, 9 defined, 103–4 by form, 106–7 by function, 99, 106–7 in microfilming, 181 when original order defective, 106–7 physical, 52, 107, 113 of records, 93

in searchroom, 153 shelf order 52, 107, 113 *see also* classification, moral defence of archives, provenance, order

Association, professional, 7, 97, 131, 138, 203–4

Association (voluntary), educational, 189, 196 federation of, 175 of users, 123, 175

Atmospheric conditions, 137–8 *see also* environmental conditions

Atomic Energy Commission, 13

Attendance book, 153–4

Audio-visual aids, 174, 176

Australia, 109

Authenticity of Archives, 105–7, 119–20, 140

Automatic data processing *see* computer

Bachelor of Education, 189

Backlog accumulations of archives, 61, 95, 98–9, 100, 131, 136

Banks, archives of, 9

Batho, G. R., 191

Benedon, W., 44

Bibliographies, 69, 228, 233–4

Binding, 139 *see also* repair

Bishop, 15, 124 *see also* church archives

Boards of studies, 70

Borthwick Institute, 124

Boundary agreements, 5–7, 8–9

Box, as unit for disposal, 90 labels, 53–4

Boxing, of archives, 22, 33–4, 38, 42, 44, 49–51, 90, 100, 107, 114, 138, 140, 146, 168, 205 of microfilm, 180

Britain, archives law of, 13–18

British Library, 2

British Museum, 13

British Records Association, 97

British Standards Institution, 205

British Steel Corporation, 13, 45–6

Browsing, 55, 145

Budgeting, for archives office, 23–4, 204 for records centre, 45–8

Buildings, for archives office, 24, 40, 137, 164–6, 205 history of, 155 for records centre, 39–42

Bulk of records, 5, 33–4, 209 *see also* appraisal

Bundles, original, 99–100, 107, 142–3

Burglar alarms, 176

Burglary, 139

Business archives, 2, 6–7, 20, 22, 32, 63, 92, 95, 109, 111 right of access to, 215

Business Archives Council, 97

Cabinet archives, 19, 207, 215 *see also* central government
Calculating machines, 168
Calendars of Archives, 118–19, 127, 130, 155, 170, 177, 204 *see also* edited texts, publications
Canada, 70, 163
Capacity, measurement of *see* archives office
Cards, index, 33, 127–8 print out on, 130
Caretaker, 176
Case records, 27, 32, 72, 88 *see also* particular instance papers
Catalogues, 120–1, 148, 155, 170 *see also* description
Census archives, 216
Central government archives, 19, 91, 122, 146, 149, 156
Centralisation of archives services *see* archives office
Chemical action on film, 180
Chemical pollutants, 137
Cheshire Record Office, 223–4
Chief executive, 58, 81–2, 112
Children, 186–8, 192–3, 195 *see also* education
Chronological arrangement, 105–7
Church archives, 3, 15, 17, 22, 122, 124, 199
Churchwarden, 15
Citation of archives, 54, 114 *see also* quotation
Cite interministerielle des archives, 40
Cities, effect on archives services, 12, 15–17, 40–1, 92, 124, 200
Civil parish, 15–16
Classification of archives, 3, 103–4, 115–16 *see also* security
Classified lists, 78 *see also* disposal schedules
Classroom, 193, 197
Cleaning, 42, 139, 205
Clerical services, 22, 205
Clerk of council, 15–16, 32, 112
Closure, of files, 33, 35, 49, 81 (*see also* retirement) periods of (*see* access)
Codes, archival, 9, 99, 114–17, 129–30, 155, 182, 210, 224 (3 n.) common standards in, 115 in microfilm, 181
Collection of archives, 2–3, 7, 22, 96–7, 115, 135–6, 199
Commercial records centre, 92
Committee minutes, 32, 124, 207, 215
Common room, 164, 166, 174
Computer, in archival description, 128–32, 170 in archives office

management, 132–4, 163 costing services of, 131–2 indexes, 123, 128, 130 output to microfilm, 130, 132, 179 paper, 130 as record producer, 132–4 time, 131 used in common, 128–9 used in research, 72–3, 89
Confidentiality, 82, 91, 157 *see also* security classification
Conservation, 4–5, 9, 14, 139, 188, 200 costs, 98 joint service, 200 of maps, 94 microfilm, 178 standards, 97
Consignments of archives, 50–2, 99
Consultants, in appraisal, 6, 86–7
Consultation of archives *see* access, issue, searchroom
Consultative committee, 12, 71
Conveyancing records, 80
Copying facilities, 4, 22, 46–8, 55, 59, 128, 136, 146, 164, 168–9, 177, 189, 192, 197–8
Copyright, 154, 192, 203
Coroner, 14, 126
Cost, of archives services, 4, 28, 33–4, 74, 76, 81–2, 92–3, 131–2, 200 of computer programs, 131–2 of education services, 192 of microfilm programmes, 177–9
Cost-benefit studies, 46–7, 66, 82, 92
County, 15–16, 173 council, 116, 125, 219 (22 n), 224 (25 n) court, 15 education, 183 record office, 6, 104, 115–17, 121–2, 146
Creating department, 3, 13–14, 25–6, 29, 53, 58–9, 62–4, 67–8, 76, 79, 88, 95, 110, 132, 173, 204, 207–9 approves disposal, 81–2 carries out listing, 38 extent of records management in, 48 functional instability of, 109 functions of, 108–9 records private to, 91
Crew lists, 73–5, 89
Cubic measurement, 33–4, 44–5
Cultural services, 12, 19–20, 26
Cumbria Record Office, 226
Custody, archival, 12, 15–16, 65, 120, 135–6, 202, 204, 210–11 breach of, 136 history of, 135–6, 140

Data, bank, 4 sheet, 51 tape, 132–4
Deacidification, 140
Decentralisation of archives services, 199–201
Declassification of archives, 149 *see also* security classification
Delegation of archival functions, 3, 20, 24, 135–6, 157

Delmas, B., 24

Departmental, archive group, 109 heads,
    19, 27, 29, 48, 203 records
    committee (*see* Grigg Committee)
    records guide for, 66–7, 206–9
    records officer, 64–6, 70, 75, 78,
    84–5, 206

Departments, as owners of records, 52
    related to administrative functions, 29,
    68–9, 82, 109, 111

Deposit, of archives, 3, 5, 8, 11, 15–16,
    20, 135–7, 149–51, 199, 202–4
    charges on withdrawal, 97–8, 210–11
    coding for, 116–17 general conditions
    of agreement, 97–8, 210–11
    miscellaneous small, 116 place of
    (q.v.)

Deposited archives, access to, 150–1
    plans 121

Description of archives, 11–12, 103,
    115, 131, 177 computers in, 128–32
    educational, 185 expository, 118–21
    machine-readable, 132–4 microfilm,
    181 structural, 121–3 *see also* finding
    aids, lists

Descriptive lists, 9, 117–18

Destruction of records, 5, 28, 37, 39,
    48–50, 56, 61, 64, 73–4, 78, 82, 84,
    90–2, 94, 134, 151, 203, 205–6, 209
    by departments, 81, 91 involving
    microfilm, 179 by records centre,
    90–1 register of, 87 *see also* appraisal,
    disposal

Devon Record Office, 224

Diazo film, 180

Diocesan archives office, 15, 124 *see
    also* church archives

Disaster plan, 43, 178

Discovery methods in education, 187–8,
    193, 198

Display, 11, 22, 42, 146, 154, 164, 176,
    193–4, 198 educational, 187–8, 197
    in museums, 195 programmes, 175–6
    by publication, 177 *see also* exhibition

Disposal, of archives, 12–13, 16–17, 27,
    35, 38–9, 42, 52–3, 73–5, 77, 82,
    203 box, unit of, 90 defined, 82
    instructions on file, 84–6 list, 78, 90 of
    machine-readable records, 132–4
    processes, 60 public discussion of, 71
    reminder system, 52–4 by routines,
    78–83

Disposal schedules, 28, 39, 43, 48,
    53–4, 78–83, 92

Documentation, 5–7, 9, 12, 17, 25–6,
    39, 48, 61–2, 66, 75–6, 92–3, 96,

131, 135, 200 centres, 92, 129, 201
    for computer programs, 133 technical,
    20, 27

Donation of archives, 97–8

Donor of archives, 100–2

Doors, 138–9

Duplicates, 4, 32, 91, 130, 133, 209

East Sussex Record Office, 223, 225

Edited texts, 118, 170, 177, 190–2, 204
    see also calendars

Editor in archives office, 147

Education, in archives office, 11, 19, 127,
    136, 146, 163, 172, 175, 183 ff,
    197–8, 203 advisers, 183, 196–7
    colleges of, 173, 188–9 joint services,
    194–6

Educational, aids in searchroom, 168,
    191 methods, 174–5

Electoral rolls, 215

Emmison, F. G., 146

Employing authority, 3, 5, 7, 10, 18–19,
    24, 43, 49, 84, 86–7, 91, 93, 131,
    135, 150, 152, 157, 199, 202

Enclosure, archives of, 121

Engineers' drawings, 6, 94, 179

Enquiries, 29, 55, 96, 157, 164, 167,
    205 policy on, 157–9, 203 record
    form, 158–9 register, 48, 55–7,
    158–9 subject-based, 69, 120, 122–3

Environment, Secretary of State for, 16

Environmental, conditions, 38, 43–4,
    135 controls, 136–8, 167–8 studies,
    197

Ephemeral records, 38, 49, 81

Essex Record Office, 116, 190, 192

Estate, archives, 3, 22 duty, 18

Estimates *see* budgeting

Evidential values *see* appraisal

Examinations, 186, 197

Exeter, 73

Exhibition, 14, 16, 136, 164, 166,
    175–6, 204–5 outside archives office,
    176 *see also* display

Exploitation, of archives, 4–5, 10–11, 20,
    28, 75, 117 of records, 38

Export of archives, 18

Exposition, 118–19 *see also* description

Facsimiles, 177, 187–8, 190–2, 194, in
    display, 176

Family archives, 22

Federal records centre, 40, 44

Fees, 151, 213

Fieldwork, 11, 21–2, 29–36, 96,
    199–200

Fifty-year rule, 14 *see also* access

File, binding, 107 bulky, 142 closure of, 64, 67 (*see also* retirement) computer (defined), 133 correspondence, 158–9 dismantling, 143 disposal instructions on, 84–6 individual, 81, 108, 178, 182 titles, 50, 56, 65, 84, 87, 112, 132 as unit of records, 65 weeding, 28, 49, 87

Filing, cabinets, 33–4, 51 centres, 82–3 (*see also* registry) index, 86 systems, 27, 31, 48, 56, 81, 84, 87, 110, 203

Film, archives, 14 maintenance, 93 (*see also* microfilm) physical qualities of, 180 storage, 46 strip, 190, 194

Filming processes, 179–82

Finance Acts, 18

Finding aids, 7, 112, 117–28, 204 access to, 156 computerised, 128–32 educational, 184–5, 187, 196 microfilm, 177, 179, 181 record provenance, 105 in records centre, 38 in searchroom, 154–6, 160, 164, 168, 202 self-explanatory, 148, 156

Fire precautions, 39, 176, 180

First review, 64–7, 75 *see also* appraisal, reviewing

Fishbein, M. H., 133

Floor space, 34–5, 44

Fowler, G. H., 61, 183

Frequency of reference, 32–3, 35, 38, 75, 133

Fumigator, 102

Games, in history teaching, 194

Genealogy, 70, 128, 151, 155, 163, 170, 209

Gloucestershire Record Office, 167

Golden rule of archive making, 61

Government *see* central government, department

Greater London Record Office, 16, 67, 226

Grigg, Committee, 13, 70–1, 73, 75, 84, 87 Report, 47, 63–7, 72, 78

Grigg, Sir J., 63

Group access, 145, 164, 168, 184, 186, 191, 193

Guides, to archives, 14, 16, 115, 118, 121–3, 130, 154–5, 157, 170, 204 educational, 184–5 selective, 121–3 specimen entries, 124 *see also* finding aids, lists

Hampshire Archivists' Group, 224

Handlist, 118, 121 *see also* finding aids, lists

Hardware, 131–3

Hayes, 40, 44, 52, 65, 78

Higher education, 70, 173

Historical, Association, 189 interpretation, 88, 192 Manuscripts Commission, 14–18 research, 151, 183 room, 198 values, 64–7, 105, 188, 208 (*see also* appraisal)

History of science, 173

Hospitals, archives of, 14, 72

Housekeeping records, 68

Humidity, 137–8, 167, 180

Hundred-year rule, 215–16 *see also* access

Impartiality of archives, 60–1, 179–80

Imperial War Museum, 8

Index, 14, 16, 38, 48, 50, 112, 117, 120, 123–8, 130, 148, 155, 157 archives in form of, 106 cabinet, 127–8, 130, 155, 168 cleaning, 56, 90 computerised, 123, 128, 130 to enquiries, 158–9 in microfilm programmes, 179, 181 to original archives, 93, 123, 156 pilot, 79–80 published, 128, 177 of registers, 103 sheaf, 127 to transfer lists, 56 union, 56, 123–8 vertical, 155 vocabulary, 123–8

India Office Records, 106, 223

Individual documents *see* items

Induction of readers, 164–5 *see also* register, users

Industry, archives of, 5–7, 22, 40–2, 44, 63, 91

Inflow, of archives, 136–8 (*see also* acquisition), records, 38, 49–54

Information, cost of, 26, 48 services, 4, 157, 201 sheets, 154–5, 157, 164, 168

Informational values *see* appraisal

In-letters, 106

Input tapes, 128–34

Insects, 138

Inspecting officer, 67, 75, 78, 96

Inspection of archives, 12, 14, 17–18

Institute of Historical Research, 89

Institutional history, 68–9 *see also* administrative history

Insurance, of archives, 176, 211 against liability, 151

Integrated studies, 197 *see also* education

Intellectual control of archives, 10, 29–30, 117

Intermediate store *see* records centre

International Council on Archives, 62, 134, 143
Inventory *see* finding aids, lists, retrieval
Ipswich and East Suffolk Record Office, 223, 225–6
Irthlingborough, 45–6
Israel, 92
Issue, of archives to users, 22, 42, 47–8, 56–8, 86, 107, 121, 145–6, 160–3, 173, 200, 205 mechanised, 163 outstanding, 55 quantity restriction on, 212 systems, 164 *see also* requisition
Items, archival, 65, 108–12, 114, 117–18, 120, 140 *see also* file

Jackdaws, 191
Jenkinson, Sir H., 9, 61, 105, 107–9
Joint services *see* archives office
Journals, 26, 69, 134, 170
Judicial archives, 12, 22
Jurisdictions *see* boundary agreements

Keeper of the Public Records, 14, 215
Kent Archives Office, 67, 116, 190, 212
Kept-out facilities, 146, 161–2, 164
Kew, 163
Keyboard operators, 129, 131
Keys, control of, 138–9
Kit *see* archive teaching unit

Labelling, 22, 31, 42, 53–4, 100, 138, 146
Lamination, 43, 140, 178
Lancashire Record Office, 165–6
Law courts, 6, 13, 106, 151–2, 211
Law of Property Acts, 14
Lecture, 174, 204, 211 room, 164, 166
Lecturer, 147, 172, 189
Legal adviser, 81–2
Legislation, archival, 10–18, 75, 96, 148–9, 152, 207
Legislature, archives of, 12, 19, 23
Leisinger, A. H., 177
Liability, legal, 151–2, 210
Library, 19, 171, 173, 200–1 in archives office, 22, 42, 55, 69–70, 164, 168–70 as collector, 2–3, 6, 8–9, 14 of Congress, 2 joint services with, 129, 148, 194–5 procedures, differ from archival, 3, 5, 103–4, 120, 146, 225 (6 n) searchroom, 169–70, 197, 202 special, 20, 26–7, 92 used by archivists, 174 *see* presidential libraries
Limbo *see* records centre
Linear measurement, 33–4, 44–5

List, archival, 17–18, 101, 115, 117–23, 155, 157 cost of, 131–2 by creating department, 38 hierarchy of, 118–19, 155 indexed, 123, 128 of microfilm, 181 order of archives in, 107 published, 170, 177 of records, 34–5 standards for, 31 structural, 118–21 summary, 117–19, 121–3, 130, 155 *see also* description, finding aids, retrieval
Listing, 114, 128, 204 by sub-professionals, 205
Lithography, 189, 195
Liverpool, 73, 191, 210
Loan of archives, 3, 14, 97, 146, 176, 211 *see also* deposit
Local archives office, 14, 16, 19–22, 24, 95, 115–17, 121–2, 146–7, 153, 165–7, 170–1, 173, 183, 191, 198–201 (*see also* archives office), standards for, 16, 202–5
Local courts, 14
Local government, 12, 32, 72, 91, 104, 125–7, 199–200, 208 Acts, 15–16, 124 archives, 3, 15–16, 109, 111, 124, 149, 215 departments, 63 (Records) Act, 16–17, 202 records centre, 40
Local public records, 13–14
Local studies, 173–4, 209
Location, chart, 53 codes, 48, 50–7, 90, 132, 138, 141, 163 index, 53 list, 121 register, 90, 102–3
Lockers, readers', 163
London, 16, 89 *see also* Greater London
Loose-leaf folders, 122–3, 127, 155
Lord Chancellor, 13–14, 214–15

Machine-readable archives, 132–4
Machine-readable records, 129
Maclean, I., 109
Magistrates' courts, 14
Magnetic, disc, 132–3 tape, 43, 46, 129, 131–3
Malaysia, 44
Manorial archives, 14, 116
Manuscripts, 2–3, 6, 8, 18 *see also* Historical Manuscripts Commission
Maps, 94, 121, 142, 163, 168, 191, 193, 195
Maritime History Group, 73
Market values, *see* archives
Master of the Rolls, 14–15
Metropolitan counties, 16, 219 (22 n)
Microfilm, 42, 72, 93–4, 163, 168, 203, 205, 213 computer, 130–2, 179 cost

of, 74, 93 in education, 189 legal
validity of, 93 objectives of, 177–9
quality of, 180 readers, 164, 168–9,
177 retrieval of, 180–1 storage of, 94,
180
Microforms, 43, 130, 178, 180–2
Minister, 207, 214 private office of,
208–9 reponsible for archives, 12, 19,
149
Ministry, archives of, 109–10 *see also*
central government
Misplacement, 139, 161
Mnemonic codes, 115–17
Moral defence of archives, 9–10, 101,
105–7, 113, 120, 130, 149, 179 *see*
also arrangement, description
Moulds, 137
Municipal Corporations Acts, 15
Museums, 3, 8–9, 19, 71, 173, 176,
186, 194–5, 201 advisory services,
175 as collectors, 14 loan services,
194

Names, spelling of, 125
National archives, 2–3, 12, 65, 75, 89,
95, 122, 146–7, 150, 153, 183, 201
of USA, 40, 44, 68, 132
National Coal Board, 13
National collections, 8, 18, 102
National Health Service, 14
National Maritime Museum, 8, 73
National Register of Archives, 17–18,
102, 125
National Standards Institution, 180
NATIS, 129, 201
Newcastle upon Tyne, 191
Newfoundland, 73
Newspapers, 26, 190, 195
Non-official archives, 22, 96, 100,
116–17, 137, 150, 163, 199 access
to, 151 *see also* private archives
Non-public records, 149
Northern Ireland, 17 *see also* Public
Record Office
Notification of transfer, 98, 100–2

Office, costs, 35, 41, 44–8, 92–3 hours,
148 space, leased, 49 superviser, 85
see also survey
Office accommodation, standards, 42
Official archives, 22, 122, 150–1, 163
Official enquiries, 163
Opening hours, 148, 154, 163, 212
Oral evidence, 9, 26, 195
Order, alphabetical, 112, 130 archival
(*see* arrangement) chronological, 112,

130 hierarchical, 112 original, 3,
98–100, 104–5, 142–3 (*see also*
provenance), slips, 146 (*see also*
requisition)
Organisation and method, 27
Original, custody of, 7
Originating organisation *see* creating
department
Out-letters, 106
Oversize archives, 50
Ownership, of archives, 97, 136 of
records, 39

Palaeography, 170
Paper, composition of, 4, 140–1, 143,
178, 180 stocks, testing, 143
Paperwork management, 27
Parchment, 142, 168–9
Paris, 40
Parish, archives of, 15, 123, 125
Particular instance papers, 64, 71–5,
87–9, 209 *see also* case records
Pens, use of, 153, 213
Permanent preservation of archives, 3–4,
80, 82, 206, 214
Permitted vocabulary, 125
Photocopies, of archives, 7, 14, 18, 55,
98, 157, 176, 187, 203, 211, 213,
216 charges for, 203
Photocopying facilities, 4, 22, 46–8, 55,
59, 128, 136, 146, 164, 168–9, 177,
189, 192, 197–8
Photographs, 18, 26, 195, 213
Photography, 166, 176, 204–5
Piece *see* item
Pilot index, 79–80
Place of deposit, 13–14, 215–16
Plans, 46, 94, 179, 192, 195
Policy, records of, 84–7, 207–8 *see also*
reviewing
Pollution, environmental, 137, 200
Poor law, 116, 126
Porters, 48–9, 205
Posner, E., 21, 23
Postal services, 41, 127, 136, 178, 225
(2 n)
Pre-archival records, 37 *see also* records
centres
Presidential libraries, 8
Primary values *see* appraisal
Printed matter, archival, 170–1
Print-out, 129–30, 132, 134
Private archives, 14–18, 26, 62, 122,
137, 178, 199, 202
Professional, associations, 7, 131, 138,
203–4 negligence, 151 standards,

5–9, 15–16, 23–4, 28, 36, 59–62, 67, 70–1, 76–7, 79, 81, 86, 89, 93, 96–7, 128, 137, 139–40, 143–5, 147, 149–52, 157, 169–70, 174, 183, 186, 188, 195–6, 198, 200, 202, 204, 210
Program, computer, 128–32
'Proper arrangements' for archives, 15–16
Provenance of archives, 3, 5, 8, 99–102, 104–5, 107, 117, 122, 223 (9 n)
Public archives, concept of, 12–14 *see also* archives
Public records, 13, 63–7, 206, 214 Acts, 13, 17, 63, 149–50, 202, 214 local, 202
Public Records Office, 2, 13–14, 63–7, 72–4, 78, 89, 106, 110, 121–2, 163, 203, 206, 214–16, 222 (16 n) of Northern Ireland, 17, 73, 191
Public relations, 154, 201
Public rights, 12, 66, 70, 152
Publication, of archives, 10–11, 14, 16, 18, 21–2, 118–19, 128, 147–8, 152–4, 175, 177, 204 educational, 185, 189–94 microfilm, 130, 178, 181 of records, 75 by owner's consent, 211
Punched cards, 129, 131
Punched tape, 130–2
Purchase grant fund, 219 (29 n)

Quarter sessions, archives of, 14, 104, 106, 116, 126
Questionnaire on readers' needs, 163
Quotation of archives, 152, 185 *see also* citation

Random sample, 88
Readers, 144–5 access to finding aids, 156 common room for, 174 confidentiality of study, 157 control of, 164 demands of, 157–8, 162–3 groups of, (*see* group access) induction of, 153–4 lockers for, 163 numbers of, 154, 163 personal advice to, 156–7 registration of, 153–4 requisitions by, 160 *see also* users, searchroom
Records, accrual of, 79 administration division (PRO), 66 assistants, duties of, 204–5 bulk of, 49, 61, 71, 88 clerks, 90, 204–5 consignment of, 50 control or possession of, 25–6 cost of, 35 (*see also* bulk) creation of (*see* creating department) dead, 33 defined, 1–2, 25, 95 duplicate series of, 32 groups,

62, 109–10 (*see also* archives group) interrelated series of, 35 measurement of, 33–5, 44–5, 48–9, 98 office, defined, 2–3 (*see also* archives office) searcher, 158 services, 2–3, 95–6 societies, 175, 192 status of staff, 64–5 store, closed, 33, 35, 82, 95, 99 systems, 64, 67, 87
Records centres, 26, 35, 37, 46, 49, 80–1, 199 accessioning in, 50–4 administration in, 42–3, 47–8 archival functions in, 39, 42–3, 55, 95 budget for, 44–8, 91, 98 building requirements for, 39–42 capacity of, 43–5, 81–2 charges for services, 92–3 costing of, 44–8, 91, 98 destroys records, 90–1 finding aids in, 38, 50–9 income from waste, 91 inflow of records to, 49–54, 84–6 as information centre, 40–1, 55 issue of records in, 54–5, 92 joint, 41, 199 location of records in, 52–3 measurement of records in, 43, 51, 57 microfilm in, 93–4 objectives for, 37–9, 46 optimum size of, 40–1, 43–4, 60 outflow of records from, 38–9, 60–1, 89–91 ownership of records in, 52–3 retrieval of records in 50–9, 92 security in, 39, 55, 57–9, 138 staffing of, 45–9, 53 storage in, 43–5, 47, 49–50 transport for, 40–1, 47
Records management, 5, 11, 19, 22, 77, 109, 199, 203–5 in archives office, 96–7 defined, 25–7 economies in, 28, 39, 44–5 microfilming in 93–4, 182
Records manager, 79, 96–7 *see also* departmental records officer
Records series, 30–6, 50, 74–6, 82, 87, 110–12 as appraisal unit, 81 defined, 31, 79–80 schedules of, 78–83 sampled, 87–9 *see also* archives series
Recycling materials, 91
Reference, to archives, 3–4, 7–8, 10, 20, 27, 92–3, 136 area in archives office, 145, 164 codes, 50–1, 99, 101, 114 instruments, 113, 117–28 (*see also* finding aids)
Regions, archives services in, 17, 92–3, 173, 200, 208
Register, of accessions, 51, 100–2 of archives, 7, 14–18, (*see also* National Register of Archives) church archives, 6, 15, 215 of companies, 215 of current records, 82 destruction, 87 of enquiries, 48, 55–7, 158–9 of

locations, 90, 102–3 of readers, 160, 163–4, 168, 212 of research projects, 156

Registrar of Shipping and Seamen, 73–5

Registration, of archives, 98–102, 117, 132, 136, 200 of case papers, 72 (*see also* particular instance papers) of records series, 110–12

Registry, 27, 32, 48, 64–5, 81–2

Regulations, 12, 152–3, 212–13

Remploy, 13

Repair, of archives, 11–12, 21–2, 43, 98, 135–6, 166, 178, 200, 204, 210–11 centralisation of, 139 emergency, 141 management of, 140–3 methods, 139–40 progress, control of, 141–2 section, duties of, 139–43

Repairer, 205

Repairers' newsletter, 143

Reproduction of archives, 177, 185, 187, 189–95, 211, 213

Requisition (*see* issue), for repair, 141–2 slips, 55–8, 146, 154, 160, 162, 212

Research, 5–6, 8, 10, 19–20, 23, 25–8, 37, 76, 93, 131, 187–8 by archivists, 9, 115 collections, 8 community, archivist represents, 136 demands on archives, 73, 149, 154, 205 in employing authority, 43, 112, 157 institutions, 97, 102, 173, 201 methods, 72, 170 predicting course of, 69–71, 89 privileged access for, 152 in records centre, 58–9 register of, 156 section in archives office, 147 values, 2, 4, 6–7, 60–1, 64–5, 67–8, 71, 74–5, 105, 206–7 (*see also* appraisal)

Researcher, academic, 66, 68–70, 74, 76, 144–5, 151, 163

Resource centre, 189, 194–6

Retention, of archives (*see* appraisal), categories (*see* disposal schedules)

Retirement of records, 27–8, 81, 85

Retrieval, 4, 27, 38, 42, 50–9, 102, 112, 114–32, 200 computerised, 73

Reviewing, of records, 16–17, 37, 59, 63–7, 75, 78, 80–1, 84–7, 90, 206 committee, 86–7 process, 84–6 *see also* appraisal

Rolls, parchment, 142, 168–9

Roosevelt Library, 226

Rural areas, archives services in, 173, 200

Sale *see* archives, purchase of

Sampling, 72–4, 78, 87–9, 207, 209

Schedules *see* disposal

Schellenberg, T. R., 61, 67–8

Schools, 70, 124, 127, 147, 183, 188, 196 *see also* education

Scott, P. J., 109–10

Scottish Record Office, 17

Searchroom, 10–11, 21–2, 42, 70, 144–7, 202 advice in, 145, 173 control of archives in, 152–3, 160–2 design of, 164–6 in education, 183–4, 187, 197 equipment, 154, 164, 167–9 exclusion from, 213 kept-out system, 161–2 in records centre, 46, 55 regulations, 151, 157, 202–3, 211–13 special purposes, 165 supervisor, 148, 156–9, 161–2, 164, 169, 183, 203–4, 210

Second review, 65, 75, 206 *see also* reviewing

Secondary values *see* appraisal

Secret archives, 91, 149 *see also* security classification

Security, in archives office, 12, 22, 43–4, 53, 82, 115, 136, 138–9, 145–7, 163, 176, 188 classification of archives, 49, 51, 59, 91, 133, 149 in microfilming, 178 national, 150, 156 in records centre, 39, 55, 57–9, 138

Selection, in archival programmes, 5, 8, 27–8, 37, 62–3, 179, 190 in educational programmes, 184–5 *see also* appraisal

Series (*see* archives series, records series), 'natural', 112 register of, 110–12

Sheffield, 191

Shelving, 22, 24, 44–5, 48, 51–2, 73, 113, 138 arrangement of archives on 52–3, 100, 107, 155 use of space on, 90

Show cases, 176 *see also* display

Signing-in book, 153–4

Silver halide film, 180

Simulations, 194

Singapore, 45

Society of Archivists, 23–4, 198, 202–3

Society of Technical Committee, 143

Software, 131, 133

Somerset Record Office, 116

Sorting archives, 107, 115, 117 *see also* arrangement

Space-saving, 93–4, 178

Staff, of archives office, 21–3, 202–5 honorary, 147 list, 154 meetings, 21, 70 records centre, 45–9 training of, 42, 174, 204–5

Stagnation, atmospheric, 137
Statistical, data, 207–8 information on
    archives office, 161, 167 records, 27,
    72–3, 88–9, 133 research, 145
    sample, 89
Stencil-cutter, 195, 197
Stocktaking, 121
Storage, of archives, 9–11, 27–8, 37,
    113, 136–8, 161, 166–7, 200, 204
    box labels, 53–4 of closed records, 33,
    35, 82, 95, 99 contamination of, 102
    costs of, 28, 74, 76, 81–2, 92–3, 98
    microfilm, 178–80
Stripping of files, 28, 49, 87
Students *see* users
Subject, arrangement by, 23, 106
    enquiries, 69, 120, 122–3 index,
    55–7, 125–6 list, 130
Subject-based archives services, 5–9
Subprofessional posts, 204–5
Summary lists, 117–19, 121–3, 130,
    155
Sunlight, 138
Survey, of archives, 11, 17, 34–6, 49,
    199, 203 of particular instance papers,
    72 of records, 28–36, 79, 133
Surveyors' drawings, 179
Sweden, 12

Tape, recorders, 164, 168, 197 storage,
    46 (*see also* magnetic tape)
Teachers, in archives services, 172, 174,
    184–9, 191–7, 205 centres, 188–9,
    195–6 instructions for, 190, 193
Teaching, aids, 168, 191 areas in
    archives office, 176 equipment, 197
    units (*see* archives teaching units) use
    of archives in, 136, 146 *see also*
    education
Teaching History, 189
Team working, 102
Technical advisory services, 143
Television, closed circuit, 148
Telex, 41, 47, 55
Temperature, 137–8, 180
Theft of archives, 115, 139, 153, 176,
    211
Thesaurus, 126–7
Thirty-year rule, 14, 149–50, 214 *see
    also* access
Tickets, readers', 153
Tithe, archives of, 6, 15
Title, card, 181 deeds, 6, 14, 80,
    116–17, 206
Tracing on archives, 153, 213
Traffic flows in archives office, 164–6

Trails, museum, 195
Training, 8, 196, 205
Transfer, of archives for repair, 141
    instructions, 50–2 list, 48, 50–4, 56,
    79–80, 90–2 list data sheet, 51 list to
    records centre, 25, 49, 89–91, 136–7
    of material to archives, 27, 48, 65, 80,
    84, 91, 98, 100, 110–12, 120,
    135–6, 200, 204 of shares, 215
    systems, 11
Transparencies, 187, 190, 194–5
Tribunals, archives of, 13
Trolleys, 42, 164
Typewriters, 103, 106, 164, 168

Ultraviolet light, 164, 169
UNESCO, 62
United States, 39–42, 44, 92, 132
Units of control *see* item
Universities, 20, 70, 73, 173 as
    collectors of archives, 6, 8–9
    extension, 174 libraries, 170 records
    of, 72
Updating of data, 128–32, 134
Urban history, 192
Users, 66, 70, 147, 167 access to
    storage for, 146–7 education of, 97,
    122, 154, 172–3, 197–8 guides for,
    122 instructions to, 168 needs of,
    119–21, 177–8 rules for, 153

Valuation, archives of, 6
Vandalism, 139
Vault, 42–3
Ventilation, 138
Verification of lists, 129–30
Victoria and Albert Museum, 219 (29 n)
Visitors' book, 153–4
Vital records, 43

Wales, 13–18, 124
Waste-paper merchant, 91
Weeding, *see* stripping
Who's Who, 88
Withdrawal of records, 54–9
Word list, 126–7 *see also* index,
    permitted vocabulary
Workcard, to control progress, 102–3
Worksheet, conventions for, 31–4
    educational, 194 repair, 142 survey,
    29–34
Writs, 106

York, 124